MEDIA EVENTS

MEDIA EVENTS

The Live Broadcasting of History

Daniel Dayan
Elihu Katz

HARVARD UNIVERSITY PRESS

Cambridge, Massachusetts
London, England
1992

This book is printed on acid-free paper, and its binding materials have
been chosen for strength and durability.

Library of Congress Cataloging-in-Publication Data

Dayan, Daniel, 1943–
Media events : the live broadcasting of history / Daniel Dayan and
Elihu Katz.
p.   cm.
Includes bibliographical references and index.
ISBN 0-674-55955-X
1. Television broadcasting of news.   2. Mass media—Social
aspects.   3. History, Modern—1945–   I. Katz, Elihu, 1926–
II. Title.
PN4784.T4D38   1992   91-23691
070.1'95—dc20   CIP

CONTENTS

Preface

====

"The live broadcasting of history? Don't they know that history is process, not events? Certainly not ceremonial events! Don't they know that media events are hegemonic manipulations? Don't they know that the royal wedding simply blotted out the ethnic rioting that had occupied the streets of London the day before? Haven't they read Daniel Boorstin's *The Image?*"

We have. We know. We even worry—intermittently—about becoming apostles of a telecommunications genre that invites politicians to perform on the stage of the world. For more than a decade, in our mind's eye, we have boarded and reboarded Anwar el-Sadat's plane for the flight to Ben Gurion Airport, trying to understand the magic of that event. We have memorized the archbishop's charge to Charles and Diana. We retake the giant steps regularly, staring down the Communist rulers of Poland with the Pope, gazing back at earth with the astronauts. When people tell us that it all would have happened without television—that the peace between Egypt and Israel was sealed before the cameras were turned on—we doubt it. That is part of what this book is about.

More than we worry about Daniel Boorstin, we worry about George Mosse. Mosse criticizes his fellow historians for identifying European nationalism, too narrowly, with the evolution of parliamentarism, while ignoring the counternormative forms that also are nurtured by nationalism. He is saying, in effect, that the evolution of what we call ceremonial politics is equally central to an understanding of European nationalism, and of the fascism to which it gave birth. "Ceremonial politics" expresses the yearning for togetherness, for fusion; "parliamentary politics" is concerned with pluralism, argumentation, and the management of competing interests. The one assumes that harmony is normal (or at least thinkable), while the other assumes the normalcy of conflict. Ceremonial politics, in this view, caters to and controls the masses who despise the bickerings of parliaments and the nagging of the press, who prefer a politics of the preverbal to dialogue and debate, who cathect charismatic leaders and spectacular displays of unity. This is Walter Benjamin's "aestheticization of politics."

Are media events, then, simply hegemonic? Are they the modern-day version of political spectacle? Of fascist rallies? When 87 percent of Israelis sit at attention in front of their television sets to view the opening ceremonies of Holocaust Day, Memorial Day, and Independence Day (forty-three years after the establishment of their state), are they victims of a yearning for unity—for that is what it is—that is undermining their parliamentary democracy? Do these events make the Knesset look bad, and the watchdog press seem subversive? Perhaps so, but we think otherwise. This book implicitly defends such events, although not uncritically.

We speak, first of all, in a neo-Durkheimian spirit that holds that "mechanical solidarity"—a sense of membership, similarity, equality, familiarity—is at the foundation of the "organic solidarity" of differentiated, to say nothing of postmodern, politics. Television enfranchises, and media events (like holidays) offer a national, sometimes international, "sense of occasion." Even highly politicized societies, such as Israel, interrupt themselves—suspend structure, as Victor Turner would say—to mark some shared occasion. Danger lurks when that is all there is to politics—if these liminal moments serve as substitutes for political structure.

Don Handelman says that societies see themselves reflected, sometimes upside down, in their ceremonies. The utility of this reflexive function is a second defense of media events, even if Mosse warns us to beware that political ceremonies invite societies to worship themselves. We think of media events as holidays that spotlight some central value or some aspect of collective memory. Often such events portray an idealized version of society, reminding society of what it aspires to be rather than what it is. In any case, the portrait must be authenticated by the public, for the elementary reason that otherwise it will not work. Moreover, democratic societies must be authenticated by professional and independent broadcasters. It is up to the broadcasters, not just to establishments and audiences, to decide which ceremonies qualify for media-events treatment. This responsibility is a form of protection against establishment predilection for a ceremonial politics.

Finally and paradoxically, we argue that certain media events celebrate not only unity but pluralism. They are ceremonial *and* parliamentary. Certain kinds of events (contests, for example) are particularly suited to societies that stress equality, achievement, and rule by law. Think of the Watergate hearings.

In *The Descent of Icarus* Yaron Ezrahi proposes that democracy, like science, requires visibility, and that the electronic media enfranchise the citizen-viewer in this respect. We agree with Ezrahi that it is futile to suppose that liberal democracy can be protected against self-aggrandizement by the absence of theatricality; "the 'realism,' 'instrumentalism' and 'publicness' of liberal-democratic regimes are equally culturally and theatrically produced," he says. We suggest that democratic and total-

itarian regimes can be distinguished by types of political ceremony, not by ceremony itself.

Admittedly, there is danger that the genres of democracy may
be subverted, participation turned into adulation, witnessing
into testimonial, persuasion into manipulation, contest into
coronation. The appeal to unity always leaves some people out;
and the renewed pledge of allegiance that is evoked by media
ceremonies may sometimes be diverted from institutions and
principles to leaders and establishments. But the opposite transformation may be equally likely, as is evidenced in the role
played by television in Czechoslovakia's "velvet revolution."

Aware of both the dangers and the possibilities inherent in
the media, we refuse to join the call for a general mobilization
against the celebratory politics of another age, or to reecho the
warning that the "aestheticization of politics" can take only one
political direction. In our analysis of the ceremonial politics of
contemporary television, we refuse to be anachronistic.

The role of media ceremonies in societal integration is discussed in Chapter 1, where we point out that such events imply
the transplantation of reality (to the "air"?) and the relocation of
public space (to the home?).

Chapter 2 analyzes the major "scripts" of media events, which
we call Contest, Conquest, and Coronation. We suggest that
these be considered enactments of Max Weber's traditional,
rational-legal, and charismatic forms of legitimating authority.

The next three chapters follow the progress of these events
through time—first, as they are "negotiated" among organizers,
broadcasters, and audiences; then, as they are "performed" by
the broadcasters; and finally, as they are "celebrated" by audiences at home. Throughout, we draw on empirical studies of
major events, on the anthropology of ceremony, the sociology
of national integration, and the aesthetics of television.

The penultimate chapter dwells on what we call shamanic events—the subset of ceremonial broadcasts that involves a "transformative" dimension—and the book concludes in Chapter 7 with an audit of the effects and functions of media events, as specific occasions and as genre.

D.D.

E.K.

MEDIA EVENTS

1

Defining Media Events: High Holidays of Mass Communication

This book is about the festive viewing of television. It is about those historic occasions—mostly occasions of state—that are televised as they take place and transfix a nation or the world. They include epic contests of politics and sports, charismatic missions, and the rites of passage of the great—what we call Contests, Conquests, and Coronations. In spite of the differences among them, events such as the Olympic Games, Anwar el-Sadat's journey to Jerusalem, and the funeral of John F. Kennedy have given shape to a new narrative genre that employs the unique potential of the electronic media to command attention universally and simultaneously in order to tell a primordial story about current affairs. These are events that hang a halo over the television set and transform the viewing experience.

We call them collectively "media events," a term we wish to redeem from its pejorative connotations. Alternatively, we might have "television ceremonies," or "festive television," or even "cultural performances" (Singer, 1984). These telecasts share a large number of common attributes which we shall attempt to identify. Audiences recognize them as an invitation—even a command—to stop their daily routines and join in a holiday experience. If festive viewing is to ordinary viewing what holidays are to the everyday, these events are the high holidays of mass communication. Conceptually speaking, this book is an attempt to bring the anthropology of ceremony

(Durkheim, 1915; Handelman, 1990; Lévi-Strauss, 1963; Turner, 1985) to bear on the process of mass communication.

Television Genres

Until very recently, television was thought to be saying nothing worthy of humanistic analysis. To propose that television—like the other media—deals in "texts" and "genres" seemed to be conferring too much dignity. Viewers were thought to be watching not programs but television. They were assumed to be passive and unselective, satisfied with stories intended for an undifferentiated audience with a short attention span. Social scientists studied television the way they had studied radio; they searched for mass response to persuasion attempts, or to the images of race, sex, or occupation, or to acts of violence. Some concentrated on long-run effects, taking note of the substitute environment with which TV envelops heavy viewers. Others focused on the effect of television on social institutions, such as politics.

Yet producers and audiences alike routinely assume the existence of television genres. The broadcasters themselves, and the TV listings in newspapers and magazines, regularly classify programs by type: news, documentary, sports, action, adventure, Western, situation comedy, soap opera, variety show, game show, talk show, children's cartoon, and the like. Researchers in mass communications employ these categories too, almost as uncritically. With the exception of soap opera that dates to radio (Herzog, 1941; Arnheim, 1944; Warner, 1962; Katzman, 1972; Modleski, 1982; Cassata, 1983; Cantor and Pingree, 1983; and Allen, 1985), very little serious work has been done on the characteristics of these forms, how they differ from one another, how they relate to corresponding forms in other media, what their messages are, and how these messages are communicated.

Systematic study of the news as a genre of broadcasting has recently begun to rival interest in the soap opera (Epstein, 1973; Tuchman, 1978; Fiske and Hartley, 1978; Schlesinger, 1978; Gans, 1979; Graber, 1984; Morse, 1985). Certain political forms—national conventions, presidential debates, political advertising—have also gained attention, and the situation comedy is having its day (Marc, 1989; Taylor, 1989). Still, until recently, and with only occasional exceptions, social studies of television have treated the medium as a whole or in terms of discrete stimuli, without paying serious attention to its component forms. The publications of Horace Newcomb (1974) in the United States and Raymond Williams (1975) in England represent major turning points in the mapping of television territory.

It is striking how different is the study of film. Cinema studies approach film with a literary perspective, as texts to be classified and decoded, sociologically, politically, and psychoanalytically.[1] The same kind of classificatory effort has been applied—although not always uncondescendingly—to the other genres of popular culture. In *Adventure, Mystery, Romance* (1976) John Cawelti elaborates on the dominant genres (he prefers to speak of formulas) of popular fiction. In adventure stories—chivalric tales, war novels, mysteries—Cawelti finds the message of triumph over death, injustice, and the dangerous enemy. The classic detective story stands out in his category of mystery and leads the reader to a desirable and rational restoration of order and of pacification of the unknown. Romance teaches the all-sufficiency of love, celebrating monogamy and domesticity.

Following Cawelti, Newcomb (1974) attempted to delve into the formulas of television. This was the first time, to our knowledge, that a scholar classified television programs systematically: he analyzed the programs in each category and generalized about what they had in common. In the process he proposed a much broader generalization: that television, as a medium, imposes an element of "familism" on each of the genres which it has inherited from the other media of popular culture. In other words, says Newcomb, the Western, the action adventure, and the detective story, not just the soap opera or the situation comedy, is domesticated by television as if to attune the medium as a whole to the nuclear family, television's original viewing group.

Television with a Halo

Even those like Williams and Newcomb, who pioneered in the classification of television genres, approach the viewing experience not in terms of discrete programs but in terms of the patterned sequences of stimuli (images, issues, messages, stories) that constitute an evening's viewing. They prefer to speak of "strips" (Newcomb and Hirsch, 1983), "flow" (Williams, 1975), compounded interruption (Houston, 1984), relentless messages (Gerbner et al., 1979), moving wallpaper, and mindless chewing gum (Hood, 1967; Csikszentmihalyi and Kubey, 1981).

Even if it is true that most of television melds into some such seamless "supertext" (Browne, 1984), there are certain types of programs that demand and receive focused attention (Liebes and Katz, 1990). Media events are one such genre. Unique to television, they differ markedly from the genres of the everynight.

Readers will have no trouble identifying the kinds of broadcasts we have in mind.[2] Every nation has them. Our sample of a dozen of these events, internationally, includes the funerals of President Kennedy and Lord Louis Mountbatten, the royal wedding of Charles and Diana, the journeys of Pope John Paul II and Anwar el-Sadat, the debates of 1960 between John Kennedy and Richard Nixon, the Watergate hearings, the revolutionary changes of 1989 in Eastern Europe, the Olympics, and others.

We have studied accounts and video recordings of these events, and have ourselves conducted empirical research into five of them.[3]

The most obvious difference between media events and other formulas or genres of broadcasting is that they are, by definition, not routine. In fact, they are *interruptions* of routine; they intervene in the normal flow of broadcasting and our lives. Like the holidays that halt everyday routines, television events propose exceptional things to think about, to witness, and to do. Regular broadcasting is suspended and preempted as we are guided by a series of special announcements and preludes that transform daily life into something special and, upon the conclusion of the event, are guided back again. In the most characteristic events, the interruption is *monopolistic*, in that all channels switch away from their regularly scheduled programming in order to turn to the great event, perhaps leaving a handful of independent stations outside the consensus. Broadcasting can hardly make a more dramatic announcement of the importance of what is about to happen.

Moreover, the happening is *live*. The events are transmitted as they occur, in real time; the French call this *en direct*. They are therefore unpredictable, at least in the sense that something can go wrong. Even the live broadcast of a symphony orchestra contains this element of tension. Typically, these events are *organized outside the media*, and the media serve them in what Jakobson (1960) would call a phatic role in that, at least theoretically, the media only provide a channel for their transmission. By "outside" we mean both that the events take place outside the studio in what broadcasters call "remote locations" and that the event is not usually initiated by the broadcasting organizations. This kind of connection, in real time, to a remote place—one having major importance to some central value of society, as we shall see—is credited with an exceptional value, by both broadcasters and their audiences (Vianello, 1983). Indeed, the complexity of mounting these broadcasts is such, or is thought to be such, that they are hailed as "miracles" by the broadcasters, as much for their technological as for their ceremonial triumphs (Sorohan, 1979; Russo, 1983).[4]

The organizers, typically, are public bodies with whom the media cooperate, such as governments, parliaments (congressional committees, for example), political parties (national conventions), international bodies (the Olympics committee), and the like. These organizers are well within the establishment. They are part of what Shils (1975) calls the center. They stand for consensual values and they have the authority to command our attention. It is no surprise that the Woodstock festival—the landmark celebration of protesting youth in the sixties—was distributed as a film rather than as a live television event.

Thus, the League of Women Voters and the two major political parties organized the presidential debates in 1976 and 1980; the palace and the Church of England planned and "produced" the royal wedding; the Olympics are staged by the International Olympics Committee. There may be certain exceptions to this rule: the European Broadcasting Union organizes the annual Eurovision Song Contest, for example, and the Super Bowl— the American football championship—involves a direct organizational input on the part of American broadcasters. But on the whole, these events are not organized by the broadcasters even if they are planned with television "in mind." The media are asked, or ask, to join.

Of course, there may well be collusion between broadcasters and organizers, as was evident in the Gerald Ford–Jimmy Carter debate in Philadelphia, for example, when the TV sound failed and the ostensibly local meeting in a hired hall was suspended until the national broadcast could be resumed. And a state-operated broadcasting system (Poland, for example; *not* England or

Israel) may be indistinguishable from the organizers. But the exceptions only serve to prove the rule.

These events are *preplanned*, announced and advertised in advance. Viewers—and, indeed, broadcasters—had only a few days notice of the exact time of Sadat's arrival in Jerusalem (Cohen, 1978); Irish television advertised the Pope's visit to Ireland a few weeks in advance (Sorohan, 1979); the 1984 Los Angeles Olympics were heralded for more than four years. Important for our purpose is that advance notice gives time for anticipation and preparation on the part of both broadcasters and audiences. There is an active period of looking forward, abetted by the promotional activity of the broadcasters.

The conjunction of *live* and *remote*, on the one hand, and *interrupted* but *preplanned*, on the other, takes us a considerable distance toward our definition of the genre. Note that live-and-remote excludes routine studio broadcasts that may originate live, as well as feature programs such as "Roots" or "Holocaust." The addition of interruption excludes the evening news, while preplanned excludes major news events—such as the attempted assassination of a pope or a president, the nuclear accident at Three Mile Island, and, at first glance (but we shall reconsider this), the so-called television revolutions in Romania and Czechoslovakia. In other words, our corpus is limited to ceremonial occasions.

Returning to the elements of definition, we find that these broadcast events are presented with *reverence* and *ceremony*. The journalists who preside over them suspend their normally critical stance and treat their subject with respect, even awe. Garry Wills (1980) called media coverage of the Pope, including that of the written press, "falling in love with love" and "The Greatest Story Ever Told." He was referring to the almost priestly role played by journalists on the occasion, and we find a reverential attitude characteristic of the genre as a whole. We have already noted that the broadcast transports us to some aspect of the sacred center of the society (Shils, 1975).

Of course, the very flow of ceremonial events is courtly and invites awe. There is the playing of the national anthem, the funereal beat of the drum corps, the diplomatic ceremony of being escorted from the plane, the rules of decorum in church and at Senate hearings. The point is that in media events television rarely intrudes: it interrupts only to identify the music being played or the name of the chief of protocol. It upholds the definition of the event by its organizers, explains the meaning of the symbols of the occasion, only rarely intervenes with analysis and almost never with criticism. Often advertising is suspended. There are variations: the live broadcast of Sadat's arrival in Jerusalem was treated differently by Israeli television than by the American networks, which had more explaining to do (Zelizer, 1981). While we shall have occasion to point out these differences, they are outweighed by the similarities.

Even when these programs address conflict—as they do—they celebrate not conflict but *reconciliation*. This is where they differ from the daily news events, where conflict is the inevitable subject. Often they are ceremonial efforts to redress conflict or to restore order or, more rarely, to institute change. They call for a cessation of hostilities, at least for a moment, as when the royal wedding halted the street fighting in Brixton and the terror in Northern Ireland. A more permanent truce followed the journeys of Sadat to Jerusalem and the Pope to Argentina. These events applaud the *voluntary* actions of great personalities. They celebrate what, on the whole, are establishment initiatives that are therefore unquestionably *hegemonic*. They are proclaimed *historic*.

These ceremonials *electrify very large audiences*—a nation, several nations, or the world. They are gripping, enthralling. They are characterized by a *norm of viewing* in which people tell each other that it is mandatory to view, that they must put all else aside. The unanimity of the networks in presenting the same event underlines the worth, even the obligation, of viewing. They cause viewers to *celebrate* the event by gathering before the television set in groups, rather than alone. Often the audience is given an active role in the celebration. Figuratively, at least, these events induce people to dress up, rather than dress down, to view television. These broadcasts *integrate* societies in a collective heartbeat and evoke a *renewal of loyalty* to the society and its legitimate authority.

A More Parsimonious Approach to Definition

Despite its heaviness, we shall argue that the elements in our definition are "necessary," and that no subset of them is "sufficient" without the others.[5] This hypothesis does not mean that the elements cannot exist without one another, but they are not then what we call media events; they are something else.

Consider, for example, the *live* broadcasting of an event which is not *preplanned*—say, the live reporting of the leaking atomic energy plant at Three Mile Island (Veron, 1981). The leakage is a great *news* event, but not one of the great *ceremonial* events that interest us. Thus, we are interested here in the Kennedy funeral—a great ceremonial event—and not the Kennedy assassination—a great news event. The messages of these two broadcasts are different, their effects are different, they are presented in quite a different tone. Great news events speak of accidents, of disruption; great ceremonial events celebrate order and its restoration. In short, great news events are another genre of broadcasting, neighbor to our own, that will help to set the boundaries of media events.[6]

Consider an event that fails to *excite* the public or one that is not presented with *reverence* by the broadcasters. Such events do not qualify according to the definition, but they are particularly interesting because they suggest a pathology of media events, of which the former is an event "manqué" and the latter an event "denied" by the broadcasters. We elaborate on such pathologies in Chapter 3.

Thus, by converting the elements of the definition into a typology—where elements are variously present or absent, or present in varying degree—we can identify alternative genres of broadcasting that differ from one another by virtue of a particular element. Examination of these alternative forms and the conditions of their occurrence will help define our own events by providing boundary markers.

One additional operation, methodologically speaking, can be performed on the definition. By transforming the elements into variables, one can note which elements correlate with which others. Doing so, one might ask whether, say, the degree of *reverence* invoked by the presenter correlates with the degree of viewer *enthrallment*.

Presentation of the genre can be formulated more elegantly, by grouping the elements of the definition into broader categories. The linguistic categories of syntactics, semantics, and pragmatics are useful for this purpose.

Syntactically, media events may be characterized, first, by our elements of interruption, monopoly, being broadcast live, and being remote. These are components of the "grammar" of broadcasting. The cancellation of regularly scheduled programs and the convergence of channels are the most dramatic kinds of punctuation available to broadcasters. They put a full stop to everything else on the air; they combine the cacophony of many simultaneous channels into one monophonic line. Of course, these elements also carry semantic meaning: they speak of the greatness of the event. And they have a pragmatic aspect as well:

the interruption of the sequence of television puts a stop to the normal flow of life.

The live and remote broadcast takes us back and forth between the studio and some faraway place. Such broadcasts employ special rhetorical forms and the technology required to connect the event and the studio. The language is the language of transportation—"We take you now to . . ." Both pictures and words are slowed to a ceremonial pace, and aesthetic considerations are unusually important. The pictures of media events, relative to their words, carry much more weight than the balance to which we are accustomed in the nightly news, where words are far more important than pictures (Altman, 1986; Katz, Adoni, and Parness, 1977). The centrality of these various elements of syntax is immediately apparent when one compares the event itself to each subsequent representation of the event—the wrap-up, the news, and the eventual anniversaries: length is drastically cut; pace is speeded up; words reassert their importance; references to the heroic logistics of the broadcast disappear. Syntactic unpredictability (that matches the semantic uncertainty) is smoothed over.

The fact that the event is situated *outside* broadcasting organizations, both physically and organizationally, implies a network of connections that differ from the everyday. The specialists of outside broadcasting deploy their OB units—as the British call them—and the studio now serves as intermediary between its people in the field and the audience, allowing some of the dialogue of stage directions between studio and field to become part of the spectacle. Their cadence is *reverential* and *ceremonial*.

The interruption, when it comes, has been elaborately advertised and *rehearsed*. It entails a major commitment of manpower, technology, and resources on the part of organizers and broadcasters. It comes not as a complete surprise—as in major newsbreaks—but as something long anticipated and looked forward to, like a holiday. In order to make certain that the point of this ritual framing will not be lost on the audience, the broadcasters spend hours, sometimes days, rehearsing the audience in the event's itinerary, timetable, and symbolics. Even one-time events can be ritualized in this way.

The meaning of the event—its semantic dimension—is typically proposed by its organizers and shared by the broadcasters—although this point requires elaboration (see Chapter 4). Of course, each event is specific in this regard. For example, the royal wedding was proposed as a Cinderella story, the moon landings as the new American frontier, and the papal diplomacy as a pilgrimage. Regardless of the specifics of each event, the genre as a whole contains a set of core meanings, often loudly proclaimed. Thus, all such events are hailed as *historic*; they strive to mark a new record, to change an old way of doing or thinking, or to mark the passing of an era. Whether it is the Olympics or Watergate, Sadat or the Pope, the turning-point character of the event is central.

The event features the performance of symbolic acts that have relevance for one or more of the core values of society (Lukes, 1975). By dint of the cooperation between organizers and broadcasters, the event is presented with *ceremonial reverence*, in tones that express sacrality and awe.

The message is one of *reconciliation*, in which participants and audiences are invited to unite in the overcoming of conflict or at least in its postponement or miniaturization. Almost all of these events have heroic figures around whose *initiatives* the reintegration of society is proposed.

Pragmatically, the event *enthralls very large audiences*. A nation or several nations, sometimes the entire world, may be stirred while watching the superhuman achievement of an

Olympic star or an astronaut. Sadat electrified the people of Israel, and the Pope revived the spirit of the Polish people. These are thrilling events, reaching the largest audiences in the history of the world. They are shared experiences, uniting viewers with one another and with their societies. A *norm of viewing* accompanies the airing of these events. As the day approaches, people tell one another that viewing is obligatory, that no other activity is acceptable during the broadcast. Viewers actively *celebrate*, preferring to view in the company of others and to make special preparations—unusual food, for example—in order to partake more fully in the event.

The genre is best defined, then, at the intersection of the syntactic, the semantic, and the pragmatic. And, as was argued above, we shall contend that all three elements are "necessary." If we chose to apply the pragmatic criterion alone, the events so defined would include television programs that enthralled very large audiences, such as the early miniseries or perhaps even key episodes of programs such as "Dallas." They might also include films that attracted large, sometimes cultish audiences such as the *Rocky Horror Picture Show* or *Woodstock*; these were indeed compulsory viewing for certain segments of the population and invited widespread participation. If syntactics were the sole criterion, major news events would demand to be included. By the same token, if the genre were defined in terms of the semantic alone, we should number among media events all those films and programs that claim to be historic, preach reconciliation, celebrate initiative, and are produced and presented with reverence. Films of the Olympics by Leni Riefenstahl, Kon Ichikawa, or Claude Lelouch, for example, might therefore qualify.

Hence our insistence on defining the corpus of events in terms of all three linguistic categories, an insistence further justified by the fact that we are dealing with ceremonial performances and that no such performance can be described in terms of its text alone. A ceremony interrupts the flow of daily life (syntactics); it deals reverently with sacred matters (semantics); and it involves the response (pragmatics) of a committed audience.

Why Study Media Events?

Implicit in this definition of the genre are answers to the question, Why study media events? The student of modern society—not just of television—will find a dozen or more powerful reasons for doing so. Let us spell them out.

1. The live broadcasting of these television events attracts the *largest audiences in the history of the world.* Lest we be misunderstood, we are talking about audiences as large as 500 million people attending to the same stimulus at the same time, at the moment of its emission. It is conceivable that there were cumulative audiences of this size prior to the electronic age—for the Bible, for example. Perhaps one might have been able to say that there were several hundred million people alive on earth who had read, or heard tell of, the same Book. But it was not until radio broadcasting—and home radio receivers—that simultaneity of exposure became possible. The enormity of this audience, together with the awareness by all of its enormity, is awesome. It is all the more awesome when one realizes that the subject of these broadcasts is ceremony, the sort which anthropologists would find familiar if it were not for the scale. Some of these ceremonies are so all-encompassing that there is nobody left to serve as out-group. "We Are the World" is certainly the appropriate theme song for media events. To enthrall such a multitude is no mean feat; to enlist their assent defies all of the caveats of media-effects research.[7]

2. The power of these events lies, first of all, in the rare *realization of the full potential of electronic media technology*. Students of media effects know that at most times and places this potential of radio and television is restricted by society. In principle, radio and television are capable of reaching everybody simultaneously and directly; their message, in other words, can be total, immediate, and unmediated. But this condition hardly ever obtains. Messages are multiple; audiences are selective; social networks intervene; diffusion takes time. On the occasion of media events, however, these intervening mechanisms are suspended. Interpersonal networks and diffusion processes are active before and after the event, mobilizing attention to the event and fostering intense hermeneutic activity over its interpretation. But during the liminal moments, totality and simultaneity are unbound; organizers and broadcasters resonate together; competing channels merge into one; viewers present themselves at the same time and in every place. All eyes are fixed on the ceremonial center, through which each nuclear cell is connected to all the rest. Social integration of the highest order is thus achieved via mass communication. During these rare moments of intermission, society is both as atomized and as integrated as a mass-society theorist might ever imagine (Kornhauser, 1959).

3. Thus, the media have power not only to insert messages into social networks but to create the networks themselves—to atomize, to integrate, or otherwise to design social structure—at least momentarily. We have seen that *media events may create their own constituencies*. Egypt and Israel were united for Sadat's visit not only by images of the arrival of the leader of a theretofore hostile Arab nation, but by means of an ad hoc microwave link between the broadcasting systems of the two countries.[8] Similarly, the royal wedding reunited the British Empire, and

Third World nations joined the first two worlds for the Olympics. That media events can talk over and around conventional political geography reminds us that media technology is too often overlooked by students of media effects in their distrust of hypotheses of technological determinism. Papyrus and ancient empire, print and the Protestant Reformation, the newspaper and European nationalism, the telegraph and the economic integration of American markets, are links between attributes of communication technologies and social structures. They connect portability, reproducibility, linearity, simultaneity, on the one hand, to empire, church, nation, market, on the other.

By extension, it can be seen that the "center" of these media-engendered social structures is not bound by geography either. In the case of media events, the center—on which all eyes are focused—is the place where the organizer of a "historic" ceremony joins with a skilled broadcaster to produce an event. In this sense, Britain is often the center of the world; one has only to compare the broadcast funeral of the assassinated Mountbatten with the broadcast funeral of the assassinated Sadat or India's Indira Gandhi to understand why.

4. Conquering not only space but time, media events have the power to declare a holiday, thus to play a part in the *civil religion*. Like religious holidays, major media events mean an interruption of routine, days off from work, norms of participation in ceremony and ritual, concentration on some central value, the experience of communitas and equality in one's immediate environment and of integration with a cultural center. The reverent tones of the ceremony, the dress and demeanor of those gathered in front of the set, the sense of communion with the mass of viewers, are all reminiscent of holy days. The ceremonial roles assumed by viewers—mourner, citizen, juror, sports fan—differentiate holiday viewing from everyday viewing

and transform the nature of involvement with the medium. The secret of the effectiveness of these televised events, we believe, is in the roles which viewers bring with them from other institutions, and by means of which passive spectatorship gives way to ceremonial participation. The depth of this involvement, in turn, has relevance for the formation of public opinion and for institutions such as politics, religion, and leisure. In a further step, they enter the collective memory.

5. *Reality is uprooted* by media events. If an event originates in a particular location, that location is turned into a Hollywood set. The "original" is only a studio. Thus conquering space in an even more fundamental way, television causes events to move off the ground and "into the air." The era of television events, therefore, may be not only one in which the reproduction is as important as the original, as Benjamin (1968) proposed, but also one in which the reproduction is more important than the original.

Sometimes the original is inaccessible to live audiences because it is taking place in London, or because it is taking place on the moon, for example. Even more fundamental are those events that have no original anywhere because the broadcast is a montage originating in several different locations simultaneously. The "reality" of Kennedy's debating Nixon when one was in New York and the other in California is not diminished for its being in the air, and in the living room. Prince Charles, at the church, is waiting for Lady Diana as her carriage is drawn through the streets of London. This is reality. But it is an invisible reality that cannot be apprehended as such because it is happening simultaneously at different places. No one person can see all of it, that is, except the television director and hundreds of millions in their homes.

6. The process of producing these events and telling their story relates to the arts of television, journalism, and narration.

Study of the rhetorical devices for communicating festivity, enlisting participation, and mobilizing consensus demands answers to the questions of how television manages to project ritual and ceremony in the two-dimensional space of spectacle. Essential to an understanding of these events—in addition to the readiness of the audience to assume ceremonial roles—is an analysis of how the story is framed, how interest is sustained, how the event aggregates endorsements, how the broadcasting staff is deployed to give depth to the event, how viewers interact with the screen, what tasks are assigned to the viewers. Media events give insight into the *aesthetics of television production*, together with an awareness of the nature of the contract that obtains between organizers and broadcasters.

The audience is aware of the genre of media events. We (and certain fellow researchers) recognize the constituent features of this rare but recurrent narrative form, and so do producers and viewers. The professional networks of producers buzz with information on the extraordinary mobilization of manpower, technology, aesthetics, and security arrangements required to mount a media event.[9] At the same time, the networks of viewers carry word of the attitudes, rehearsals, and roles appropriate to their celebration. The expectation that certain events in the real world will be given media-events treatment is proof of public awareness of the genre. Israelis appealed to the High Court of Justice demanding that the war-crimes trial of John Demjanjuk be broadcast live.[10]

7. Shades of *political spectacle*. Are media events, then, electronic incarnations of the staged events of revolutionary regimes and latter-day versions of the mass rallies of fascism? We think not, even if they might seem to be. It is true that media events find society in a vulnerable state as far as indoctrination is concerned: divided into nuclear cells of family and friends, disconnected from the institutions of work and voluntary association,

eyes and ears focused on the monopolistic message of the center, hearts prepared with room. This is reminiscent, mutatis mutandis, of the social structure of a disaster that strikes at night, or of a brainwashing regimen. The threshold of suggestibility is at its lowest the more isolated the individual is from others, the more accessible he or she is to the media, the more dependent the person is, the more the power to reward conformity or punish deviation is in the hands of the communicator.

Nevertheless, media events are not simply political manipulations. Broadcasters—in Western societies—are independent of, or at least legally differentiated from, government. They can, and sometimes do, say no to an establishment proposal to mount an event. Journalists need convincing before suspending professional disbelief, and even commercial interest sometimes acts as a buffer. Second, public approval is required for an event to succeed; official events cannot be imposed on the unwilling or unbelieving. Third, individuals are not alone, not even alone with family, but in the company of others whom they invite to join in the thrill of an event and then to sit in judgment of it. Some societies provide public space for such discussion and interpretation; others provide only living rooms and telephones. Family friends, home, and living-room furniture are not a likely context for translating aroused emotion into collective political action. Fourth, the audience, too, has veto power. Oppositional readings are possible and hegemonic messages may be read upside down by some. These checks and balances filter the manipulative potential of media events and limit the vulnerability of mass audiences.[11]

Still, the question of hegemonic abuse must be asked continually. Almost all of these events are establishment initiated, and only rarely, one suspects, do the broadcasters say no. Instead, journalists—sometimes reluctantly—put critical distance aside in favor of the reverent tones of presenters. Broadcasters thus share the consensual occasion with the organizers and satisfy the public—so we have hypothesized—that they are patriots after all.

8. When media events are seen as a *response to prior events* or to social crisis, the link to public opinion is evident. Thus, certain media events have a commemorative function, reminding us—as on anniversaries—of what deserves to be remembered. Others have a restorative function following social trauma. The most memorable of them have a transformative function inasmuch as they illustrate or enact possible solutions to social problems, sometimes engendering yet further events which actually "change the world." In the restorative domain, media events address social conflict—through emphasizing the rules (as in Contests), through praising the deeds of the great in whom charisma is invested (Conquests), and through celebrating consensual values (as do Coronations).

9. At the same time, certain events have an *intrinsically liberating* function, ideologically speaking; they serve a transformative function. However hegemonically sponsored, and however affirmatively read, they invite reexamination of the status quo and are a reminder that reality falls short of society's norm. Taking place in a liminal context, evoking that climate of intense reflexivity which Victor Turner characterized as the "subjunctive mode of culture," their publics exit the everyday world and experience a shattering of perceptions and certainties. Even if the situations in which they are immersed are short-lived and do not institutionalize new norms, at least they provoke critical awareness of the taken-for-granted and mental appraisal of alternative possibilities. They possess a normative dimension in the sense of displaying desirable alternatives, situations which "ought to" exist but do not. These are previews, foretastes of the perhaps possible, fragments of a future in which

the members of society are invited to spend a few hours or a few days. Activating latent aspirations, they offer a peek into utopia.

10. One wonders whether the media-events genre is not an expression of a *neo-romantic desire for heroic action* by great men followed by the spontaneity of mass action. In this sense, media events go beyond journalism in highlighting charisma and collective action, in defiance of established authority. The dissatisfaction with official inaction and bureaucratic ritualism, the belief in the power of the people to do it themselves, the yearning for leadership of stature—all characterize media events. We can join Sadat or the Pope and change the world; the people can unite to save Africans from starvation by supporting "Live Aid." The celebration of voluntarism—the willful resolve to take direct, simple, spontaneous, ostensibly nonideological action—underlies media events, and may indeed constitute part of their attraction. The desire for spontaneous action, of course, recalls the erratic rhythm of arousal and repose predicted by the theory of mass society (Kornhauser, 1959). In the telling of media events, establishment heroes are made to appear more defiant than they actually were. But media events and collective action may be more than a dream. The escalation of interaction among public opinion, new or old leadership, and the mass media fanned the revolutions of Eastern Europe in the fall of 1989.[12]

11. The *rhetoric of media events* is instructive, too, for what it reveals not only about the difference between democratic and totalitarian ceremonies, but also about the difference between journalism and social science, and between popular and academic history. The media events of democracies—the kind we consider here—are persuasive occasions, attempting to enlist mass support; they take the form of political contests or of the live broadcasting of heroic missions—those that invite the pub-

lic to embrace heroes who have put their lives and reputations on the line in the cause of a proposed change.[13] The ceremonies of totalitarian societies (Lane, 1981) are more commemorative. They also seek to enlist support, but for present and past; the First of May parade was a more characteristic media event in postwar Eastern Europe (Lendvay, Tolgyesi, and Tomka, 1982) than a space shot.[14] Terrorist events contrast with both of these in their display not of persuasion but of force, not of majesty but of disruption and provocation.

The rhetoric of media events contrasts—as does journalism, generally—with academic rhetoric in its emphasis on great individuals and apocalyptic events. Where social science sees long-run deterministic processes, journalism prefers heroes or villains who get up one morning resolved to change the world. Where academic historians see events as projective of underlying trends, journalists prefer a stroboscopic history which flashes dramatic events on and off the screen.

12. Media events *privilege the home*. This is where the "historic" version of the event is on view, the one that will be entered into collective memory. Normally the home represents a retreat from the space of public deliberation, and television is blamed, perhaps rightly, for celebrating family and keeping people home (Newcomb, 1974). When it is argued that television presents society with the issues it has to face, the retort, "narcotizing dysfunction"—that is, the false consciousness of involvement and participation—is quick to follow (Lazarsfeld and Merton, 1948). Yet the home may become a public space on the occasion of media events, a place where friends and family meet to share in both the ceremony and the deliberation that follows. Observational research needs to be done on the workings of these political "salons." Ironically, critical theorists, newly alert to the feminist movement, now see in the soap opera and other

family programs an important "site of gender struggle," and their derision of the apolitical home is undergoing revision.

But there is more to politics than feminism, and we need empirical answers to the question of whether the home is transformed into a political space during and after a media event. In fact, we need basic research on who is home and when (in light of the growing number of one- and two-person households), who views with whom, who talks with whom, how opinion is formed, and how it is fed back to decision-makers. These everyday occasions of opinion formation should then be compared with media events. It is hard to believe, but nevertheless true, that the study of public opinion has become disconnected from the study of mass communication.

13. Media events preview the *future of television*. When radio became a medium of segmentation—subdividing audiences by age and education—television replaced it as the medium of national integration. As the new media technology multiplies the number of channels, television will also become a medium of segmentation, and television-as-we-know-it will disappear. The function of national integration may devolve upon television ceremonies of the sort we are discussing here. By that time, however, the nation-state itself may be on the way out, its boundaries out of sync with the new media technology. Media events may then create and integrate communities larger than nations. Indeed, the genre of media events may itself be seen as a response to the integrative needs of national and, increasingly, international communities and organizations.

Certain multinational interests have already spotted the potential of international events and may sink the genre in the process. Some combination of the televised Olympics and televised philanthropic marathons inspired the effort to enlist worldwide aid to combat famine in Africa. Satellite broadcasters already transmit live sports events multinationally (Uplinger, 1990; but see Mytton, 1991). Aroused collective feeling must be a great lure to advertisers, and one wonders whether the entry of the commercial impresario into the arena of these events does not augur ill for their survival as necessarily occasional, and heavily value-laden, "high holidays."

2

Scripting Media Events: Contest, Conquest, Coronation

As we have said, the corpus of events can be subdivided into Contests, Conquests, and Coronations. These are story forms, or "scripts," which constitute the main narrative possibilities within the genre. They determine the distribution of roles within each type of event and the ways in which they will be enacted. Venturing beyond the exposition of this typology, we shall propose that the three story forms are dramatic embodiments of Weber's (1946) three types of authority; in other words, that rationality, charisma, and tradition are inscribed respectively in Contest, Conquest, and Coronation.

Certain events do not altogether correspond to any one of the three dominant scenarios, while other events appear to switch in midstream, as if they were conceived in terms of competing scripts. All media events, finally, even those which strongly adhere to a given script, nevertheless contain echoes of other scripts which loom in the background or are given secondary status. The questions of how such scripts are chosen will also occupy us in this chapter and the next.

Three Basic Scripts

It was television's Sadat who first aroused our interest in media events. Initially, it was the specifics of this rare example of media diplomacy that seemed worthy of analysis. But the similarities between the Sadat journey in 1977 and the earlier moon journey were irresistible, and we soon found ourselves comparing Anwar el-Sadat and Menachem Begin with the astronauts (Katz, 1978). Here were heroes pushing back a frontier, overcoming ostensible laws of nature and society. There were similarities in the ceremonies of departure and arrival, in the dramatic tension of risk of life and reputation, in the moments of triumph, in the use of biblical quotations, and not least, in the epic prose and pictures provided by television to accompany progress in real time. And soon we were comparing both the moon landing and Sadat with the journeys of the Pope.

This is the formula we call Conquest—the live broadcasting of "giant leaps for mankind." These are rare events, indeed, both in occurrence and in effectiveness. Life is not the same after a televised Conquest—because of the great achievement itself, and because of the great broadcast of the great achievement.

Contests range from the World Cup to presidential debates, from the Olympics to the Senate Watergate hearings. Their domain is sports and politics. They are rule-governed battles of champions. They enlist hundreds of millions of spectators. Sometimes they are defined as play, sometimes as real, but the stakes are always very high. The political conventions of 1952 were among the first events of this kind in the United States,[1] while the televised hearings of Senator Estes Kefauver's subcommittee investigation of organized crime were an early pretest (Friendly, 1967; Russo, 1983).

Coronations are parades (funerals, for example). While both Conquests and Contests include strong ceremonial ingredients, Coronations are all ceremony. The genre is spiced with royal events from the coronation of Elizabeth II to the wedding of Prince Charles.[2] The homecoming of General Douglas MacArthur in 1951 was the first television coronation (Lang and Lang, 1953).[3] The funeral of John Kennedy, probably the most moving of all events of this kind, brings to mind other state funerals such as those of Lord Mountbatten and Indira Gandhi. Mutatis mutandis, minor events such as Hollywood's annual Academy Awards (Arlen, 1979; Real, 1977) are included here as well.

As we proceed, it will be shown that these three forms are closely intertwined. Indeed, the most dramatic cases speak of an initial Contest, then a Conquest, and finally a Coronation— just as in fairy tales (Propp, 1968; Bettelheim, 1975). Consider the moon landings, for example. They began as a Contest between the United States and the Soviet Union when the first Sputnik was launched into space. Ten years later, as advertised, came the American Conquest of the moon. Finally (but long anticipated) the astronaut heroes were crowned and recrowned by society and the media (Wolfe, 1980). Less spectacular events also display this merging of forms. The Academy Awards are a Coronation, but their origin is in Contest. Sometimes all three phases are the subject of a television event or series of events. More often, however, only one phase is celebrated in a live broadcast, which anticipates or recalls or reconstructs the other phases.

Heroic Events and Play

Television uses these formulas to tell its stories, but television obviously did not invent them. Neither did literature. They are on view in myth, in children's games, in history books. The events that concern us are situated close to the border between play and reality. They are constituted of elements of both. Watergate, John Paul II in Poland, and the royal wedding were undeniably real and influential, although they were also cere- monially enacted and ceremonially witnessed. The Super Bowl, the setting of an Olympic record, and the crowning of Miss

America—playful as they may seem—also have a bearing on society and culture. The most dramatic events appear at moments of crisis and speak to a conflict that threatens society. The more routine events, like all ritual occasions, recall and reiterate basic values of the society and offer a shared focus of attention and at least vicarious participation.

"The two ever-recurring forms in which civilization grows in, and as, play are the sacred performances and the festal contest," says Johann Huizinga (1950), arguing that competitive games (our Contests) and exhibitions (Coronations) do not proceed from culture but precede it in the play forms of animals and children. In adopting these forms, societies invest them with religious meaning and use them to placate gods and ancestors, to mark the seasons, to accumulate and boast of honor through heroic deed and display, to promote unity and collective memory.

Contests are a training ground for the construction of social institutions based on rules. Disputing Jakob Burkhardt, who thought that the contest was unique to Greece, Huizinga sees the play principle of "agon" (contest) as universal.[4] This "agonistic" phase of Greek culture is said to be a sublimation of an earlier "heroic" temper that expressed itself—but also spent itself—in real battle.

Huizinga suggests that even exhibition may originate, ultimately, in Contest. The bragging of the peacock, "a stepping out," says Huizinga (p. 13), sometimes accompanied by dance steps, or the triumphant victory parade are representations of contests, or allusions to them. In this sense, the splendid funerals of heroes—Kennedy and Mountbatten, for example—may be read as defiant declarations. For Huizinga, then, our formula of Coronation is also associated with Contest.

Stories of Conquest are equally primordial.[5] Students of folktales, such as Propp (1968) and Greimas (1966), incorporate

Conquests in their semiotic schemes for analysis of the journeys, trials, and triumphs of heroes in the process of restoring
order. Reformulating Propp, Greimas identifies three turning
points in the career of the hero that correspond to our three types
of events. One serves to "qualify" the hero (our Contest); a second shows the hero reaching beyond human limits (Conquest);
the third sets the stage for recognition and "glorification" of the
hero (Coronation).

Stephenson's (1967) "play theory of mass communication"
anticipates our discussion. Almost alone among students of
opinion and communication, Stephenson's theory views the
media as agents of play, and play as an agent of socialization.[6]
In a passage on the deaths of President Kennedy and Pope John
XXIII, Stephenson says (p. 59):

> Here was a tragedy, and a goodness, each on an Olympian
> scale, gripping the world—transcending creed, color or ide-
> ology. Each was universal. The one touched youth and the
> other age, and both pulled at the deepest primitive feelings
> . . . One may doubt the reality of these men; one can be sure
> that myth more than truth surrounded Kennedy's impact. But
> that both touched the world massively and deeply cannot be
> doubted.
>
> The cynic will say the mass reactions to the deaths were
> mere emotional binges, weekends of sobbing and pathos sig-
> nifying nothing. I would rather think of each, instead, as an
> example of primitive communication, of primitive comrade-
> ship, of primitive communication pleasure. Each was en-
> joyed, as a wake is. Surely, too, the events seemed to make
> little difference, everyone going on his way afterwards, as
> before. But was the self of anyone quite the same afterwards?
> . . . We are indeed not a little self improved.

Given the borderline status of these narrative forms between
documentary and fiction, the televising of such events serves to

highlight the way audiences are provoked to teeter between reality and play, and being there and being home. Television, the medium of popular fiction, invites us on such occasions to approach the screen in a different mood, as if to transform the set into a ceremonial object in the way that the dining-room table is made festive on holidays by adding extra leaves and the best tablecloth. But the very framing of these events on the nonetheless familiar small screen, and the "as if" invitation to "be there," qualify the reality of the events by miniaturizing them, embroidering them in the narrative form of fairy tale and romance, and asking us to suspend disbelief. "Hurry, they are just landing on the moon!" Or are they? "You are there!" Or are we? Realists such as Boorstin (1964) dismiss these as pseudo-events, theatrical games manufactured for and by the media, and critics such as Edelman (1989) warn that all dramatized events are distractions from the gnawing truths of chronic problems. Romantics consider them an alternative, maybe even a higher, form of reality. Sadat's gesture would find strong support among students of "the play element in culture" and students of the role of ceremony in politics. Edelman notwithstanding, the most interesting of them—as we shall show—speak to basic values and social arrangements. Yet they do so in rhetorical forms that are associated with fantasy.[7]

On the Retelling of Heroic Events

The story of an event cannot be told without form, and the form carries meaning. History cannot, apparently, be separated from its own retellings (White, 1973), nor can journalism escape this truth.[8] It follows that the retellings (and retellings and retellings) that characterize television's great events deserve careful analysis. Sometimes the organizer of an event "names" it; sometimes television does; sometimes various labels are applied. And the naming has strong bearing on the telling, although there is a tension here as well; the Pope's visits are called "pilgrimages," but television does not always present them that way.[9]

When critics of television say, too mightily, that news is entertainment and entertainment is news, they mean in part that the two genres often draw on the same narrative forms and consequently transmit the same messages. Indeed, they are on view not just on the special occasions with which this book deals, but every day and night. The heroic Contest, for example, underlies the quiz, the game show, the beauty contest, the sports match. The rules are well known, the form is familiar, and such programs are sometimes broadcast live. What makes an event new, and electrifying, is the enhanced status of its personae: the two nominees for the presidency of the United States, for example, or the two contestants for heavyweight champion of the world.

Conquests, too, find a daily echo in the "missions impossible" of television, in the exploits of dashing, daring heroes acting singlehandedly against all odds. The images of Sadat's entry into Jerusalem or the Pope's first minutes in Poland are already familiar to viewers of Westerns. These are heroes of a new sort entering the enemy camp unarmed, relying against all odds on the sheer strength of their convictions, confident in their power to redefine the situation, ready to submit themselves and their charisma to an ordeal.

Coronations might seem a less easy fit; but that is not the case. The rites of passage of heroes—their weddings, deaths, appointments to office—have their mundane echoes in the soap operas that melodramatize the vicissitudes of lesser notables as they make their way through the stations of life. The British royal family, for its part, has provided us with a steady flow of such events, beginning with the abdication of Edward for the love of a commoner, through the coronation of Elizabeth in 1952—the first great television event—and continuing to the investiture of Charles as Prince of Wales (Blumler et al., 1971), the Queen's silver jubilee, the Mountbatten funeral, and the royal wedding.

When the television networks mount a great event, they do not typically mobilize their entertainment division or drama department; they turn, rather, to the department of news and public affairs—for, officially, it is in charge of reality. Ostensibly the narrative resources are different; but, as we have already noted, this is not the case. The wars and the shootouts, the climbings of Everest, the red carpets at the airport for visiting heads of state, are nightly staples in most of the world. These mundane events are the Contests, Conquests, and Coronations of the eleven o'clock news.

In employing these forms to script the major events, television can count not only on their familiarity to audiences but on the expectations of audiences. In his discussion of the aesthetics of live television, Umberto Eco (1989, pp. 119–121) ponders why the director prefers to tell an unfolding story in a familiar (closed) form rather than treat it as open, as chancy, as not-yet-known. "The interpretation of something that is happening to us now and to which we must immediately respond—or that we must immediately describe televisually—may well be one of those cases in which the more conventional response is also the most effective," says Eco. "The public will demand it, and the TV director will feel compelled to give it to them."

The difference, then, between the special events that concern us and everyday television is not in the unfamiliarity of their scenes or their underlying themes, but in their proclaimed historicity. They are events narrated—but supposedly not created—by television; their origin is not in the secular routines of the media but in the "sacred center" (Shils, 1975) that endows them with the authority to preempt our time and attention. It is in this sense that they constitute high holidays connecting us to the center. The public is invited, but they are events that would presumably take place even if there were no television audience—the prince would be married, Kennedy would be buried, Sadat would come to Jerusalem. We are interested, of course, not just in what these events do to and for television, but in what television does to them, and to us.

A Typology of Television Events

Table 1 looks more closely at the characteristics of these three types of events. As an example of Contest, consider the presidential debates; for Coronation, think of the funerals of Mountbatten or Kennedy; for Conquest, recall the case of Sadat, or the Pope's first trip to Warsaw. (The following discussion—all of which refers to Table 1—is better served by the sequence Contest, Coronation, Conquest than that of Contest, Conquest, Coronation.)

Contests pit evenly matched individuals or teams against each other and bid them to compete according to strict rules. Such games, say Huizinga (1950) and Caillois (1961), are freely entered into by the contestants; typically, participation is not obligatory unless the Contest is a ritual or a mandatory event such as a trial. They are circumscribed in time and place, and thus represent a certain stepping out of everyday life. The rules are known both to the competitors and to the spectators, who are as much a part of the game as the contestants or the referee. Indeed, Caillois insists that every competition is also a spectacle that proceeds according to dramatic rules and requires the presence of an audience to "crowd about the ticket windows" and applaud "for each point being scored" (p. 74). Most Contests are regularly recurrent, in the sense that the Olympic Games or the national political conventions are held once every four years at a given season. The televised Contests between Senator Joseph

Table 1 Dimensions of Contests, Conquests, and Coronations

Dimension	Type of event		
	Contest	Conquest	Coronation
1. Periodicity	Fixed (cyclical)	Not fixed (one time)	Not fixed (recurrent)
2. Rules	Agreed rules	No rules	Custom, tradition
3. Locus (stage)	Arena, stadium, forum, studio	Thresholds of social space, frontiers, limits	Streets, church aisles, urban itineraries
4. Opponents	Man *vs.* man	Hero *vs.* norms, beliefs, nature	Ritual *vs.* reality; persons *vs.* symbols
5. Odds	Even	Against hero	Against ritual
6. Drama	Who will win?	Will hero succeed?	Will ritual succeed? Is principal deserving of these sacred symbols? Can reality be kept out?

7. Role of principal	Playing by the rules. Best man will prevail. Loser has another chance	Recasting the rules. Allowing discontinuity. Giant leap for mankind	Embodying the rules. Symbolizing continuity
8. Role of TV presenter	Nonpartisan	Bardic	Reverent, priestly
9. Role of audience	Judging	Witnessing: being awestruck; investing hero with charisma; withholding disbelief	Renewing contract with center; pledging allegiance
10. Message	Rules are supreme	Rules can be changed	Rules are traditionbound
11. Form of authority	Rational-legal	Charismatic	Traditional
12. Relation to conflict management	Frames, miniaturizes, humanizes conflict	Overcomes conflict via suprapartisan identification	Offers intermission from conflict by invoking basic values of society
13. Time orientation	Present	Future	Past

McCarthy and the United States Army,[10] or the Senate Watergate hearings, on the other hand, are obviously not cyclical events; only their grandeur distinguishes them from the routines of regular congressional hearings and courtroom sessions. Students of play would include juridical events among the Contests (Huizinga, 1950), as would we.

Presidential debates, for example, meet the criteria of periodicity, agreed rules, evenly matched opponents.[11] The debates pose the dramatic question, "Who will win?" Their message is that the rules reign supreme, that the rules are more important than the will or status of the opponents, that the best man will prevail, that the loser will have another chance. They transpose conflict from an actual but vaguely defined field of battle, one where direct confrontation rarely takes place, to a framed arena in which the rivals face each other to sharpen, but circumscribe, their differences. The 1960 debates dramatically showed that political institutions could be designed to overcome the process of selectivity, whereby politicians were able to reach and persuade their own partisans (Katz and Feldman, 1962).[12] Contests communicate that the other side, too, deserves to be taken seriously.

Like Contests, *Coronations* proceed according to strict rules, dictated by tradition rather than by negotiated agreement (see Table 1). Since they deal in the mysteries of rites of passage, they pit society and culture against nature. The leader is dead, says the funeral, but society will not succumb.[13] Freedom of choice has brought the prince and his lady together, says the royal wedding, but they cannot unite without the ceremony which society will witness. The tension of Coronation has to do with the magic of ritual: "Will it work?" Or will it be undermined by some ceremonial slip?

Huizinga (1950, p. 56) says that this tension also applies to ritualized contests whose smooth running relates, magically, to the smooth running of societies. Coronations, more than other events, keep their distance from reality, since time and place and ceremonial symbols must all be kept unpolluted. Coronations remind societies of their cultural heritage, provide reassurance of social and cultural continuity, and invite the public to take stock. The weekend of mourning after Kennedy's assassination was a reaffirmation of basic American values, raising reflexive doubts about the direction in which the society had been going, and giving tangible evidence that the succession was assured. The Mountbatten funeral meant to show the restraint and elegance with which British society responds to threat, with a sidelong glance toward the once glorious dream of Empire, which had to be buried again.[14] It held up for admiration a man whose greatness embodied strands of ascription and achievement, of victory and martyrdom.

Conquests are one-time events (even if we are stressing their repeatability as genre). Unlike Contests and Coronations, Conquests tend to break rules (see Table 1). The great man defies the heretofore accepted restrictions: he proposes to visit hostile enemy territory; he surmounts known human limitations; he aims a slingshot at a giant. "Will he succeed?" is what everybody wants to know as he crosses the frontier.[15] The message of Conquest is that great men and women still reside among us, and that history is in their hands. Some people get up in the morning, decide to do or say something, and the world tomorrow is a different place. The principals of Conquest, of course, are not just anyone. They are endowed with charisma and submit themselves to an ordeal, whose success multiplies their charisma and creates a new following. Thus, what we call Conquest may be defined in terms of the two dimensions of this type of ordeal: (1) the reaching beyond known limits through an act of free will, and (2) the resulting charismatic seduction.

The Role of Television

Television not only confers roles upon principals and viewers, but serves as simultaneous commentator and subtitler of the event. The more remote the viewer from the event—physically and psychologically—the more the broadcasters help to "bring home" its meaning and enliven that meaning with interest and relevance.

In the case of Contests, television typically underscores the rivalry between the competing sides. Research has shown that the same match narrated as a drama of long-standing animosity between the players can increase the excitement of the television audience (Comiskey, Bryant, and Zillman, 1977). It is no coincidence that national rivalries play such an important part in the narration of the Olympic Games. The way in which television leaves the podium of a national political convention to wander the floor of the auditorium and the lobbies of the various hotels in search of its own convention has been widely commented upon and often severely (and, in our opinion, unjustly) criticized (Gurevitch, 1977).

In the case of Coronations, television rehearses the audience in the ceremony they are about to witness, carefully spelling out the meaning of the symbols, framing the event by separating it from daily life, monumentalizing it, upholding its official definition, and offering a story line and commentary to shape its interpretations. Thus, television scripted a Cinderella story for Lady Diana and a Lincoln story for Kennedy. Television's performance of these events is elaborated in Chapter 4.

In Conquests, television broadcasters invite the public to witness an almost impossible undertaking. They spotlight a deadlocked situation that requires extraordinary measures, stressing the immensity of the task and the huge risks involved—all in the form of an open-ended suspense story.

We should not be so blinded by the integrative function of media events as to overlook their relation to conflict. Many of these events, as we have shown, speak directly to acute conflicts. Some speak to long-lasting crises or to deep rifts within societies. Each of the forms of events speaks to conflict in a different way. Thus, the live broadcasting of Contest—the Olympic Games, for example—is in effect a symbolic transposition of political conflict. As has been suggested, televised Contests frame conflicts and miniaturize them. Coronations demand that conflicts defer to shared symbols of tradition and unity.

Conquests are a process whereby conflicts—the Middle East before Sadat, for example—evaporate in the aura of a hero who proclaims a new symbolic order. As a result, peaceful gestures, not only hostile ones, entered the realm of Middle Eastern possibilities. The hero's daring seems to invite admiration and identification even from those who are disadvantaged by his triumph.

Principal Performers

Continuing with Table 1, we note that each type of event has its own players. The competitors in Contest are fighting for themselves and their group, but ironically they are the least charismatic of the great men who feature in television events. Unlike the less ceremonial conflicts of the daily news, they symbolize the equality of opposing forces and, above all, the predominance of the rules. Contests are thus rather rationalistic events, in which the loser is seen to have certain of the winner's qualities. While the victor is presented as a potential candidate for Coronation or Conquest, Contest offers the chance of a "next time" to the defeated side—and no more than temporary reign to the victor. Still, the winners of Contest often receive great acclaim, all the more when the underdog wins. But this is when Contest borders on Conquest; recall Kennedy's unexpected victory in the 1960 debate.

Coronation, on the other hand, puts a great man on view, sometimes as the product of ascription, more often as the product of achievement. But this is a great man acting a ritual role, in which initiative is minimized, dwarfed by the august setting of cathedral or cemetery. Ironically, these are great men and women stuffed with the symbols of achievement and voluntarism, but unable to act: the dead Kennedy or Mountbatten or Indira Gandhi are pressed into the service of rhetoric. Minwalla (1990) says:

> During the television broadcast of the ceremony, Indira Gandhi was built up into a martyr for democracy. A week before she was killed, Indira Gandhi had made a speech in Orissa in which she had said, "I will fight for my country with the last drop of my blood." During the telecast of the procession, her words were constantly replayed and mentioned, to enhance the aura of a woman who died for her ideals.[16]

In the live broadcasting of Conquest, the odds against the hero are so great, and the risks so real, that humanity holds its breath to witness the challenge and its outcome. Consider the Pope in Poland or Sadat in Jerusalem. Each of these stories begins with the hero's climb from humble origin to great stature, culminating in a deliberate decision—carefully calculated—to try to change the world. In both cases, we find the "enemy" actually daring the hero to try. In both cases, the hero talks over the heads of his rivals to enlist the attention of the rival's ostensible following—the Polish and Israeli peoples—inviting them to invest him (the hero) with the charisma that will allow him to charm them. Of course, the rivals—the governments of Poland and Israel—stand to benefit too, albeit reluctantly, if the hero succeeds. Risking failure, and perhaps his life, the hero offers himself as a sacrifice by the very act of making the journey. In response, he is offered a show of welcome whose pomp and ceremony are difficult to exaggerate. But the hero wants more—and gives more to get it. There is a consequent escalation of demands—on the principle of potlatch—and of gestures of largesse.

With certain modifications this is also the story of the astronauts, except that they did not have to negotiate their access to the moon. It is the story of de Gaulle in Quebec, hailing "le Québec libre" over the heads of his Canadian hosts.[17] It approximates the story of the Ayatollah Khomeini, who, however, managed to dispatch the most important of his putative hosts prior to his arrival at Tehran airport. In certain ways it is also the story of the self-sacrifice of Kate Smith in her marathon warbond drive (Merton, 1946),[18] and of the breaking of a world record by an Olympic hero. And as we shall see, the television retellings of Conquest push these stories even further in the direction of symbolic exchange, away from rational calculus.

The Audience

Contests enlist the audience in two roles that are, in fact, contradictory. One of these is the role of partisan—to root for the home team as a committed loyalist. The other is to decide who won, to act as a referee. Both roles involve "choosing." One choice is particularistic, the other invokes universalistic criteria. Implicit in the juridical role is a reflexive attitude. The audience is invited to act as a critic, to judge not only the winning but the playing with reference to the wisdom and beauty of the rules. It is this reacquaintance with the spirit of the laws that gave the American presidency renewed status after Watergate.

The polity rose above the President's appeal to frame the hearings as partisan Contest.

In daily life we are much more suspicious of the rules, wondering whom they benefit. We know that there are many who work their way around them. In the liminal period of sacred Contests, the rules reaffirm their civilizing function.

The audience for Conquests watches in awe. It is dazzled by the daring of the hero as he jumps over the wall that unjustly separates them. Israelis held their breath from the moment Sadat landed to the moment of his departure. He was invested with trust for unraveling the double bind that both beckoned Arab leaders to Israel and kept them away. He was perceived—perhaps correctly—as risking his life and reputation to make a historic gesture. Pope John Paul II was watched just as eagerly by the television audience of the world when he arrived in Warsaw to confront the Polish leadership. The same awe and suspension of disbelief characterized the vast audience of the astronauts as they landed on the moon.

Coronations also require audience approval. The mass audience is invited to attend and answer "amen" at the crowning, or wedding, or funeral service of a national leader. It is an occasion to repledge allegiance, to recall the contract between leaders and led, to reaffirm the values of the center which they, together with us, uphold. "Television viewers who watched the cremation were actively participating," says Minwalla (1990). "Most people prayed as Indira Gandhi was consigned to the flames."

These audience roles—to be further elaborated in Chapter 5—complement those of the principals. The audience applies the rules, or watches the rules applied, to the heroes of Contest. It invests the heroes of Conquest with the right to be charismatic. It invokes sacred values to justify the hero's crown.[19]

Ceremonial Enactments of the Bases of Authority

If students of folklore can attest to the primordiality of these story forms, students of politics provide evidence of their applicability to real life. The ceremonial enactment of the relations between rulers and subjects has long been a matter of scholarly interest (Bagehot, 1927; Nicolson, 1955; Edelman, 1964, 1989; Kertzer, 1988; Kantorowicz, 1957; Gross, 1986; Abeles, 1988; Lane, 1981; Myerhoff, 1977). Shils and Young (1953) analyzed the meaning of the 1952 coronation that ushered in the television era, and Geertz (1980) has studied the forms of "royal progress" in Morocco, Thailand, and England. Careful study of Lincoln's funeral cortege also serves as a point of comparison (Lewis, 1929). "The triumphus," claims Huizinga (1950), "is far more than a solemn celebration of military success; it is a rite through which the State recuperates from the strains of war and re-experiences its well-being." Analyzing the postwar victory parade of 1946 in Britain, Chaney (1983) argues that the BBC altered the event by narrowly scripting its military aspect, thereby failing to transmit the utopian and universalistic motifs in its civilian aspect. All of these authors are concerned with the fit between a particular political situation and a specific ceremonial form.

We wish to suggest further that the three scripts of the live broadcasts of Contest, Conquest, and Coronation enact different models of authority. Clearly, there is a match between the ceremonial forms we have so far described and the bases of legitimate authority proposed by Max Weber (1946): rational-legal, traditional, and charismatic. Thus, ceremonial contests seem best suited to highlight the nature of a rational, legal, political system and the criteria of achievement that give access to leadership in such a system. As Aron (1957) says, commenting on Weber, "The legitimation of power may be rational when it is based on a belief in the legality of the rules and of leaders chosen in accordance with them." The agonistic element in parliamentary democracy is evident.

Coronations, on the other hand, enact traditional authority, the second of Weber's bases of political legitimacy. "They rest on the belief in the sanctity of traditions and in the necessity of obeying those who are called upon to rule by those traditions" (Aron, 1957). When they are more than celebratory jingles, Coronations act as reminders of a time when authority was anchored in tradition. Depending on their match with the situation being addressed, Coronations may highlight areas of continuity between traditional structures and rational-legal ones, thus demonstrating the persistence of traditional forms in modern societies (Abeles, 1988), or they may be seen as nostalgic fictions.

The third form in Weber's system is charismatic authority—the active ingredient in Conquests—"where the subject submits, in exceptional emotional states, to the heroism, sanctity or outstanding merit of an individual's personality" operating outside the rules (Aron, 1957). Conquests represent the eruption of the charismatic model onto a political stage. They address a deadlocked situation and introduce the possibility of change. Turning their protagonist into a "shaman" of sorts, Conquests are closest to the rituals of archaic societies. They allow the "trying on" or "modeling" (Handelman, 1990) of a new symbolic order in response to the contradictions of the existing system.

Reference to Weber (1946) helps to specify the roles imparted to the audience within each type of script (see Table 1). The audiences of Contests judge the participants on the basis of rationalized criteria; they check, like an umpire, to see whether the performances are in conformity with the applicable rules.

The audiences of Coronations pledge allegiance to traditional forms of authority and do so in ways that are themselves codified by tradition. The audiences of Conquests echo the proposed rearticulations of the symbolic order, often in the form of spontaneous social movements (Lewis, 1978).

Fitting Events and Forms

It follows that the story form in which an event is scripted carries its own latent message: legal, traditional, or charismatic. Obviously, such forms must be attuned to the events they celebrate.

Most events are already "named" before they reach the broadcaster; the royal wedding does not easily lend itself to scripting as Contest or Conquest. And yet, even this is possible. Eco (1989) says of the wedding of Grace Kelly and Prince Rainier of Monaco that "it could have been approached as a political event, a diplomatic meeting, a Hollywood parade, an operetta, a Regency romance." Even a contest, says Eco, leaves some room for interpretation. "The focus of a football game must be the ball," he says. "But . . . a camera that tends to focus on the particular contributions of individual players is telling us something different from the one that prefers to stress teamwork."

From our own corpus, we know that the parties to a broadcast event do not always agree on its definition. For example, broadcasters circumnavigated the Polish government's designation of the Pope's journey as a pilgrimage. In the case of Begin and Sadat, the principals wrestled to tilt the definition of the ceremony to particularistic advantage: Begin preferred Coronation, hoping to pay as little as necessary for the long-awaited act of recognition; Sadat strove for Conquest, seeking the realities of territory and peace in return for a spellbinding gesture. Sometimes, as in the case of space initiatives, essentially the same type of event was scripted as Conquest by the Americans, who broadcast the takeoff, and as Coronation by the Russians, who broadcast the homecoming—reflecting a difference in the "openness" of the two regimes.

From this point of view, Conquest, Contest, Coronation are not equally open to negotiation, nor do they allow their actors comparable amounts of freedom. Coronations would seem least open to negotiating since variations in their scripts would be more strictly controlled by tradition. The fact that traditions are often reorganized in the process of being transmitted (Myerhoff, 1977), or sometimes even invented (Hobsbawm and Ranger, 1983), suggests, on the contrary, that they allow a broad range of choices on the implementation of their formal scenario.

Contests, and political debates in particular, involve the most extensive forms of negotiating. Negotiations are conducted in a legalist manner and in public, often calling for a debate over the rules according to which the contestants will conduct their confrontation. Far from increasing the protagonists' freedom, negotiating over rules results in the drastic curtailment of freedom. Once decided upon, no matter how strenuous the bargaining, these rules are irreversibly attached to the event and will control, often pedantically, the range of acceptable behaviors.

Conquests also rely on prior negotiations, such as those by which the Polish government required of Pope John Paul II that he submit the itinerary of his intended visit and the texts of his scheduled speeches. Yet these negotiations are typically secret, as we have shown. Conquests are the least predetermined of our three categories. They lend themselves perfectly to renegotiation while in progress, to ad hoc scripting. This rescripting does not prevent them from being clearly identified, however. In fact, it is quite relevant to the charismatic story they tell. Pictures of the arrival of Sadat at the Tel Aviv airport, long before the words came, represented the recognition by an Arab leader for which Israel had waited so long.

The next chapter will consider the politics of this type of negotiation. Our aim here is to illustrate how story forms convey latent messages that echo the manifest message of an event. Consider, for example, the ceremoniality of the Watergate Contest, which elevated a routine confrontation between the two political parties to a legislative challenge to executive authority, and transposed it further into a tragic but just exposé of the failure of a leader in the face of the law. Consider how the Pope's conquest of Poland might have looked if it had been scripted as pilgrimage. It is both the fact of the festive, live broadcast—proclaiming the extraordinary—and the script in terms of which it is narrated that underline its meaning. The moment Czech television turned its live camera on Wenceslas Square, people knew that the revolution had the upper hand. When the cameras returned to the square, it was to express a sense of outrage that the Communist Party had still not relinquished power. "The camera cut to a pained close-up of the forum's leader, Vaclav Havel, appearing on the balcony . . . The smiling revolution was suddenly wearing a frown" (Newman, 1989).

Consider the narrative form called shuttle diplomacy, made famous by Henry Kissinger. Although the coverage of Kissinger does not qualify for our corpus because it was not broadcast live, it is an instructive example of how a story form not only underlines a message but itself constitutes a force for change. Descending from the sky and surrounded by the journalists who had won coveted places on his plane, Kissinger would announce that the crisis he had come to unravel was all but impossible for human solution. Moreover, he would say, he had only three days to spare for the mission, as equally worthy crises elsewhere were demanding his attention. Thus, he portrayed himself, and was portrayed by the media, much as Weber (1946) would have hoped: self-appointed, self-confident, an "outsider" who is "called" to the mission, rejecting "rational" administrative conduct in favor of the "particularistic" dispensation of power and justice, leaving implementation and routinization to disciples and successors, achieving and maintaining authority by putting extraordinary talents to use in the performance of miraculous feats, deriving prestige by the seizing and effective use of power, thus demonstrating "strength in life" (Schwartz, 1983).[20]

Thus, the afternoon newspaper and the evening television news offer us the melodrama of a hero setting out on a journey in which he will face an almost insurmountable obstacle, accompanied by storytellers who will announce to readers and viewers, from day to day, even from hour to hour, what the hero is doing and saying and, above all, whether he is succeeding. Note that the journalists have all but excluded themselves from access to outside sources, depending very heavily on the reports of the hero. Manipulated into this situation by the deus ex machina himself, and by the norms of journalistic praxis, they have been invited aboard as members of the wedding and will tell their story in typically breathless, awestruck fashion. When the story form is fixed, it becomes a standard which reporters employ to relate, and evaluate, subsequent activities.[21]

It is evident from this example that the story form itself—the discourse of Conquest invoked by journalists to report on a heroic mediator commuting between embattled parties—is an essential part of the message. We are arguing, in other words, that the particular manner in which the hero, his personality, and his actions are packaged is essential to an understanding of their effect.

Collective Actors and Unscripted Events

Certain media events do not fall neatly into the tripartite classification of Contests, Conquests, Coronations. Their distinguishing mark, we believe, is that they do not have individual actors but collective protagonists. This is not a problem when teams can substitute for individuals, as in the moon landing, for example, or in sporting events such as the Super Bowl or the World Series. The script of collectively enacted events becomes more difficult when the collective actor is too diffuse to be seen in terms of either individuals or teams. The extreme case—but increasingly on view—is where half the population, at home, is watching the other half, live on camera.

The New York City marathon, broadcast nationwide, is a good example. It is primarily a collective affair and not a contest at all. The great metropolis is cleared for the run, traffic is interrupted and made to digress, throngs line the streets of the five boroughs, and everybody—as the ABC commentator notes— "has" somebody who is running: his mailman, her doctor, their priest. The cameras and helicopters posted along the route show magnificent pictures of the comradely crossing of streets and bridges, celebrating the city and displaying its potential for the convivial integration of its diverse inhabitants. Gradually the media and some of the contestants turn it into a race, and there is talk to the effect that "the object is to get to the finish line first." Very few of the people lining the sidewalks can have this as their primary interest, but for the members of the television audience who have followed the marathon for two hours, the contest aspect looms ever larger as the finish line comes into view. Thus the media relabel as Contest what started out as Communion.

Even last-minute labeling becomes impossible in the case of certain events that seem to have a different format altogether. The most extraordinary of these was a telethon of sixty-five hours over an eight-day period in 1983, in which the Korean Broadcasting System served as an intermediary for people searching for lost relatives.[22] Separated traumatically by civil war, a very large number of Koreans were in total ignorance of the fate of their families. A show that began as the final two-hour episode of a series commemorating the war turned into a procession of individuals who appeared on camera for about fifteen seconds with inscriptions of their names and the names of the persons for whom they were searching. Persons who answered their description, or hoped to, made contact with the studio by special telephone lines, and later from regional and even international video hookups. While the viewing audience looked on and wept, both as potential participants and as observers, the program electrified the country. The appeal to use the service was so overwhelming that a twelve-hour broadcast each Friday night continuing the format became "by far the most popular TV show in South Korea."

Here we see an innovative variation on the power of television: to open audiovisual channels not between the few and the many but between the many and the many—with even more looking on in the dual role of potential addressees and witnesses. Beyond its instrumental function, this use of television as a tool to search for lost relatives and reunify families acquired the symbolic dimension of a "healing ceremony" celebrating the will of the Korean people to overcome the traumas of war (Jun and Dayan, 1986). But this healing ceremony was neither Contest nor Conquest nor Coronation. It was an event with definite political consequences for the Koreans' perception of their postwar identity. It had no main actors, no leaders, no teams. It was a grass-roots, spontaneous event, one that escapes our classification of ceremonial possibilities because it does not openly address the problem of authority and legitimation, and because in its anarchic celebration of private values it circumvents the political sphere altogether, ignoring rather than embodying or confronting the "center" of society. An event of this type escapes our classification inasmuch as its interactive connection of periphery with periphery short-circuits the representative sphere. Such a short-circuiting is conceivable only when an event of this amplitude is unscripted. One wonders whether this is not the event that launched the era of "interactive TV."

As a final example, let us consider the extraordinary live broadcasts of the demonstrations in Prague, in the fall of 1989. When the massive rallies were underway in Wenceslas Square, broadcast-journalists of Czech television insisted that it was their duty to present them live. Their demand was refused, the journalists declared a strike, and security forces took over the building to restrain them from reporting the protest meetings. Two or three days later, however, the situation in the country was so anarchic that the broadcasts were made possible with the concurrence of the faltering government. Czech viewers, especially those living outside the capital (where half of the population were in the streets) saw the sight of their lives, night after night, on the single government-operated channel.

Different from all other events in our corpus—even those that played a part in a process of change—the first broadcasts from Wenceslas Square were not transmissions of well-tailored ceremonies, but live representations of a revolution-in-progress. Television obviously did not cause the "velvet" revolution, or incite it; television entered into it well after the alternative media and the revolutionary groups had gone into action. Yet it did more than celebrate the revolutionary accomplishment, for success was by no means assured when television entered the situation.[23] We should say, rather, that television "intervened" in the revolution, became a part of it, and affected its outcome in several perhaps unique ways.

The television cameras at Wenceslas Square revealed the mammoth scale and intensity—but yet the discipline—of the protest rallies. These were broadcasts of the many to the many; they showed the people demanding change, calling for resignations and further resignations, and investing charisma in their leaders (Ash, 1990). The first role of television, then, was to bring the big news—not in the disaster-oriented genre of major *news* events, but in awe, revealing that the opposition were winning the day. Recall that the opposition had not been shown before, certainly not in full strength or in a live broadcast! And as the live broadcasts continued, they signaled that protest and radical change were thinkable and, surprisingly, that there would be no suppression from Moscow. The broadcasts proclaimed that television itself was free to say and to show what needed saying and showing.

A few days later, television covered a major rally in Letenske Gardens, where not only the opposition leadership spoke but also the prime minister himself. Here was a semblance of ceremony—well advertised, and by now anticipated—cast in the genre of Contest. Again, following the most dramatic of the revolutionary actions—the total shutdown of all work for two hours on November 27—there was a further television ceremony, a live broadcast of the special session of Parliament on November 29, in which the party, in effect, unanimously voted itself out of office.

Thus, television served as a herald, reporting on the revolution in progress; it served to temper the threat and anxiety of outside intervention; it offered itself as evidence that civil liberty and freedom of speech were now reinstated; it moderated a debate between old and new leadership; it celebrated the "de-coronation" of the Communist Party and the promise of free elections. In short, especially in the later events but in aspects of the earlier ones as well, Czech television punctuated the revolutionary process with live broadcasts of political ceremonies, akin to those with which this book deals. For all of the differences between the real-world action in Czechoslovakia and Romania, and the symbolic action of most of the other events in our corpus, ceremonial television amid the Eastern Euro-

pean revolutions had important symbolic work to do. Television
displayed the last stages of a popular Conquest that would usher
in a new leadership. Conquest, in turn, paved the way for Contest, in which new and old leaders could engage in debate. The
two sides to the historic confrontation were talking to each other
within the arena of the new rules. The enthralled audience in
the square could now signal those who had stayed home that it
was all right to come out, while television broadcast the coming
attractions of democracy for all to see. Liberated, its very presence at the event modeled the new era that was being proclaimed. Thus, television itself enacted the revolution before
the crowd and the cameras. Totalitarianism was vanquished, the
new leadership was hailed, and the business of democracy
began.[24]

3

Negotiating Media Events

Television events have three partners: the organizers of the event who bring its elements together and propose its historicity; the broadcasters who re-produce the event by recombining its elements; and the audiences, on the spot and at home, who take the event to heart. Each partner must give active consent and make a substantial investment of time and other resources if an event is to be successfully mounted for television.[1] Indeed, it is useful to think of such events as constituting a kind of "contract" among the three parties whereby each side undertakes to give something to the others in order to get something in return.[2]

Agreement on the scripting of an event may be difficult to obtain, however. The great television events radiate political and ideological consequences, and it is little wonder that choice of script is often the subject of considerable debate. Even events that call explicitly for one script or another—the way a state funeral calls for Coronation or presidential debates call for Contest—engender debates over the nuancing, and this holds true, a fortiori, for events that can be fit to different scripts. Is the New York City marathon a Contest or a Coronation? Is the Pope's first visit to Poland a pilgrimage or a provocation? Is Sadat's journey a Coronation or a Conquest? And, to anticipate the Archbishop of Canterbury—to whom we shall return—is the royal wedding a fairy tale or a Christian marriage?

Organizers and principals may differ among themselves on the scripting. Organizers and broadcasters whose interests diverge may differ too. Different audiences—as we saw in the case of the marathon—may provide different readings. These differences are mostly ironed out backstage, but they may persist into the event, to erupt onstage and at home. In other words, what we see and hear is the end product of political, aesthetic, and financial bargaining, from which it follows that (1) each of the partners is a free agent, independent of the others, and (2) there is a process of "negotiation" among the partners that begins prior to the event and continues throughout. These propositions are the subject of the present chapter.

The Sociology of Producing Media Events

It is not trivial to insist that the three partners are, in principle, free agents. It is the addition of the broadcaster as a third party to the contract that most clearly differentiates media events from public ceremonies prior to the era of radio and television. Broadcasting has transformed public events, rhetorically and politically, by adding the voice and technology of a commentator who is independent of the organizer even if (in the case of ceremonial events) he is also his authorized agent. In the West, the broadcaster—drawing on the freedom of the press—is neither the employee nor the slave of the organizer. Even if one believes, as many communications theorists appear to do, that the press prostitutes its freedom, it is nonetheless important to reiterate that such freedom exists in principle. This is what makes a contract necessary and negotiation possible. Of course, whether this freedom is in fact exercised is equally important.

The nearest analogy to this kind of tripartite affair may be found, perhaps, in the classical relationship of church, state, and audience. The church, acting as a free agent, often places itself at the service of political events, lending its cathedrals, its priests, its sacraments, to occasions of state. The event, thus augmented, takes on a wholly different aura. This enhancement is obvious in the case of state funerals or weddings, but it is also present in the religious invocation prior to the opening session of the Congress, for example. Here again, cynics will say that the church is a mere agency of the state, hiding behind a pretense of independence. We suspect otherwise: even ostensible independence creates bargaining power. But for all the similarities between church and media, there is a difference. When the church is a partner in the construction of public events, it shares in the "original" production and is therefore much more directly subject to the control of the initial organizer. When television becomes a partner in an event, it has considerably more independence and influence, for it deploys its own equipment and manpower to re-produce and re-state an event before an audience to whom the organizer does not have direct access.

The notion of contract is implied in the discussion of traditional events and of communication forms generally (Cawelti, 1976). It serves to remind us that even the most sacred and ancient of holidays are designed and redesigned to meet the requirements of the various parties. It is incorrect, that is, to think of traditional events as "nonnegotiable," to assume that weddings and funerals and ritual occasions are unchanging and unchangeable. We know they are not; liturgical reforms are introduced in every generation. In the old days, they must also have had producers, people whose job it was to integrate the elements of the ceremony into a coherent whole, to assign roles to celebrants and audience, to choose the music and the players. No less than modern media events, it is useful to think of the earliest of holidays and the most traditional of ceremonies as products of some kind of "symbolic engineering," even if the records are sparse (Fogel, 1989).

Media Events and Political Spectacle

In contrast with the media events of democratic societies, the events of traditional societies (as well as events mounted in the nondemocratic sectors of modern societies) may be characterized as two-party contracts. Typically, only organizers and audiences are involved; the producer is usually in the employ of the organizer. Even the audience may not be free to opt out or disapprove. Thus, Mosse (1980) tells us of Charles Ruggieri, pyrotechnist to Charles XII, who sought through public festivals "to renew the link between the people and their monarch, and to make them forget for a short time the misfortunes and sorrows of the human flesh . . . [But] these festivals were popular diversions rather than liturgical rites centered on a national symbol." In France after the revolution, says Mosse, a concerted effort was made to mobilize symbols that would substitute for the symbols of the church and serve as themes for popular festivals. The Jacobins chose the tree of liberty, the goddess of reason, and the early-morning rays of the sun as symbols for the republic. The point was "to make the people live the Republic and to ensure the maintenance of order and public peace."[3] But none of these efforts was a success.[4] According to Mosse, they lacked an organic link to deep-seated rituals and traditions and failed to express the mystique of the movement or the nation. The audience, in other words, failed to grant charisma to these events; the audience refused to enter into the contract. Successful events, Mosse believes, cannot break with tradition altogether, because they thereby fail to arouse the voluntary cooperation of the audience.

The difference, then, between the media events discussed here and these past examples of symbolic engineering is in the emergence of three distinct partners. The Western media, in particular, are free to join in the event or not, and may agree to present the event in the spirit proposed by its organizer, or not. Broadcasters can actually say no and survive, even if they do not often do so. When the broadcaster is less free, he takes his orders from the organizer, as Polish television did when the Pope first came to visit, in 1979. Reflecting the mixed feelings of the Polish government, the official hosts, Polish television followed the Pope on his journey through the country but understated the euphoria of the crowds that thronged to see him. We have been told that government ordered the broadcasters who were in its direct employ to focus close up on the Pope in his role as "pilgrim"—the agreed logo for the event—and to avoid showing the crowds. [5]

A review of the production of public festivals inevitably brings to mind the political spectacles of the fascist regimes of twentieth-century Europe. Although we have said that audiences must agree to allow themselves to be enthralled, it is also true that certain external conditions are particularly conducive to the acceptance of such proposals. The merging of the self into the nation that characterized the early twentieth century was one of these circumstances. Uprooted from traditional ties and equally abandoned by the organizations that were designed to replace them (such as trade unions and parliaments), millions of individuals turned to the state and the strong leader to redeem their sense of dishonor—personal, economic, and national. The new technology of radio, plus the uniformed, choreographed, spellbinding mass rallies in which tens of thousands of people assembled in a stadium to salute the leader and await his command, expressed the social organization of fascism in which the leader established a direct connection between himself and the atomized masses. Such events, according to Mosse (1980), serve as alternatives to parliamentary democracy by binding masses to their leaders far beyond the leader's personal power to persuade or terrorize or oppress. Walter Benjamin (1968) warned us of such events, writing of the fascist tendency "to aestheticize politics."[6]

The independence and ultimate professionalization of the media in the United States, and in others of the Western democracies, make it less likely that a political regime can transform a public event into a frenzied political spectacle, even if the public were willing. Indeed, television may be said to "contain" public events in several ways. The most elementary of these is that television keeps people at home. Even to ask whether media events might be considered political spectacles is to make the assumption that television is capable of whipping up a frenzy.[7] Social movements take place outside the home, not inside.

We are suggesting, in other words, that television depoliticizes society, both because it keeps people at home and because it contributes to the false illusion of political involvement (Lazarsfeld and Merton, 1948). On the other hand, to return to our main theme, free television acts as a brake on the temptation of government to mobilize mass support through political spectacle. To the extent that the institution of broadcasting is normatively differentiated from government (Alexander, 1988)— at least enough to take a critical stance vis-à-vis the choice of media events or the forms of their representation—we are protected from some of the excesses of political spectacle that marked the days of Hitler and Mussolini. The freedom of the broadcaster to negotiate such matters, to threaten noncooperation or to say no, is central to an understanding of the dynamics of producing media events.[8] In the language of mass-society theory, free media protect individuals from the intrusion of elites (Kornhauser, 1959).[9]

Yet on certain rare occasions—as illustrated by these events—television may substitute for the experience of "being there." It cannot quite replicate the anonymity or the single-mindedness of vast crowds, or simulate the physical or the ludic elements of thronging, or make effective channels available for feedback to decision-makers, but it can and does provide ways of "participating" in an event even in the small-group settings in which the audience is dispersed. Moreover, by their intermediation, broadcasters offer us professional protection—never guaranteed—against crass or malevolent manipulation.[10]

Successive Endorsements

Negotiating a contract and producing a media event may be thought of as a series of successive endorsements by the three partners to the enterprise—and by partners of the partners. So far, we have talked about the endorsement of a proposed event by the audience and by the broadcasters. But it is more complicated than that.

Consider once more the case of an unemployed youth and a pretty girl who decide to get married, as Walter Bagehot (1927) might have put it.[11] The boy's parents, the queen and her consort, propose that the event might be of interest to the kingdom. After due consideration, the government decides to endorse the event, declaring the wedding day a public holiday and offering to put various national resources—such as a delegation of the armed forces—at the disposal of the event. The national church does the same, offering an appropriate venue and the person of the archbishop. The capital city and its lord mayor do likewise. Thus, the endorsement of the event by municipality, church, and government gives a ceremonial frame to the event, endowing it with the full spectrum of symbols of the center (Shils, 1975).

The crowd, arriving the night before to ensure a good place in the line of march, throngs the event and gives its endorsement in turn. It, too, frames the event, placing inside the frame not only the original proposers and principals of the event but also its first endorsers, Mrs. Thatcher, the armed forces, the archbishop, the lord mayor, and their teams.

Next come the broadcasters, who by their endorsement include the in-person audience in their frame. Thus transformed, all previous endorsers become television actors and are presented as integral to the event by hundreds of technicians, cameramen, directors, producers, and commentators mobilized for the occasion. In the framing by television, the elements of the event are so recombined and so subtly mixed and amplified with material produced by the broadcasters that one begins to wonder whether the true locus of the event has not subtly been removed from the streets of London to another realm of reality available only to the television viewer. Thus, the television audience must consider the event and find it worthy of the special form of attention that it demands. The TV audience includes the broadcasting personnel and the in-person audience in its framing of the event.

And that is not all. Foreign television companies may wish to add their own endorsements, framing not only the pictures offered by the local broadcasters but also the home audience viewing the event on television. This may be presented either live or as news to foreign viewers who, in turn, may accept or reject the event as proposed to them. Thus, in a further iteration, American sailing enthusiasts were offered a live glimpse of members of the Melbourne Yacht Club viewing the live broadcast of their team's victorious race off the coast of New England.

Each successive framing of the event invites endorsement by a new social entity. Government, army, church, and municipality bring their bureaucracies into the picture. In-person audiences organize themselves in queues and crowds. Television organizations provide professional frame-makers. At-home audiences, composed of family and friends, gather for the occasion under the auspices of household heads. Each new partner to the contract places previous endorsers inside the frame.

Endorsement and Negotiation

Of course, each successive endorsement implies negotiation. The potential partner may refuse to endorse the event, may wish to script it otherwise, may even attempt subversion or sabotage. But why bargain over the endorsement of an event? Why should one of the partners wish to subvert an event? What does negotiation look and sound like?

The most painful negotiations probably take place within the organizing agencies themselves and among the principals; sometimes, however, they loom inside the broadcasting organization, sometimes among the audience, and often between organizers and broadcasters. An example of dissension in the ranks of the organizers occurred at the time of the Sadat-Begin meetings, as we have noted. Both men were anxious to have the event televised, and both were interested in a scenario of exchange. Begin was eager for the diplomatic recognition of Israel implied by the visit of the vanquished leader. He apparently hoped to get Sadat's support for Israel's continued occupation of the West Bank in exchange for relinquishing the Sinai to Egypt. Sadat, for his part, wished to place before the world a picture of Israel's indebtedness for his heroic gesture; he wished to use the occasion to enlist American support for himself and for Egypt; he wanted the Arab states to acknowledge his leadership and to realize that the Arab cause against Israel, particularly the return of territories, would be well served by his journey.

Such Conquests are constantly in danger of being turned into Contests between visiting leader and host. This is equally true of the Pope's first visit to Poland. In principle, all of these began as situations of "no contest," wherein the host leader chooses to step down to allow the visitor to unleash his charisma. But the visitor, live on television, is liable to transgress the agreed limits, in which case the script may be rewritten—as Begin appeared to do (or perhaps played at doing) at the end of Sadat's visit, when he assumed an agonistic stance and engaged his guest in an oratorical confrontation before the Knesset.

The scripts proposed by the organizers of an event do not necessarily coincide with the enacted event, or with the event as shown on television, even when the organizers come to an agreement among themselves. The travels of John Paul II, for example, are announced as pilgrimages. And, indeed, the Pope may be seen as a pilgrim, considering how he prostrates himself before the holy places, inviting his adherents—in person and on television—to follow vicariously (Dayan, Katz, and Kerns, 1984). But the message of these events strays far from pilgrimage. Recall not only the Pope's Conquest of Poland, but the dramatic confrontation with the leaders and priests of Chile, Brazil, and Argentina. This blurring of definitions may be blamed on how the event is retold by television, but it may also stem from the principals' uncertainty over the appropriateness of the script selected to structure the event. An announced script may prove inadequate. It may also be chosen in spite of, or because of, its inadequacy. It may be a mere facade, a protective shield, or even a Trojan horse. Despite their common labeling as pilgrimages, each of John Paul II's journeys involves a different story; all of them are political, aimed not at commemoration but at taking sides in an ideological dispute, restoring order, or encouraging social change.[12]

Another more explicit example of dispute among the organizers is evident in the royal wedding of Charles and Diana. In his sermon to the couple, the Archbishop of Canterbury publicly challenged the definition of the event as a fairy tale, as will be discussed in the following chapter.

The Watergate hearings provide an instructive example of all three forms of internal debate (Lang and Lang, 1983)—that is, among organizers, among broadcasters, and within the public. The Senate committee was divided in itself over whether to permit live coverage of the hearings, and the division was not always along expected partisan lines. There were sharp counterattacks from the Nixon administration on the committee's inclination to broadcast its hearings, and a variety of attempts to convince the Senate and the courts to accept the principle that the presence of television cameras would impair the performance of witnesses and subvert the search for truth. "The Committee disagreed," say Lang and Lang, "holding with Woodrow Wilson that, in the case of corruption of the executive branch, the public-informing function of Congress was more important than its legislative function." The President himself entered the fray in a nationally televised speech on August 15, 1973, which was to be his public "testimony" before the court of the American people. "After two weeks and two million words of televised testimony . . . we have reached a point," said Nixon, "at which a continued, backward-looking obsession with Watergate is causing the nation to neglect matters of far greater importance to all of the American people."[13] By this time, the committee had concluded its work, after 237 hours of television coverage that reached nearly 90 percent of the American public at least some part of the time, consistently outdrawing regular entertainment programming (Lang and Lang, 1983, p. 63).

The media were hesitant too, always reticent about interrupting regular programs. Helped in their decision by the publicity anticipating the hearings, they consented to mounting the broadcasts live. After the first five days, they further agreed among themselves to rotate the coverage, keeping options open to rejoin whenever the testimony proved unusually interesting. Thus, in every city, at least one major station broadcast the hearings by day while the network of public television stations rebroadcast them at night. "Whatever transpired during the day inevitably made the evening news, the next morning's headlines and everyday conversation, and few people could extricate themselves entirely from their pervasive influence" (Lang and Lang, 1983, p. 62). Recalling our definition of media events, we note again that the unprecedented sharing of network facilities communicates at the syntactic level the urgent, centralizing, and ultimately unifying message that underlies such events.

The audience also divided over the event, splitting differently at different stages. There was concern among the public that the media were giving Watergate "more attention than it deserved," but the work of the Ervin committee was continually praised by a majority of the public. Most critical of the fairness of the committee and of the media were the nonviewers, who tended to be Nixon voters in 1972 and distrustful of politicians. Ironically, persons with such attitudes did not seek to confirm their mistrust by viewing the televised hearings, preferring to spare themselves the ordeal of confronting their fears. More than half of the public supported continuing live coverage of the committee after its recess in August. Fifty-two percent said that the hearings had been "a good thing." Interestingly, Die Welt sided with those who opposed the broadcasts, calling it a "show trial" by television, an allegation that echoed the White House's objection that the hearings had tarnished America's image abroad.[14]

Negotiation among the Partners

While the internal debates of organizers, broadcasters, and audience, within their own organizations, are of high importance for an understanding of the battles over the representation of public events on television, even more interesting are the negotiations among the partners.

Consider the arguments between broadcasters and organizers over the presidential debates of 1976 (Seltz and Yoakam, 1979).[15] The broadcasters insisted on their right to show reaction shots not only of the dueling candidates but of members of the audience. The broadcasters insisted on controlling the sound in the auditorium where the debate was held, even though they were legally enjoined from doing so. Indeed, the myth that the League of Women Voters was the organizer of the event— together with the national committees of the two political parties—was created in order to relieve the broadcasters of their responsibility, under the Federal Communications Act, to open the airwaves to all parties if free time were given to the two major parties.[16] Yet the broadcasters threatened to quit the production if they did not get their way. The fight was over definition and control of the event.

Threats that an event will not be broadcast live unless broadcasters' conditions are met have been a regular feature of party political conventions since the inception of television (Russo, 1983). The British Gurevitch (1977) conducted a study of television coverage of political conventions in Britain and the United States and found a difference of opinion between the organizers, who think (or thought in 1964) that the TV audience ought to hear and see more of the speeches delivered from the rostrum—while the TV producers were priding themselves on roaming the convention floor and reporting from behind the scenes. There were, and are, two rather different conventions, the one proposed by its organizers and the one seen on the television screen. To state it this way is to oversimplify, of course, since the organizers take account of the presence of live television in their planning of the event in the first place.[17]

Or consider the tension between broadcasters and organizers

over the Olympic Games. Members of the International Olympics Committee are said to wish to represent the games as part of an unbroken tradition that stems from classical Greece, celebrating individual achievement, healthy minds in healthy bodies, the striving to accomplish more than humans can be expected to accomplish. It is dubious, of course, that they really want this, given the emphasis on national Contest in the organization of the games. For their part, the broadcasters explicitly prefer national over individual competition, thus taking sides with the national rather than the international organizing committees. The fight is over the representation of the event.

The audience is a negotiating partner, too, even if it does not take part in formal negotiations. Football fans, for example, dissatisfied with the concessions made by the producers of Monday night football in order to attract a prime-time family audience, are said to take their revenge by turning down the sound of the television commentary and tuning in the radio broadcast of the game (Breitrose, 1980). Audiences demand that certain events be broadcast live—an example is the insistence on more and more hours of broadcasting for the Korean reunion event; as a result, regularly scheduled programs were canceled and the reunion telecasts continued. It was express audience interest that helped decide, too, on continuation of the live Watergate broadcasts.

Inversely, the joint decision of organizers and broadcasters to give media-events treatment to some public occasion may fail because the audience refuses to attend, or to celebrate, the event. Thus, the live broadcast of President Nixon's visit to China fell flat for lack of audience participation.[18] By preempting scheduled programs, other major events have antagonized certain segments of the viewing public; Sadat's arrival in Jerusalem, for example, interrupted the live broadcast of an all-star football game in the United States and caused one of the American networks considerable concern lest football fans be offended.

A Pathology of Events

The failure to reach consensus among the partners negotiating over the production of a media event may result either in cancellation of the broadcast or in one or another aberrant form of broadcast. Contemplation of the range of these possibilities suggests what might be called a "pathology" of media events, resulting from a veto or refusal to endorse the event by one or more of the partners. Consider Table 2, where we assume that two of the partners endorse an event and the third does not. The results are "events manqué," "events refused," and "events denied."

Thus, when the audience refuses its endorsement of an event, the event will fail, however gloriously it is produced. The live broadcast of the Nobel Peace Prize to Begin and Sadat simply did not fly, because the audience demurred. It was a Friday afternoon in Israel, Sadat had chosen not to attend, and there was a sense of dissonance about the event as the Egypt-Israel peace talks began to sour. Yet the event was broadcast live from Oslo, a result of cooperation between the Israeli broadcasters and the Swedish Academy, the organizers.

Table 2 A "pathology" of media events

Event	Organizer endorses	Broadcaster endorses	Audience endorses
Manqué	Yes	Yes	No
Refused	Yes	No	Yes
Denied	No	Yes	Yes
Reluctant	Yes/No	Yes/No	Yes/No

The signing of the peace accord between India and Sri Lanka in 1987 presents an even more radical example. For the Sinhalese this was an imposed event, where staying home to view was not dictated by a social norm or even by edict, but by curfew (Nesiah, 1990). The parade of Russian tanks and troops into Czechoslovakia in 1968 was also broadcast live.

Or consider an event that is refused by the broadcasters and, as a result, is not transmitted at all; for example, when the President wishes to deliver a live presidential address to the nation. Such requests are rarely refused. On some occasions, however, one or another of the networks may decide that it will not make free time available. A similar misfortune befell President Ronald Reagan's effort in 1981 to organize a day of "solidarity" with the Polish people when only PBS, among the networks, saw fit to respond.[19] Such episodes add weight to the proposition that, potentially at least, the media are free to say no.

Yet another example refers to the gigantic assembly of 400,000 people in a Tel Aviv square in 1982 to demand that a national commission of inquiry investigate the massacre in the Palestinian refugee camps in Lebanon after Israeli troops had withdrawn. Organizers of this event tried to persuade Israeli television to give at least some moments of live coverage to an event they correctly perceived as "historic," even though they could not know how dramatic the turnout would be when they made their (unsuccessful) request. Media events directly critical of establishments are rare or nonexistent—almost by definition—even in Western democracies.

Of course, broadcasters are continually refusing events. Every group feels that its anniversary celebration, or its particular achievement, is historic, and tries to persuade broadcasters that the entire society wishes to join in the celebration. Often, broadcasters refuse initiatives from within their own organization, as when CBS refused to give live coverage to the Senate hearings on organized crime, insisting that the hearings were not sufficient reason to cancel the afternoon soap operas (Friendly, 1967; Russo, 1983).

In the most radical case, the organizer may be petitioned by audience and by broadcasters to permit the live broadcasting of an event, yet fail to be persuaded. This possibility sounds very prudish in the age of mass communications and evokes thoughts of events that may embarrass or compromise the organizers. Much ceremony attends summit meetings, for example, but the meetings themselves are not broadcast live.

Mutatis mutandis, another case of organizer recalcitrance is the return of Khomeini.[20] The audience certainly wanted to see him—and so, apparently, did the broadcasters. But the putative organizers, the shaky government that was acting as caretaker following the shah's departure, obviously did not want to permit a live broadcast of the return of the exiled leader. And so it was that after a few minutes the live broadcast was interrupted by the intervention of loyalist officers. A picture of the shah appeared and the national anthem was played (Sreberny-Mohammadi, 1990).[21]

Consider, too, the historic uprisings in Eastern Europe in the fall of 1989, when governments suffered mass rallies to be held and heard petitions for political and economic liberalization. On one such occasion, as already noted, journalists of Czech television declared a strike in the name of freedom of information, insisting on their duty to give live coverage to the demonstrations. The government—prior to its capitulation—promptly intervened, sending in the police to take control of the television station. When this restraining action somehow failed, there were hours of live broadcasting of protest and even of Contest between opposition leaders and government (a rare example) heralding the collapse that followed soon after. It is no surprise that live media events in totalitarian states are reserved for establishment initiatives. But it is also the case that ceremonial events do not go forward without appropriate endorsement even in democratic societies. These are events denied.

A different example comes from the Catholic church, which persistently denies permission to broadcast the mass. It is true that certain great events (the Pope's journeys, for example, or the Christmas Eve programs) include celebration of the mass and are broadcast. But none of these "count" for believers—except, authorities say, those unable to leave their homes. The church steadfastly insists that television does not permit true participation. And thus, quite knowingly, the Catholic church elects not to compete with the burgeoning electronic pulpits of the evangelist movements.[22]

"Reluctant" events take their place alongside events "denied," "refused," and "manqué." These are events that are mounted live but reflect the lack of, or fear of, total commitment on the part of organizers and/or broadcasters and/or audiences. We have already referred to the funeral of Sadat. Egyptian and foreign networks were on hand to transmit the ceremony as it was taking place, but it was soon apparent—indeed, the French presenter said so explicitly—that there was very little enthusiasm for the event. First, no in-person audience was permitted to assemble, whether for reasons of security or for fear of embarrassment. Second, the ceremony was so awkward that one could not but infer that the expectations it disappointed were perhaps those of Western audiences who regarded Sadat as a hero, but perhaps not those of the Egyptian audiences, organizers, or broadcasters.[23] In other words, some events may be given media-events treatment only reluctantly. The same holds true for an audience that is compelled to participate against its will, or against its inclination. Country after country gives the day off to its schoolchildren or advises government offices to give leave to their staff, in return for lining the parade route for some visiting dignitary or joining in an anniversary celebration. "Enthusiasm barometers" have yet to be defined for public events, but it is not difficult to sense the difference between the in-person audience for the Pope or the royal wedding and those to be found on more reluctant occasions. As to the television audience, it takes and understands its role accordingly.

There is yet another aspect of pathology that must be considered here—"hijacked" events. By definition, media events attract the attention of the world: the cameras are mounted, the lights are turned on, the ceremony begins. There is no stronger temptation to advocates of some revolutionary cause than to turn these lights and cameras on themselves. Such were the Munich Olympics of 1972, when Palestinian terrorists held Israeli athletes hostage and murdered them in cold blood.[24] Such was the 1968 Democratic national convention in Chicago, when students marched on the convention in protest against United States policy on the issues of the '60s.[25] Such was the case in the signing of the Indo-Lanka peace accord, when a Sinhalese navy ensign struck out at Rajiv Gandhi with his rifle as he was reviewing a military unit that had been assigned to the honor guard of the ceremony. Mirroring the rage of his people, the ensign became a hero and catalyst for a subsequent Sinhalese uprising against the Indians (Nesiah, 1990).

In hijacked events such as these, broadcasters look uneasily to their contracts. Their pledge is to be faithful to the agreed definition of the event as a ceremony, but here is breaking news that needs to be covered as news that violates ceremony, no less than would an assassination attempt on the President or the Pope. Should the broadcasters revert to their role as journalists, or should they remain faithful to the agreement? When protesters massed near the White House to denounce the signing of the Camp David accord between Israel and Egypt, the networks had to ask themselves that question.[26] One network sent a camera crew to the protest meeting and cut away from the ceremony to the news event; the other two networks remained true to their ceremonial role.

Functions and Dysfunctions

It is clear by now that the calculus guiding the partners to the negotiation process is based on a desire to control the definition and the character of an event, and to maximize the profit (or minimize the loss) of association with it. This is true no less for hijackers than it is for organizers; but it also is true of broadcasters and audiences.

Organizers promote events that embody those values around which society, or some large portion of it, can be rallied, and with which they can associate themselves. Thus, in World War II, the United States Treasury proposed a special drive for the sale of war bonds in the name of the American soldiers fighting for their country. It enlisted Kate Smith, at ostensibly great personal sacrifice, for a marathon radio program; the treasury certainly did not proclaim that the event would also serve the anti-inflationary function of withdrawing currency from circulation (Merton, 1946). The moon landings were proposed by the National Aeronautics and Space Administration to celebrate man's ability to conquer outer space; the agency refrained from proclaiming that it was seeking a renewal of its funds and its mandate (Wolfe, 1980). The royal family proposed the wedding of Charles to Diana as a national celebration of the glorious traditions of Great Britain, not as an effort to distract attention from the troubles besetting the British economy and polity.[27] Organizers of events seek to focus attention on the most appealing and most traditional of the values involved, and to reaffirm them. They also attempt to make certain that they are acknowledged as the rightful custodians of those values.

Hijackers, on the other hand, wish to protest those values, to explode the myth of value consensus implied by the event. They reach out, not only for attention, but for potential recruits whose "false consciousness," shaped by the ostensible consensus, prevents them from identifying their true interest (Coleman, 1980; Katz, 1981; Noelle-Neumann, 1984).

We know what the gains may be, but entering into a contract with others implies compromise. What do organizers have to lose by contracting with broadcasters and audiences? The answer, of course, is exclusive control. In times prior to the differentiation of media from government (Alexander, 1988), the sovereignty of the organizer over the locus of the event was uncontested and uncompromised, as was the orchestration of its program and deployment of the audience. The representation of the event by broadcasting threatens this control of the organizer over the mix of moralizing and entertainment, of politics and passion. A commentator may explain the meaning of the event, or of some gesture, in a manner unintended by the organizer; the broadcaster may project his own symbols onto the event. The audience, for its part, may refuse to prepare itself for the solemnity of the occasion, or give the event its hegemonic reading.

Even if faithfully broadcast, a message may fail to get through because the demeanor of the audience is beyond the control of the organizer, or because there is no way to maintain continuity of contact with persons who were moved by it. It is easy to see why the Catholic church fears the loss of community implicit in the private consumption of religious television; the loss of ritual propriety in the living-room posture of prayer; the loss of appreciation for the intermediary role of the church in communication with God (Guthrie and Grand, 1988). Even when the organizers have direct control over their own broadcasts—as is the case for evangelical TV—they cannot easily control the audience at home.

The primary actors in the drama (Sadat, the Pope, Prince Charles) also have something to gain and something to lose in the contractual process. Such events associate their principals with sacred values and inspire them in the knowledge that millions, sometimes hundreds of millions, have endowed them with the right to act in the name of those values. Television knows how to dramatize their gestures. Potentially, the actor can do things he could not have dreamed of doing otherwise. Thus, in public and on television, the Pope accomplished more than he could have through the traditional channels of papal diplomacy (Guizzardi, 1981). Begin and Sadat acted more decisively, and perhaps more dangerously, than they would have outside the live television event. The charisma of the moment overrides the restrictions of normal political dealings, hemmed in as they are by the cautious, complex, and contradictory advice of ministers, party leadership, and relevant reference groups.

But participants also have something to lose. They are in danger of losing the right to interpret their own gestures. The media make them into symbols, far beyond their power to control. Sometimes this approach helps, as the media "helped" the astronauts to look more like the test pilots they would have liked to be than the passengers they actually were (Wolfe, 1980). But just as often, it hurts; after all, Sadat was perhaps deprived of the subtle image of himself he was simultaneously trying to address to his fellow Arabs. Being part of the organizing agency, leaders gain and lose by being subjected to the broadcasters' representations.

The in-person audience gains an association with the center of society by attending the original event, and consequently joins the broadcast event as actors. They feel potent because their presence has an effect on their hero—on the football field, at the airport in Warsaw, on the launching pad, or in the convention hall. They will be seen on television and acknowledged long afterward as persons who took part in the experience of being there. But from where they are standing they get only the most fragmentary glimpse of what there is to see, compared with the orchestrated ensemble of events seen by the television viewer. And sometimes it is cold and wet outside.

Television broadcasters also have much to gain and lose. By offering their endorsement to a public event, they are catapulted into the center. They become full-fledged members of the wedding, suddenly welcomed by all. Walter Cronkite, Barbara Walters, and John Chancellor flew from Egypt to Israel with Anwar Sadat. Playing its priestly role in a consensual event, television is perceived as a public service that annuls the everyday dissatisfactions targeted against it. The small screen becomes the authorized historian, inviting its vast audience to take part in the chronicling of modernity. Television rivals the elite's control of the locus of the event, and of its meaning.

But even if the broadcasters are pleased to get such good box seats at the event, their intervention has unanticipated consequences. It raises the question of where the "real" event is actually taking place. Is it on the playing field chosen by the organizers, or is it in the air and at home? In their pleasure to be counted among the principals, the broadcasters may fail to realize that they have recast themselves as actors, rather than observers, in a new event. What they lose in the process is their critical distance. By agreeing to play a role in the representation of public events, broadcasters thereby suspend something of their professional roles as independent critics. In the mutual exchange of status—whereby organizer and broadcaster give legitimacy to each other—there is also a blurring of the broadcaster's identity (Levy, 1981).

If the broadcasters are not certain of the true locus of the event—coveting their free seats to the Olympics as much as others in the primary audience—we cannot expect more from the home audience. There is a pervasive uneasiness, at least for those events that have some real locus, that one is missing out on something better. The in-person audience, it should be remembered, is also unsure about whether it should not be at home, watching TV. So are some of the organizers, for that matter.[28]

To sum up, it can now be said that successive endorsements by the partners to the negotiations over media events relate not only to the problems of control of the event, its values, and its meaning, but also to a quiet but powerful uprooting of the locus of reality. There is still considerable ambiguity about whether "public space" has not moved from the forum where it originated, from the theaters and stadia and churches, to the living room.

Blessed, then, are the television viewers for they (may) have inherited reality. We say this not in the sense that television is a substitute for everyday reality, but because these great events may have their primary effect, and certainly their place in the collective memory, not in the form in which they were originally staged but in the form in which they were broadcast. Most events are radically transformed by television, often becoming unrecognizable to people who attended them in person. All the more reason, therefore, to be concerned with the way in which the event is scripted.

4

Performing Media Events

The televising of public occasions must meet the challenge not only of representing the event, but of offering the viewer a functional equivalent of the festive experience. By superimposing its own performance on the performance as organized, by displaying its reactions to the reaction of the spectators, by proposing to compensate viewers for the direct participation of which they are deprived, television becomes the primary performer in the enactment of public ceremonies. Such performances by television must not be considered mere "alterations" or "additions" to the original. Rather, they should be perceived as qualitative transformations of the very nature of public events.

It is conceptually distracting to ask whether this type of broadcast offers a "true" rendition of the original event. Given the openly "performative" (Austin, 1962) nature of television's role, the problematics of "truth" and "falsehood" become almost irrelevant here. The issue is less one of truth than of loyalty. Television enacts a commitment to the event, not merely its reproduction. It bets on the event's importance and ties itself to its fate, repudiating journalistic detachment.

The commitment is not only moral or ideological; it is also a commitment to the form of the event. It is an effort to repudiate the truism that if the original event is ceremony, its retextualization by television must unavoidably flatten it into a spectacle.

The rhetoric of television then consists in developing an aesthetics of compensation by trying to reinject the lost ceremonial dimension, by offering a substitute for "being there." The commitment is expressed in the striving of the medium to overcome its own limitations.

Three aspects of television's performance are implicit here, and this chapter will take up each in turn. First we ask, what does it mean to say that a broadcast is faithful to the ceremony as organized? We examine television's loyalty to the event, its efforts to uphold its original definition. Then, in a second section, we explore television's vain attempt to provide a channel through which viewers and celebrants can actually reach out to each other, trying to multiply the reality of the ceremonial event as if it were loaves and fishes. From this more nostalgic use of the medium, we turn, finally, to an analysis of television's ability to provide its own event. Neither reproduction nor access, it offers an experience in its own right, different from the original, and probably more important.

Television as Wedding Photographer

Television's commitment to an event is, first of all, definitional. It recognizes the event, conveys its distinctive features, and exposes what Searle (1971) would call its constitutive rules. A second aspect of definition is "hermeneutic." Beyond identifying the event, television explores what the event is about and offers "instant interpretation" (Nora, 1972). One might say that television proposes the event's "ascribed" meaning, as opposed to the meaning the event will eventually "achieve" through the retrospective assessment of historians. Third, television is protective of the event. It makes clear the event's absolute priority and, in particular, its precedence over other news of all sorts. It gives resonance to the event's specific mood. An aesthetic watchdog, television makes sure that the event's unity of tone and action are preserved from interference.

Upholding Definition

Unlike physical objects, ceremonies are self-defining; their performance consists in the proclamation of their identity. Television serves to relay the pertinent features through which this identity is proclaimed, allowing viewers to identify the nature of the event. Given the contractual character of public events and the equally important role of principals and public, these features are to be found both in the realm of reaction and in the realm of performance.

The very nature of a ceremony implies the existence of a response. Television underlines this response, first by highlighting the reactions of the audience of spectators who are present at the event in person. Directors select the "relevant" reactions for transmission and emulation.[1] They stress the communal nature of the experience, the unanimous adhesion of the crowd to the values and symbols being celebrated. What is stressed is not only unanimity, but unanimity within diversity. Consensus is portrayed as a process, as an overcoming of differences. The event requires that rivals suspend their feuds and strangers their particularisms to join in the effusive, contagious mood of the moment. As in the Roman Adventus—the ceremonial welcome of a distinguished visitor at the town gate—care is taken to assure the presence of representatives of all groups that are constituent of the community; the absence of any group might seem to imply rejection or defiance.[2] The event must therefore be shown to be adequately representative of the entire community.

Television also provides means for identifying the event

through the tone and cadence of the narrator's voice. Some presenters have become famous—indeed, some have become indispensable—for their specialization in the narration of public events. Their reverent tone, eloquent silences, strangled or contained voices, are essential elements of the event. Like the cheering crowd, they have over the years become part of the event's prerequisites. In fact, narration and cheering are so similar in function that one can be substituted for the other. In the coverage of the royal wedding by both British channels, the roaring of the crowds was permitted virtually to drown out the voice of the presenter, as if the narration was but a more articulate form of cheering.

The absence of a responding crowd, and in some extreme cases the unavailability of a narration, may leave viewers in doubt about what type of reaction is called for, and ultimately about what is going on. Recalling an earlier example, the decision by Polish television to focus on the Pope's ritual functions and (deliberately) to play down public reactions resulted in a blurring of the event's definition as the reunion between a people and the representative of the spiritual heritage from which it was forcibly separated. Technical instruction in the nature of Catholic liturgy was not what Polish viewers needed from television. Similarly, the funeral of President Sadat caused obvious embarrassment (and hardly disguised irritation) to the narrator of the event's French broadcast. Ambiguity concerning the type of response expected, and uncertainty about whether any response at all was expected, ultimately backfired on the performance itself, casting doubt on the nature of what was taking place. In this particular case, the event remained "mute." While lending a hand to the technical tasks of burying his president, Hosni Mubarak abstained from making any decisive statement, thus further preventing the burial from becoming a "full" public event and, as such, the state funeral of an assassinated leader. Television was unable to uphold a definition which the event itself was reluctant to provide.

When events are less ambiguous, television can come to the rescue of their self-definition, reiterating the features by which their organizers wish them to be identified. Emotional displays, for example, are not supposed to be part of a hero's funeral. In the case of Lord Mountbatten's funeral, therefore, British television resisted the temptation to display "private" emotions: the fact that Prince Charles was apparently fighting back a tear during his reading of scripture was not shown in close-up. Emotion, however, is quite compatible with the ethos of a wedding. Therefore, when the expression of emotion took the form of a newlywed kiss on the balcony of Buckingham Palace, it was perceived and presented by television as a public gesture.[3]

With respect to the definition of the royal wedding, television deliberately overlooked not only the deviations of the performers from their scenarios, but also the antics of the would-be performers among the spectators. The carnival ambiance which could be observed along the procession route led many observers (including novelist John Fowles) to comment on the contrast between what they perceived as English playfulness (that of the crowd) versus British arrogance (the procession), and between Elizabethan jocularity (street behavior) and Victorian etiquette (behavior of the principals). Only the Victorian or British in tone survived the broadcast, leaving little place for the ironic dimension of many a patriotic gesture. Chaney (1983) notes this same tendency—and its social and moral cost—in the BBC's preference for military formalism over civilian expressiveness in its live broadcast of the victory parade after World War II. The spontaneity and universalistic mood of the informal marchers was sacrificed thereby. Tact, good taste, and restraint guide the BBC broadcasters as custodians of an event's definition.

Loyalty to definition is probably the essence of that which makes broadcasters performers rather than observers. As loyalty often does, it may render the broadcasters blind to the non-scripted aspects of the very event they are transmitting. This was strikingly illustrated at the queen's silver jubilee, when a mock attempt on the life of the queen was noticed by those present at the event but not by the television team which was unwittingly recording it. Of course, the dilemma of whether to transmit an aberration or a "hijacking" of an event (such as Sadat's review of troops turned assassination, or the Munich Olympics turned massacre) involves an uneasy editorial choice. As we have seen, it requires a decision to violate the integrity of the contractually agreed event by reintroducing journalistic considerations that may go beyond the authority and competence of the special teams charged with the broadcasting of ceremonial events.

Providing Interpretation

Television serves as a guide to the meanings of which the event is a carrier. It does so first by imposing a narrative coherence on the event, by endowing it with a story line; indeed, it constrains even its organizers to think of the event as a whole. Its participants are invested with roles and attributes which interpret and add depth to the identity of the event.

Television also relies on connotations by highlighting those elements—generally nonverbal ones—which illuminate the "why" of an event from the perspective of its organizers. The ostensible discovery by the cameras of visual messages "inlaid" in the faces of participants or the windows of the cathedral tends to mask the fact that such messages are made available by a deliberate decision. Television's reading is, thus, more "expositive" than interpretive. In a sense, it is an exercise in authority.

These two processes take place simultaneously; they reinforce each other and are often indistinguishable. Consider the royal wedding once more. The messages of the wedding were organized in eloquent dramaturgies and spelled out in the articulate voice of the Archbishop of Canterbury. Television's performance joined that of the archbishop and the other organizers—palace, church, armed forces, police—in a way so strikingly complementary that while the three performances were organized independently, so we were told, there lingers an insistent feeling of "collusion"—call it teamwork. The archbishop explicated the themes which the organizers tried to communicate in protocol and ceremony. The messages later made articulate in the archbishop's speech were also visually or gesturally offered to the spectators throughout the occasion, in flickering, discontinuous cueings.

The archbishop's speech fulfilled an editorial function. Constituting an event within the event, it referred to the main themes of the occasion and, in the process, proposed additional messages of its own. Reciprocally, television abandoned its role as observer and commentator, and reverently assumed an "observant" role. Organizers, for their part, preempted the directorial role, planted photo opportunities, and offered a choreographed ceremony, anticipating the metamorphosis of the heroes of the day into televised images. In short, the organizers were putting on a show; the priest was commenting upon it; television was leading the amens.

We perceive television as a chorus, underlining on the surface of the event the messages the archbishop spoke from its depths. While the meanings proposed by the archbishop were authentic by virtue of his authority over the event (because, in a "performative" act, he simply made them so), the meanings proposed by television were not openly ascribed to the event but rather revealed during its unraveling. It is striking that, with the exception of one message, these several meanings were identical.

The archbishop firmly established the fairy tale theme in the very act of brushing it aside. "Here is the stuff of which fairy tales are made," he began. Having thus ushered in Cinderella, the archbishop continued by rejecting the sufficiency of the metaphor. He dismissed the idea that the time had come for the newlyweds to live happily ever after.

Cinderella, however, was much on the minds of the organizers, who made sure that Lady Diana would be accompanied to Saint Paul's by ordinary policemen, but be escorted back to Buckingham Palace by the household cavalry. The same organizers dutifully displayed the roommates of her brief working career now seated in the church's front pews, where television cameras could easily underline their presence. The narrators continued from that point. Announcing that the bride's gown was a "fairy tale" gown, that the state carriage in which she rode was a "glass carriage" (indeed, there were windows), they evoked a narrative metamorphosis which, for a moment, demoted the granddaughter of Lady Fermoy to a fairy tale "commoner." She was a kindergarten teacher, an Earl's Court boarder—the better to celebrate her promotion.

The archbishop's second theme redirected attention from the institution of royalty to the institution of family. Pulling an aristocratic, wealthy, and outrageously privileged couple out of its leisure class, the orator pointed to it as an embodiment of the universal image of youth and of the drama of everyman's marriage. "There is an ancient Christian tradition," said the archbishop, "that every bride and groom, on their wedding day, are regarded as a royal couple." The archbishop thus translated the extraordinary status of this particular couple into something equally extraordinary, but no longer "above" ordinary: the universally shared, but once-in-a-lifetime experience of marriage. In Turnerian (1969) terms, the archbishop transposed the originality of the event from the realm of "structure" into that of "antistructure." He switched from particular to universal in order to recognize the ceremony of marriage as the foundation of the institution of family, and to proclaim that family holds the potential for social change. "Our faith sees a wedding day, not as a place of arrival, but as the place where the adventure really begins . . ."

Obviously, there is a difference between the progression of royal family events and soap operas, in that the former have a public face offered only intermittently and in ceremonial settings, while the latter expose private life as a continuous performance. Both, however, deal with the interaction between individuals and norms; both are concerned with the fate of families and the transmission of values from generation to generation. The organizers of this event did not need to emphasize its family dimension—it was visible throughout. Television's performance echoed this attitude, highlighting the archbishop's concern. BBC close-ups subtly stressed the theme, pointing rapidly to a worried mother, a proud father, an emotional grandmother. These domestic figures told a story that paralleled that of the royal personae, providing a frame which, at least superficially, competed with the Cinderella story.

The third theme stressed the power of marriage to improve society in accordance with God's will. "We, like them, are agents of creation," said the archbishop, to indicate the similarity between a "we" (the people) and a "them" (the princely couple). The statement "We are like them," or more exactly, "We, like them, are agents of creation," invited the overcoming of distance. But despite the overcoming, distance was maintained. The royals will move closer, but only if you imitate them. Their approachability is not physical but moral. They are approachable insofar as they are embodiments of norms to which any one of us may subscribe. The archbishop's rhetorical gesture was particularly interesting in that it offered a solution to the paradox highlighted by Blumler et al. (1971) in their analysis of the contradictory attitude of the British public toward the royal family. The royal family, in the Blumler study, was expected to meet the impossible requirements of both dropping and maintaining decorum; of abolishing protocol and perpetuating it; of keeping its distinctiveness, while renouncing the thought of being different.

The event's organizers catered to this ambivalence of the British public vis-à-vis monarchical distance, but less subtly than the archbishop. The rhetorical core of the event consisted in a series of back and forth motions stressing two antithetical themes: "Now they are like us . . . Now they are not . . ." Relayed by television, the pomp and pageantry served to establish distance, but they were also used as a continuous background for discrete signs of approachability. Such was the "Just Married" sign painted in lipstick and naughtily stuck on the back of the state carriage, together with a flock of balloons echoing those in the hands of myriads of well-wishers, or the departure at Waterloo Station, where cameras showed the honeymooners delivered into the realm of public transportation from a six-horse carriage on a red carpet.

Television was faithful to the organizers' view of the problem of monarchical distance. Humanizing devices were stressed as often as possible against the background of the event's definitional grandeur. The "Just Married" sign received full attention. Royal children were celebrated as childlike, the princely couple as young, and biology was generally allowed to obliterate caste. Such details may seem pedestrian, compared to the archbishop's elevated message. They provide a translation of its gist, however. Television highlighted messages that were in fact the wedding's raison d'être, proving itself something more than a reliable wedding photographer.

To take an example from another event, consider President Sadat's arrival at Ben Gurion Airport. The particular way in which he disembarked was hailed by almost every narrator as "symbolic" of the trip as a whole. While crew members opened the door of the Boeing aircraft, impressively decorated with the emblem of the Arab Republic of Egypt, an El Al gangway was pushed alongside. Unthinkable until that very minute, this juxtaposition was the paradigmatic example of what the television teams were there to film. Missing that image would have been a minor catastrophe (as it was for the ITV to have missed the royal kiss on Buckingham Palace's balcony, and for the BBC to have failed to show it in close-up).

Television directors are constantly on the lookout for situations which express the purpose of an event in a condensed way. Television narrators have to make sure that the significance of such images will not pass unnoticed and will be correctly assessed. In other terms, television's interpretive function consists in making sure (1) at the image level, that the significant features of the event, its visual messages, are properly highlighted; and (2) at the narration level, that these features, once noticed, are correctly interpreted—that is, within a frame of reference consonant with that of the organizers.

The highlighting process has an importance which goes far beyond its technical achievement. It diminishes the role of exhortations and announcements emanating from the organizers of the event or its principals while exalting the event's visual or gestural aspects. By displacing audience focus from explicit statements to visual clues, television "naturalizes" the event; it authenticates its inlaid message, transforming the performative aspects of ceremonies (utterances emanating from figures of power) into visual anecdotes. It also makes audiences active partners in the reading of the event by inviting interpretation, by encouraging hermeneutic pleasure in the deciphering of indexes and the scrutiny of "symbols." Television converts pronouncements of authority into exercises in seduction.

Protecting Tone and Prerogative

Unlike the roving glance of the cynical journalist, the glance of the media-event broadcaster is stubbornly focused. Unlike the equally single-minded glance of the security agent, the broadcaster's glance is participatory, actively involved in the official meaning of the event, busy endorsing and conveying its definition. The security glance is blind to meanings.[4] The journalistic glance is cynically receptive to all meanings. The broadcaster's glance, helping the event to spell its name, enacts its meaning. The event is given absolute priority over all other programs; it is placed above all competing concerns and tightly protected from any interference with its political content, its temporal sequence, its tone, its mood.

Television's power lies not only in the way it structures the flow of daily life, but in its consequent ability to interrupt this flow. Media events are an example of this interruptive dimension. They cancel all other programs, bring television's clock to a stop, and while they are on the air, cannot themselves be interrupted. Their performance belongs to "sacred time," bringing all social activity to a standstill. For a while, the event occupies society's "center." No matter what happens, the event has to go on. Thus the riots at Toxteth during the royal wedding ceremonies are not mentioned until the ceremonial occasion is over. This protectiveness toward the event goes to such extremes that it inspires plans for the continuation of the broadcast even if a terrorist incident were to affect some of the principals. The BBC preparation for the royal wedding included contingency plans and alternative editing routes. The occasion can go on while the crisis is being dealt with.

The only reality which can compete with a media event is another media event. We have already noted how one major American channel chose to commute between the Rose Bowl and Sadat's arrival in Jerusalem. The result was that both events were robbed of their symbolic resonance, of their mood. The Jerusalem event looked unbearably slow and pompous; the American event looked gratuitously frenetic.[5] Television's double commitment in this case failed to protect an essential dimension of such events: their tone.

While anthropologists keep stressing the messy and often chaotic dimensions of rituals they have attended, media events are characterized by an almost pedantic concern with unity: unity of time (related to the duration of the live broadcast) and, of course, unity of action. Only in news broadcasts—never in media events—does one juxtapose and give equal importance to, say, the peace moves of President Sadat and the bellicose declarations of rejection-front leaders among the Arabs.

The Dallas assassination of President Kennedy was a "tragedy," and as such, an occasion to invoke fate and to turn the youngest President into an effigy of human suffering, the central figure of a "tableau": *Pietà* in a convertible. But tragedy was also an aesthetic concern. Television's homage to the departed President stressed the dignified stoicism of the principals, particularly the Hecuba-like composure adopted by Jacqueline Kennedy after a few seconds of petit-bourgeois dismay. Once this tone was established, it had to be maintained throughout the event. Hence the uneasiness felt by television teams over the assassination of Lee Harvey Oswald and expressed in the CBS tribute to Kennedy, "Four Dark Days." There were now two assassinations, two corpses, two funerals. The second corpse could not be brushed aside for the duration of television's requiem. A stylistic problem received a rhetorical solution: if the first assassination was a tragedy, the second would be a farce, a caricature, a travesty. Illustrious examples notwithstanding, Kennedy's crucifixion could not take place in bad company. Genres are not to be mixed.

Television's protective role stems from the fact that it is not reporting an event, but actively performing it. In view of this fact, one can hardly expect broadcast journalists to display a penelopean abnegation and to coldly dissect what is largely their own creation. They are not simply transmitting an event or commenting upon it; they are bringing it into existence. Thus, broadcasters double as monument makers or apostles.[6]

Something takes place in the symbolic realm which might affect reality. This something is akin to the medieval dramaturgy of "mysteries." Giving media-event status to a proposed event implies a belief in its mystery. As in all religious rites, attendance cannot be neutral and uncommitted. Television here is not simply an observer or a producer. Its presence reactivates an ancient function: the act of attending, of "being there," and of being an eventual propagator, a subsequent medium. Those present at early Christian events were used as such "media." They were called "witnesses," or, in Greek, "martyrs."

Agreeing to promote a political occasion to media-event status thus implies a willingness on the part of television organizations to accept an apostolic mission. It involves an endorsement of the event's goals and an affirmative assessment of the event's power to achieve these goals. This power inheres in the ceremony—in its appeal and evocative character—and in the ability of the media to produce the ceremony. This is still show business, of course: producers have to assess the potential of an event before placing their bets.

Once the commitment is made, it is not easy to switch back again to journalism, as in the hijacking of an event. In the face of media events, the journalistic paradigm of objectivity and neutrality is simply irrelevant. The choice is either to maintain an agonistic role, treating the event as "news" and addressing it within a news broadcast, or to enter the mode of media ceremonial and become the event's witness. A journalist assigned to a media event must undergo a temporary conversion, one which is not always to his liking (Levy, 1981).

An Aesthetics of Compensation

Striving to go beyond its upholding of definition and even beyond its role of witness, television dares to give viewers the feeling that they are "there." Refusing to be reconciled to its essential inability to provide a phatic channel (Jakobson, 1960) for the actual interaction between celebrants and home audiences, television insists at least on trying to simulate ceremonial participation.

Walter Benjamin (1968a) asks what becomes of the public's relationship to art when works of art are copied and diffused through mechanical reproduction. As students of mass communication, we wish to raise a similar question: What happens to ceremonies when, instead of being attended in person, they are delivered to each of us at home? Is it possible, we ask, for television to do more than make a spectacle of a ceremony, a show of a performance? How can television give a sense of ceremonial participation? How can it compensate viewers for the absence of interactivity?

Consider some distinctions among the modes of interaction between performers and audience which characterize different kinds of occasions (MacAloon, 1984). *Spectacle* stands at one extreme, with cinema as its ultimate form. *Festival* is at the other extreme, almost entirely free of spectacle. *Ceremony* takes a middle ground between the two. We suggest that these forms differ according to (1) specificity of focus; (2) specificity of response; and (3) the nature of interaction between audience and performers.

Spectacles—such as sports and theater—share a narrowness of focus, a limited set of appropriate responses, and (excepting certain modern forms of theatre) a minimal level of interaction. What there is to see is very clearly exhibited. Spectacle implies a distinction in role between performers and audience. Performers are set apart and audiences are asked to respond cognitively and emotionally in predefined categories of approval, disapproval, arousal, or passivity. Audience reaction may enhance the performance, but it is not meant to be part of its definition. (In the case of cinema, such an interaction becomes so irrelevant that audience response is almost entirely internalized.)

Festival, on the contrary, is diffuse in focus. No simple picture or pageant is imposed monopolistically on participants. The occasion offers many different foci and much room for ad hoc activity. Appropriate responses may be many and varied. Indeed, creative responses are typically welcome. Interaction is obviously called for, since the roles of performers and spectators are neither fixed nor irreversible. Equally obvious is the observation that the nature of the resultant "performance" is altogether dependent on the audience "response."

Ceremony shares features with both spectacle and festival in that, on the one hand, it offers a clear focus, a definite distinction between performers and respondents—the latter being expected to respond in specific (and usually traditional) ways—while, on the other hand, its existence consists in interaction between audience and performers. Audience response is one of the constitutive features of ceremony. Without it, a ceremony is empty.

If an event as organized contains elements of both ceremony and festival, it is reasonable to assume that the event as televised can only be spectacle; its focus is irremediably narrowed, reactions are highly limited, and they can in no way affect the performance. But is this really so? Television says no—at least it tries to. The media-events viewer, claims television, has *better* access; the event *is* "three dimensional"; the audience *can* respond. Let us see how.

Equalizing Access

First and most obvious, television equalizes access to the occasion. Nobody need (or can) pay more for a better seat; nobody need spend the night in a queue hoping to secure a better vantage point. There is some loss in this, as we have noted. Ostensibly, the festival aspect of the experience is lacking. Being jostled by a crowd, or rising as one person to cheer, has its attractions. But television offers compensation by removing invidiousness; neither power, nor money, nor dexterity gives advantage. As far as access is concerned, the structure of the broadcast audience is altogether different from the socially stratified audience on the spot. Moreover, the event is in better focus at home. The home audience "sees" more—not only because the view is not blocked, but because television, as we have shown, underlines the definition proposed for the event by its organizers and adds interpretation. The television viewer is drawn into the symbolic meaning of the event even more than is the primary audience on the spot.

Reinjecting Unequal Access

Not satisfied with the magic of equalizing access, television also attempts to reintroduce differentiation of participation—not in the audience but among its representatives.

In-person attendance at a public event or ceremony means attending part of the event. One cannot view a procession from all vantage points unless one moves along with the procession (and therefore loses one's place), or unless one is part of the procession (and therefore totally unable to focus on it as spectacle). An event is seen from a given place; this place and its distance from the center of the event tells you (and others) who you are. In the case of the royal wedding, either you are in the church (that is, a guest of the royal family) or you are outside the church, where a place with good visibility has to be paid for (in terms of rising before dawn or spending the night on the pavement). As in theater, distance from the stage and placement in regard to the center of the event are obvious reminders of one's place in society.

With the introduction of television, everybody can attend the whole of the event. The very notion of the totality of an event is new; it is a concept inherited from the domains of spectacle, on the one hand, and narrative structure, on the other.

Traditionally, an event such as a royal wedding was a string of smaller ceremonial units, featuring the same actors (the royal family, the newlyweds) but different audiences, and the dramaturgy of each of these units was oriented to the nature of its specific audiences. With television, the distinctive self-presentations of royalty to the different constituents of the British public are no longer exclusive of one another. The several groups now form one audience. The several subevents now form one narrative (and one of the tasks of the broadcaster is to organize the rhythmic continuity of the performance). By turning the event into a single spectacle, TV acts as an enfranchiser; ironically, only the audience in person is privileged to see a part of the event, thus experiencing the deprivation as the event's "aura."[7] The equidistance introduced between the event-as-a-whole and the various segments of the public is compensated for, however, by a television-performed reintroduction of distance.

This new distance is that which separates members of the broadcasting organizations involved in the event. A clear distinction is made between those television people who are part of the event (for example, Tom Fleming at the BBC wedding) and those television people who are in the studio and out of the event (Angela Rippon, also for the BBC), as evidenced by Rippon's interview of Fleming. Similarly, when the stars of American TV disembark with President Sadat on his historic visit, they are observed from the tarmac by the special correspondents of their respective networks. The less elevated status of the latter means not only that they are out with the crowds, while their prestigious colleagues are "in" with the principals, but also that they see less of what is taking place than either the telespectators at home or the studio anchors.[8]

Being pressed in the crowd, with no monitors at their disposal, they have to guess a large part of what is happening from visual deductions or audio clues, and their commentaries seem to corroborate the images on screen by a continual miracle. In such an extreme case, one wonders why these special or local correspondents are used at all, since they know less than the stars accompanying the President and see less than their studio counterparts who monitor the output from many cameras. One might answer that their function, perhaps, *is* to know less, to be pressed in the crowd, elbowed, pushed around, frantically trying to perceive, see, or guess. Their function is an aesthetic one (even though it is probably not planned that way). They are there to *restore* the sense of distance, of specific involvement in this or that partial aspect. They are performing that archaic dimension of events which is specific to audience participation and which disappears when a ceremony is indifferently offered to equidistant glances, evenly soaked in banalized knowledge. By their frantic and futile attempts to see and know, they are in charge of reinjecting the lost aura of the event. It is within this framework that one can understand the reference made to "rumors" in so many media events. Rumors reinject depth into a televised event, differentiating those who know from those who do not know yet. They suggest the existence of physical volume in the event: they counterbalance its pedagogic cool, its ironed-out flatness.

The Model of Contagion

Television simulates what its presence has abolished: status difference among spectators. Simultaneously, it tries to erase the actual distance which separates them from the physical celebration. Thus, in the carefully planned royal wedding, the point was to deny any discontinuity between the celebration in London and the audiences who were receiving the broadcast, to ignore the transformation of celebration into spectacle. In order to achieve this, an image was proposed: that of an epidemic, a contagion of celebrations which progressively merged into one another until the viewer was plunged into a vast party involving the whole of England.

Such tactics threaten to become permanent features of media events. On the day of the investiture of President François Mitterrand, French television's second channel (Antenne 2) chose to transport its studio to a village, away from the Paris-based ceremonies.[9] In this bucolic setting (possibly chosen for its affinity with the Rousseauist ethos of the festivals that followed the French Revolution), local ceremonies and celebrations transformed the reception of the broadcast into an event in its own right. The spectacle of a celebration was immediately converted into a focus for another celebration. The result was not very convincing: differences in celebratory styles tend to act as cruel reminders of the importance of props and pageantry. The broadcast of the royal wedding, too, included a village celebration during which children stuffed with ice cream waved little flags in the direction of majestically displayed TV sets. Despite the ice cream and flag-waving, TV sets remained TV sets, and the model of contagion remained a wish.

Contagion was more explicit the night before the wedding in the broadcast devoted to the festive fireworks in Hyde Park. This broadcast began as a sequence showing fire-signals traveling over the countryside, from hilltop to hilltop, from beacon to beacon, until the last of them came into view of the royal party, signaling Prince Charles to start the fireworks. The use of beacons suggested a progressive unification of England, a string of parties situated in a line of sight, a physical contagion of mood modeled on that of a forest fire. It is, of course, ironic that the progression of the beacons had to be conveyed electronically, but this metaphor was used by television to absolve itself from the sin of "representing" a celebration rather than diffusing it. Television could offer its services as a phatic channel, as an instrument of spatial continuity, rather than as an intermediary.

This was manifest also in other ostensibly secondary features of the event, such as the breakfast menu or the gown of Lady Diana. Thus, the British public was not simply informed that the queen would offer her guests a breakfast party: rather, the menu of the breakfast was widely advertised, and advertised as one which included no especially "fancy" item. Anyone who wished could prepare the breakfast being served in the dining room of Buckingham Palace. The culinary suggestion, however, was only implicit, compared with the huge publicity given to the copying of Lady Diana's gown. Organized as a suspense story, the reproduction of the dress became one of the threads which helped unify the wedding day as a continuous event. By the end of the day, the copy was displayed in a London window and a number of young women were interviewed saying they would buy copies for their own weddings. A few days later, the dress was mass reproduced and for sale.

The projects provided to viewers by both the breakfast menu and the gown served as unifiers of dispersed celebrations. Symbolically, television served as a continuer of the tradition which requires a young bride on her wedding day to distribute fragments of what she is wearing to the brides-to-be who surround her, in order to associate them, by some sort of magical contagion, with the *mana* which inhabits her on that day. Instead of fragments of her veil, Lady Di circulated television images of her dress, thereby offering to share her good luck with all the maidens of England. Television overcame distance, performing as a medium of physical contiguity.

Once more, television reinstated distance in the process of abolishing it. The breakfast menu was publicized, but the recipe for the wedding cake was emphatically kept secret. The wedding dress also was kept hidden until the last moment, and all sorts of stratagems were used to maintain this secrecy, including the announcement that many gowns had been prepared and that any leak would lead to the choice of a different one. Characteristically, the woman who busied herself with copying the dress for the television audience had no access to it, except by television. All her decisions were professional guesses based only on what she could see on screen (with the help of an instant-replay videotape). Television interfaced two versions of the gown, and they were presented as nearly identical. One was the "original" and destined to remain that, and that only. The other was the matrix for mass reproduction.

The activity of copying was encouraged, publicized, and submitted to an intricate mise-en-scène, the point of which was to

assert the "aura" of Lady Diana's dress, as opposed to the availability of its master copy. Thus television was reinstated as an
instrument of distance and defrocked as a medium of participation. The simulation of participation was looked upon benev-
olently as long as it did not infringe on the "aura" that distinguishes originals from reproductions and royalty from movie
stars. As soon as it did, television was sent back to the realm of
copies, of images, and "lesser realities." The would-be festival
reverted to its true status: that of spectacle.

Retextualizing the Event

Try as it may, television cannot succeed in transporting us
"there," or delivering the whole of an event to everyone's home.
The model of an electronic agora—however thrilling to con-
template—is not likely to be successfully achieved. In trying to
do so, television is being defensive and almost nostalgic, trying
to persuade viewers to reconcile themselves to a simulated participation in the "real" ceremony which is, alas, very far away.
Failing to maintain this phatic pose, television proceeds next to
compensate viewers for the secondhandedness of the experience, by offering a variety of consolation prizes such as those
we have just reviewed. But television has yet another strategy in
its repertoire, something more intrinsic than trying to persuade
the viewer that he or she is "there." What we offer you, says
television, is not just an unobstructed view of "there," but a
wholly different experience that is available only to those who
are *not* there. Making full use of the powers of spectacle, television presents its viewers with new, modern modes of participation in lieu of the old.[10] Instead of a pale equivalent of the
ceremonial experience, it offers the uniquely televisual "experience of not being there." As a matter of fact, says television,

there may not be any "there" at all. In any case, ours is the ceremony of record.

Nobody ever saw a royal wedding or an Easter mass from a blimp or from a fish-eye hanging from the ceiling of a cathedral. The new images do not correspond to any previous experience, except perhaps that conjured by visionary writers such as Victor Hugo. Modern television spectators are offered unexpected ways of participating in the ritual experience. New aesthetic avenues are opened which no longer stem from the apologetic need to exorcise spectacle, but from the decision to maximize the power of spectacle.

Tracing the Boundaries of the Event

In order to accomplish this goal, television's essential task consists in separating the event as figure from ground and, within the background, sorting what will remain inside the event's frame from what will be dropped as irrelevant. It is in the periphery of the event that television's role is most inventive, for it literally consists in recreating the event's environment. This creation serves three main purposes: it gives mastery over meaning, it differentiates among networks, and it provides liturgical interruption of the world's daily business.

Producers highlight the meanings of an event by surrounding it with human interest stories, small features originated by the networks and not the organizers. Forming the event's textual suburbs, these sideshows—interviews, documentaries, panel discussions—allow the networks independence in proposing and reinforcing their readings. Such sideshows seem secondary and anticlimactic. They are often greeted with impatience, semi-indifference, or mild amusement. Yet they play an important semantic role as parables cut to the size of crucial messages; they are little constructions which allow producers, in a process reminiscent of Freudian displacement, to say all they wish to say about the event without visibly altering it or remodeling it. This procedure solves a problem which is specific to the televising of live events, and which stems from the network's obligation to renounce the mastery over meaning that normal editing provides.

Filmed live, the event has to be displayed as a continuum, that is, without temporal cuts. It cannot be preedited at the level of scripting, since television, at least theoretically, has no access to the event's dramaturgy (which is the organizer's responsibility). Television's editing thus must assume an original form: it is cumulative rather than subtractive. It consists in adding extensions to the event, rather than taking off parts of it.

This cumulative editing ("authorship," in one of the original senses of the word) gains in importance when one moves from the center toward the periphery of the event. It is here that television regains the control is could not exert over the main figure. The Gandhi funeral, for example, was preceded by a program on the life of Indira Gandhi, "followed by three devotional songs sung by Lata Mangeshkar, the most popular singer in India. This created a solemn mood. The viewers were then 'taken live' to the ceremony" (Minwalla, 1990).

Thus, peripheral stories are generated, surrounding the event with a vast textual package that often consumes much more time than the event itself, giving the impression that the event serves only to promote the rest of the package. In view of the existing competition between networks, the rest of the package is far from secondary. Live broadcasts of events are electrifying, but they tend to resemble one another. The rest of the package permits more distinctiveness and may consequently enhance the ulterior image of the channel or network which puts it together. Each competing network makes a point of being more exhaus-

tive in its treatment of the event than its rivals, an ambition which often leads to the Sisyphean task of "exhausting" the event by taking each element in it and transforming it into an independent story. Starting from a live center, the event thus spreads in all directions, in an endless process of fragmentation and cloning which reminds one of the fate of medieval relics. Even if the event itself may still be described as genuine, it is nevertheless framed in a persistent background of "pseudo-events" (Boorstin, 1964).[11] Through metonymic contagion, these pseudoevents may acquire the look of authenticity.

Building the Event's Liturgical Context

In addition to constructing the semantic frame of the broadcast event, television builds a frame around the frame. It organizes the circumstances of viewing, surrounding the event with other programs—before and after—which make the event appear as the only important reality. Thus, television submits its spectators to a complex rite of passage, subverting the usual definition of what is "important," "real," or "serious."

Building the event's liturgical context is a two-step process. The first step is one of decontextualization. Television reproduces within its own programming the state-endorsed disruption of social rhythm that characterizes public events, thereby inverting the everyday distinction between work as public and leisure as private. As on holidays, leisure becomes public and work, if present at all, is conducted in private. Within this new framework, the seriousness and importance of the news as the main definition of social reality (as opposed to the "futile" world of entertainment) disappear in favor of a new reality, which is neither news in the usual sense of the word nor entertainment. Both are made to look distant, unreal, and shabby.

The second step is one of recontextualization. Time is now

structured as expectation and rehearsal, in order to allow full ritual involvement in exceptional and therefore unfamiliar ceremony. During the royal wedding, for example, the world of news lost its immediacy; the everyday became unreal and anachronistic echoes from another planet. When news bulletins were reinstated at the end of the wedding day, they showed, among other things, riots in Toxteth following the accidental death of a young man run over by a police van.[12] But the horror and absurdity of the incident seemed far removed, as if the death of a young man had become less important than the shape of a lackey's bicorne. This perception went so far as to create sentiments of rejection when a character belonging to the realm of the everyday was filmed and interviewed within the frame of the event. Despite her deliberate self-effacement and the perfectly proper wedding-guest answers she gave to her interviewer, Margaret Thatcher seemed out of place.

Somehow the reality of the everyday had been replaced by another, stronger, more convincing one. Superseding the news, the event was something other than entertainment; it was perceived as essentially serious. The royal wedding gave England an opportunity to enter a "liminal period," Victor Turner's (1969) name for this compelling, if ephemeral, shift in the definition of reality, during which social life is characterized by the suspension of usual norms and structures and irrigated by the overflowing of communitas. In Turnerian terms, such periods are characterized by a shift from an "indicative" definition of reality (reality as what is) to a "subjunctive" one (reality as what could or should be). Indeed, this shift was perfectly perceptible, as skinheads addressed the celebrants in the streets, convivially sharing the joyful spirit of the moment, even while warning that hostilities would resume once the event was over. Spectators in the street suspended doubts and avoided negative judgments when interviewed on television, preferring to reiterate platitudinous "certainties" that the young couple were conforming or would conform to traditional norms. Deliberately, people decided to see in the occasion only what ought to be seen. They had no doubt that the emperor was wearing his new clothes, and that Lady Diana would in due time be a good cook.

The event was separated from the unwelcome intrusion of everyday concerns by being placed under the aegis of nonnews teams at both BBC and ITV. During the days that preceded the wedding, the rest of reality was dwarfed by television via a pyramidal growth of wedding-related features. When Wednesday morning arrived, switching to the event appeared not as an interruption, but as a culmination. "At last," gasped some of the Tuesday evening headlines, expressing the tension which had been built up and defining the wedding itself as a release. The media, especially television, had organized a world hypnosis focused on what *Broadcast*, the magazine, called Wednesday morning fever. They had acted as ceremonial leaders, removing us all from mundane concerns and enacting the entry—the *rite de passage*—into the domain of the sacred.

Mutatis mutandis, compare the contextualization of the Gandhi funeral:

> The days between the assassination and the funeral passed in a kind of limbo. Few people left their houses, and much of the day was spent watching television. Doordarshan [Indian television] contributed to the atmosphere of depression that permeated the country. Throughout the day, television covered the "lying-in-state," focusing alternately on the body and on the distraught mourners. In between, short programs touched on Indira Gandhi's life and covered tributes of various world leaders. Gaps were filled by devotional songs. Constant announcements were made on television about the cre-

mation preparations. In fact, all media, including press and radio, were drawing attention to the cremation. (Minwalla, 1990)

Once an event is launched, television faces another problem: how to negotiate an exit from it. While the wedding crowds massed on the parade grounds had to improvise the return to ordinary reality for themselves, television choreographed its spectators' departure from the enchanted realm. Television again played the part of a ritual limbo, of a threshold between worlds, offering progressive reinsertion into ordinary patterns, ordinary norms, ordinary rhythms.

Television's about-face began immediately after the appearance of the royal family on the balcony of Buckingham Palace. The time had come to disengage from the event and to adopt a retrospective stance. Television guided spectators through the anticlimax of the after-event by proposing a new range of attitudes. Crowd members were deliberately prodded into a reflexive attitude by interviewers who asked them which images they thought especially worth remembering. Fragments of the event were played back, recalling its flamboyant pageantry while withdrawing it from the present tense. It was already a record in the archives, the videotape of a spectacle, no longer imbued with the magnetism of a live broadcast. It was an architecture of signs inhabited by intentions but deserted by life. The event was discussed by studio panels and on talk shows (thus removing us a step further from it). It was then decomposed into its constituent elements. Despite a convivial party mood, we were introduced to a melancholy knowledge of the backstage machinery. We met the wedding-cake baker, the parents of the dress designers, and the presenter whose disembodied voice had been, for a while, the instrument through which the event spoke. From an increasingly peripheral point of view the event itself was also split into parts, with the queen's guests having breakfast at Buckingham Palace, the newlyweds driving to Waterloo Station, and the cast in the process of disbanding. In short, we were offered a cheerful but anticlimactic anatomy lesson: the magic that had added parts into a whole was now fragmented into a mosaic of ordinary talents, special effects, and expertises.

This anatomy of the event served as prelude to a series of fluctuations between what remained of it (the newlywed couple being driven to Waterloo) and visits to its outskirts, the real world of the everyday, whose unwelcome presence continually nagged until the event was reinserted, after the final wrap-up, into the evening news broadcasts.

Everyday life was claiming its rights, and we were introduced at last to some of the manifestations organized to protest, reject, deride, or "ignore" the wedding—such as the champagne trip to Boulogne of a boatload of antiroyalists. Still, the countercelebrations now placed on display were yet another way of highlighting the mood of the event. The celebration was protected—at least for a while longer—from an intrusive reality. In the very criticism of the event, its liminality was reaffirmed. Criticism indeed, but ritualized with champagne. We had not quite reentered the ordinary.

Television again acted as a threshold, helping the audience through the task of readjusting to a world no longer characterized by the alternative reality of "antistructure" (Turner, 1969). Typically, this helping took the form of a play between live images of the postevent and recorded images of the event itself, thus allowing a tapering off of its intensity.

Having performed the end of the event, having ritually declared it over, television assumed a new task. After stressing what was worth remembering, it organized forgetting. The event was evoked in shorter and shorter wrap-ups, reduced to images that functioned in almost ideogramic patterns, seen through the reactions of increasingly distant observers (Argentinean, Russian, Chinese). It became a small dot on the horizon and disappeared from perception. Time was now ripe for abstraction and, a week after the wedding, this object of pleasure and fascination had officially become an object of knowledge: in a BBC program directed by Michael Lumley (who directed and produced the wedding coverage), Alistair Cooke proposed his interpretations.

We have tried to show here how television served not only as a model-provider for the reactions expected from the spectators, but as an icon of the event, modeling involvement in, then disinvolvement from, the "other" reality constituted by the event; how television superimposed its own *rite de passage* upon the ritual contained in the event (Van Gennep, 1909); how, within the construct of liminality, it had the essential responsibility of constituting the limen.

Heightening Spectatorial Receptivity

Television's commitment to providing a different experience is audible in the reverent tone of the narrator's voice. It affects the contents of the narration and leads to the use of elevated or ornamental language. The ordinary, concise, terse, matter-of-fact style of the journalist opens itself to cosmic lyricism. It is a "beautiful October night" when Sadat lands in Jerusalem. A "magnificent summer day" enhances the celebration of the royal wedding. The arrival of John Paul II in America brightens the atmosphere, like a "sun coming out of the clouds."[13] The informative prose of the commentary switches to celebratory poetry, but these new panegyrists usually content themselves with short-lived effusion. Narration is not simply an expressive tribute paid by television to the event through the conspicuous consumption of lavish metaphors; it plays an important part in laying the ground for spectatorial participation.

A public event has a table of contents which we must memorize, and it relies on a cultural repertoire with which we must become acquainted. Spectators are helped to prepare themselves for the ceremony. Narrators offer them an introduction to the program, a description of its itinerary, a rehearsal of its highlights, and profiles of its participants. Once it starts "for real," the event repeats an already-known pattern, as if it were a melody which the viewers can already hum for themselves.

This rehearsal is also performed visually. Before broadcasting the Easter-time ceremony during which John Paul II closes Saint Peter's monumental doors to conclude the "holy year" (in April 1984), Italy's national network (RAI) offers in grainy black and white a flashback to the same ceremony performed in 1975 by Pope Paul VI.[14] This flashback transforms television spectators into instant "connoisseurs." Such connoisseurship parallels a thriller technique familiar to moviegoers who are rehearsed in a decisive suspense sequence so that they will anticipate all the expected moves and be properly mesmerized by the unexpected ones. In the domain of ritual, the technique points to the importance of tradition, to the fact that rituals must be repeated.

When rituals happen too infrequently for their components to be memorized, emphasis is placed on their connection to tradition. Spectators are offered access to a dimension of which on-the-spot audiences may feel deprived: the sense of cultural continuity. Television narrators provide their viewers with a running exegesis, underlining what the event means to say and reinfusing it with cultural depth.[15] Thus, the BBC offers bibliographic services to foreign narrators of the royal wedding. When President Sadat is seen praying at Jerusalem's Al Aqsa mosque, a brief lecture on the Moslem festival of Al Adha is interjected.

When the Pope visits Poland, the life of Saint Stanislaus is submitted to scrutiny. When the same pope leads the Easter mass in Rome's Saint Peter's Square, the Catholic tradition of concluding "holy years" with Easter "pilgrimages" to Rome is traced to its postmedieval origins and associated with eminent pilgrims such as Dante Alighieri or Giotto. Throughout the event, philologically-minded narrators are expected to whisper erudite commentaries on various aspects of the ceremony.

Television substitutes for tradition by proposing a crash course on protocol, and by offering instant expertise on the event's components. This pedagogic role aims to ensure better participation, and it usually does. But it may also defeat its own purpose when its obtrusive presence succeeds in distancing the event by interrupting its flow and immediacy. Polish viewers of the papal masses in Warsaw, Cracow, or Yasna-Gora became incensed over what they perceived as deliberate attempts by narrators to break the spell of the occasion. Why—they ask—deliver a course on Catholic ritual to an audience known for its fervent piety? Television's exegesis was perceived as an intentional faux pas, the deliberate projection of a museographic frame on a living faith. Indeed, it was almost a literal application of the Brechtian principle that "instead of identifying with the characters, the audience should be educated to be astonished at the circumstances under which they function" (Benjamin, 1968b). Whether justified or not, the anger of Polish spectators stresses an important characteristic of the genre of media events: narration tries to encourage participation when it is lacking. Pedagogic or not, narration must remain unobtrusive, self-effacing. It must be heard but not noticed; it must flow with the event, never obstruct it.

The narrator's voice and what it tells are clearly defined as secondary to the event. The voice must be hushed. The statements should be reverent, brief, and grammatically simple. They may be interrupted at any point by voices and pictures from the event. Visual continuity has definite precedence over that of narration. In media events, the editorial function is performed inside the event and not by the narrator. The narration provides clarification, footnotes, or "in petto" remarks, but its status is essentially that of a lubricant. Media events are expressive occasions, forms of discourse. Television commentators are expected to avoid superimposing their own messages on those which constitute the event. The narrators' performance must frequently step aside in order to give precedence to the acts of communication within the event. When it fails to step aside, the director may drown the commentary in the cheers and murmurs of the crowd, to the point of depriving it of any intelligibility. The narration should not only be ancillary to the event's performance, it should be so in an almost invisible manner. This invisibility extends to the very nature of the narrator's voice.

The narrator's voice is important in its tone, its accent, its connotation of a given generation or social group. This last, apparently secondary feature differentiated the two parallel broadcasts of the royal wedding by pointing to the difference in the styles of narrators Alastair Burnett (ITV) and Tom Fleming (BBC).[16] Both narratives were reverent. Both echoed its main values. The difference between them was less a question of attitude (slightly more journalistic in one case, slightly more celebrational in the other) than of vocabulary, cadence, and tone of voice. Young people and members of groups less attached to establishment values were said to find Fleming's voice irritating, comical, or pretentious. Being alien to their generation, the BBC voice stood between them and the event; they could not "flow" with it or make it their own. The voice acted as a reminder of distance, preventing them from immersing themselves in the occasion. Burnett's alternative was therefore a means to augment the narrator's invisibility, to heighten audience participation in the ceremony.

Physically contained and culturally compatible, the narrator's attitude actively enacts the phatic definition of television's role. This attitude is matched by television's visual treatment of the event, one which actively calls for spectatorial participation while simultaneously trying to direct attention from itself, to remain inconspicuous and unnoticed, as if it were simply "transporting" us.

Dramatizing the Event

A heightening of receptivity is not always synonymous with an aesthetics of effacement. Indeed, on first look, media events strike the observer by their directorial flamboyance, by their display of visual rhetoric. They strut their arrogant monumentality, their uninhibited reliance on special effects, striking compositions, montages, and juxtapositions. An equivalent of ceremonial Latin, television images remodel and stylize the situations they represent. Often the event is used as raw material, as a jump-off for virtuoso exercises. Michael Lumley, for example, treats the royal wedding in a style reminiscent of Busby Berkeley. Franco Zeffirelli, filming the 1984 Easter mass in Rome, superimposes the figure of the Pope on the huge mosaic of faces turned toward him, merges the august body with the crowd, provides rhyming effects that equate the Pope's tiara to Saint Peter's dome, celebrates in a long series of closeups the faces of the younger members of the crowd—their youth, their innocence, their diversity, their beauty. In true pindaric tradition, the point is to find striking images, unexpected metaphors; to express in a startling way what spectators already know or expect.

The true monument makers of the twentieth century may be television directors. Their ambition, however, is not above mannerism. While usually anonymous—with the exception of Zeffirelli, who owes his fame to previous cinematographic achievements—they are heirs to the church architects, the great frame makers of collective experience.[17] The RAI Easter mass uses the architecture of Bernini as its decor and somehow is functionally equivalent to that architecture. It has the same intimidating ambition—that of heightening sensitivity to a message. The monumentality of media events serves a purpose. So does their attempt at achieving a rhythmic structure.

Rhythm, in music and speech, plays a role in converting an assembly into a community. George Mosse (1980) has considered the rhythmical quality of speech of the great mass-electrifiers such as Adolf Hitler, Benito Mussolini, and Charles de Gaulle. Rhythm creates a feeling of togetherness, of one-bodiness which easily translates into—or may be confused with—consensus. Cinema, especially silent cinema, has attempted to make use of the contagious, overwhelming power of rhythm, and we are left with landmarks such as the "Marseillaise" sequence in Abel Gance's *Napoleon* or with the explosive beat of *Battleship Potemkin*. Started by a protest about rotten meat, the rebellion of a few sailors receives symphonic treatment and, spreading in successive waves, makes converts of all who come to subdue it. Eisenstein's montage offers the equivalent of a mass rally and conveys the tense feeling of crowds in formation, creating the atmosphere of what Alberoni (1983) describes as the "statu nascendi" of collective movements. The Eisenstein montage represents a masterly manipulation of visual motives, which is anything but unobtrusive. Still, by managing to convey the contagious rhythmical power of the live crowd, he is one of the founding fathers of the media-events genre.

In most cases, however, except for isolated fragments or

sequences, media events have opted for a radically different aesthetics, an aesthetics of realism based on invisible editing rather than brilliant montage; an aesthetics inherited not from silent cinema but from the "talkies," and more specifically, from American cinema in its classical period. This is an aesthetics which provokes spectatorial participation by not calling attention to itself, by rendering itself almost invisible. Thus, the aesthetics of media events is syncretic in nature, and often inconsistent.

Fictionalizing the Event

The thrust of media-event aesthetics is best revealed by analyzing the transformation it imposes on the familiar dramaturgy of the news broadcast. The conferral of media-event status on a given occasion consists in pulling it away from the news and translating it in a fictional register. The result is a text which neutralizes the opposition between fiction and news.

The same public event may be treated as a media event by networks or channels in one country and as news by those of other countries. The same public occasion is thus submitted to two different textual treatments, an ordinary treatment (news) and an extraordinary one (media event). Opting for the news treatment flatly rejects the event's aim of being experienced as an occasion. News broadcasts distance the event. They offer a cold look at its ideological claims, denying their spectators any possibility of "flowing with" the event. If the event itself—as we believe—is a performative address, it is ironically turned into a performative-in-the-third-person, a "constated" performative (Austin, 1962). Even when a news broadcast adopts a sympathetic attitude toward an event, the latter's participatory features are lost. On the other hand, media events come very close to fiction films, especially when one considers the nature of the broadcast's temporal sequence and spatial continuity; the "enunciative" role imparted to the audience in attendance; the fact that principals avoid direct address and almost never look into the cameras; the tension established between these principals as symbols and the indexes which point toward their private feelings or emotions.

Temporally, media events treat a given occasion as a happening to be related in continuous manner. The syntagmatic coherence of the broadcast derives from the progression of the event itself, a characteristic of fiction made all the more salient by the fact that the event is broadcast live. This sequential progression is absent in the news, where one generally finds what Metz (1968) calls descriptive syntagms. The same event in news is usually stripped of its temporal dimensions; its images are withdrawn from their sequences. Serving now as illustrations or emblems, they are encased in a staccato flow of shots that do not really need to display a clear spatial relationship to one another.

Media events, on the contrary, allow their spectators to follow the event from within. The spectators are invited to inhabit the event through the mediation of the primary audience in attendance, to see through the eyes of those directly involved. Images depict the situations perceived by "spectators in the text." These spectators may also be performers, momentarily turned audience. Menachem Begin, Ezer Weizmann, and Moshe Dayan listen intently to Sadat's speech in the Knesset. A composed Queen Elizabeth watches her son pronouncing the vows of marriage. But the principals are only rarely used as vantage points. On-the-spot spectators, rather, are exactly in the position required to suggest that the shots selected by the director are expressions of their own attention. Thus, those in attendance represent the main enunciators of media events, so that spectators at home can watch a public event as they would a fiction film. In this process of fictionalizing media events, television downgrades the role of the studio, with its metacommunicative dramaturgy. The television personnel do not vanish; they are transferred from their usual discursive position outside an event to a new one that is immanent to the event. Thus Walter Cronkite, Barbara Walters, and John Chancellor are on Sadat's plane flying to Jerusalem. They no longer talk *of* the principals but *to* them. Joining the event's prestigious cast, they have been turned into supporting actors, while the networks' special correspondents also join the cast but in the less prestigious company of studio extras; they have more modestly become part of the crowd. Television's enunciative team, no longer above and outside the turmoil, have been cast in their own roles, swallowed by the event. [18] We are only one step removed from a blossoming genre: films about television people, photographers, and journalists.

Translating Myth into Novel

The attempt to fictionalize the event is also manifest through a characteristic inflection of the ceremonial domain. Ceremonies are based on the explicit invocation of myth and on the display of symbols. While stressing these symbols and providing a gloss on them, media events switch our attention to cues. Ceremonial performers assume hieratic "personae." Television, however, points to the person underneath the persona, to the tension between the one and the other. Sadat visits the Israeli memorial to the holocaust (Yad Vashem). Has he or has he not covered his head as required by Jewish etiquette? He is seen praying in a Jerusalem mosque. Why the sweat on his brow? Is Lady Diana nervous? Is the stare of John Paul II unusually "blunt"? Is Richard Nixon sick? Television treatment takes us away from the official gestures and into the feelings of those who

perform them. Symbols become almost obtrusive, an imped-
iment to television's intimate diary of the participants' emotions.

Ceremony is what the event is about, but ceremony stands in
the way of fiction. There seems to be no recourse when the
ceremony is a funeral and its silent hero no longer a person. His
existence then is exclusively as a symbol. In such cases the fictionalization of the broadcast may seem an impossible task. Yet
it is achieved even if it takes some narrative readjustment. Jackie
Kennedy is projected as the main figure of her husband's
funeral. Her behavior and that of her children allow for affective
identification; her struggle with her imposed role points to the
young woman beneath the black veils. To take another and
striking example, Lord Mountbatten's funeral is narrated by
none other than Lord Mountbatten himself. In an eerie effect,
his voice hovers over the casket transporting his remains; the
event is reinfused with the uncertainties of life, its hesitations
and accidents made to confront the rigorous destiny assigned to
the symbol. "I always wanted to be a sailor . . ." confides the
old man's voice, and the slow progress of his body toward the
grave fades into a childhood dream, evoking the youthful,
expectant mood of a bildungsroman. Ceremony is there, but
respect and admiration are overwhelmed by the discovery of an
unexpected intimacy.

Cinematographic Ceremony

The uncertainty of the status of media events may be part of a
larger phenomenon. Ceremonies are turning into fiction texts,
and fiction texts are consumed in an increasingly ceremonial
fashion. Turner's (1977) description of liminality as a laboratory
of forms is directly to the point. It is indeed through liminality,
either in its subjunctive form (media events) or in its carnival-

esque form (cult movies), that a new type of public event may be entering our lives.

Catering in flamboyantly freakish displays to a largely adolescent or postadolescent public faced with the difficult problem of identity, the genre of cult movies is obviously different from that of media events, by the nature of the register each invokes. Yet both may be characterized by a similar blur of the distinction between ceremonial performance and fiction text. With their midnight processions of costumed spectators, of look-alikes duplicating the main character in the film; with the collective singing, dancing, miming by which their audience greets the sequences displayed on screen, cult movies start as fiction texts but move from mere spectacle toward the realm of performance. They are turned into ceremonies.

Public events are not fixed in a given form once and forever. Throughout history they have tended to adapt themselves to the prevailing modes of making an event public. The dominant mode of publicness is changing now. We are witnessing the gradual replacement of what could be a theatrical mode of publicness—an actual meeting of performers and public in locations such as parliament houses, churches, convention floors, stadiums—by a new mode of publicness based on the separation of performers and audiences, and on the rhetoric of narrative rather than the virtue of contact. Born with cinema and first described in aesthetic terms by Walter Benjamin, this new mode of publicness culminates in television, which transfers it to all areas of public life including the most traditionally sacred—the political and the religious—thus profoundly affecting the nature of public ceremonies and occasions. Separated from the large majority of their public, these modern rituals display the texture, internal coherence, narrative "beat," and visual gloss which used to characterize Hollywood spectaculars.

5

Celebrating Media Events

Media events are rituals of coming and going. The principals make ritual entries into a sacred space, and if fortune smiles on them they make ritual returns. The elementary process underlying these dramatic forms is the *rite de passage*, consisting of a ritual of separation, of entry into a liminal period of trials and teachings, and of return to normal society, often in a newly assumed role (Van Gennep, 1909). Such liminal periods, according to Turner (1977), evoke the subjunctive—thoughts of what might be, or what should be, rather than what is.

These transitions in and out and between are dangerous, and evoke anxiety and enthrallment in believers and well-wishers, too. Indeed, it is of us that the hero is taking leave; it is for us that the hero is undergoing great risk; it is to us that he will return. Lift-off and splashdown, even more than what happened on the face of the moon, are the drama of the moon landing, says Stanford (1979). We are not surprised that leave-taking moved us at the Kennedy funeral, but even antagonists and agnostics were moved by the leave-taking from Nixon after his televised resignation speech (Lang and Lang, 1983) or from Pope John XXIII upon his death (Gritti, 1966).[1]

No less than the principals, we—the witnesses to these events—traverse the same ritual stages. If we accept the invitation to assume a ritual role, we take leave of everyday routine together with our heroes; experience the liminality of their sojourn; hold our breaths awaiting, or despairing of, their return; and reposition ourselves to resume everyday reality when the event is over.

The "text" itself ushers in and out of these stages. Preparing us for the great event, television gradually evacuates us from our everyday roles as routine viewers, and makes the living room into a festive place. From casual, tired, consumer-oriented, pleasure seekers we are transformed into expectant witnesses of a historic moment. But television cannot do this alone. Its call to prayer—if it is to succeed—must be echoed in the words of national leaders, by our friends, by the newspapers, by the schools that declare a recess, by employers who allow us to view on company time, by the flickering lights in all the neighbors' windows.

In short, media events require not only the consent of the viewer, they require his or her active involvement. The previous chapter explored the ways in which the aesthetics of television events invite ritual participation, by (1) offering free and equal access, (2) creating a liminal space, (3) rehearsing the ritual order, and (4) positioning the viewer so that he can both identify as an observer and respond as a participant. In the present chapter, we consider how the viewer accomplishes this. Wherever possible, we draw on empirical studies of "real" viewers in order to contrast them with the implied viewers of the discussion so far. But since there are only a few studies of living-room celebrations of media events—presidential debates, the Kennedy funeral, the Watergate hearings, the 1984 Olympics, the Super Bowl—we continue to draw on the folklore of collective experience as well. We begin by contrasting the festive viewing of events with daily, routine viewing, and explore the way in which the living room is turned into a public space. The primary focus of the chapter, however, is on festive viewing roles, on the identities that viewers assume to complement those of the personae of the events, the social context of reception, and the social psychology of identification and interactivity.

Routine and Festive Viewing

Festive broadcasts of media events contrast so sharply with everyday broadcasts that it is useful to think of them as different media. True, both propose to transport the viewer from his armchair to the world outside. But the similarity stops there. Routine, nighttime viewing positions the tired viewer in front of a range of recuperative choices—among channels, among programs, among products. It addresses him as family member, consumer, sensation seeker, and sometimes as information user, in the apolitical living room.

Evening television tells family members, first, that they want to feel comfortable with one another at home, and, second, that they wish to be amused by the antics and crimes of familiar story characters who are typically remote from their world. It tells them that they have a "right" to be entertained any time at their own choosing, and that they have freedom of choice among channels and genres. It invites them to consider the advertised products and the dreams or needs these fulfill.

Some theorists think that this kind of sun-never-sets television is a pervasive tease. It engenders an aura of familiarity and warmth and promises a fulfillment that is never consummated. Commercial advertisements punctuate the flow, offering products to sublimate aroused desire. The viewer is lulled into erotic semiconsciousness. The "text" is not a program but the flow (Houston, 1984), and the experience is relaxing, soporific, but unchallenging (Kubey and Csikszentmihalyi, 1990).

Gerbner et al. (1979) also think of the viewer as victim. Surrounded for hours on end by the substitute reality of the television world, he comes to disbelieve, or disconnect from, his own personal experience. The message of television is that the world is a frightening place; it mobilizes the viewer, unconsciously, to give ideological support to the forces of order that keep the impending crisis at bay (Gitlin, 1980). The shows may be organized in thirty- or sixty-minute programs, but this message inundates each and every viewing hour and creates only one composite story. Choice, therefore, is merely an illusion, a hegemonic device used to perpetuate the myth of freedom.

Other scholars treat the viewer as freer, more awake, and more adult. His viewing role is shaped by needs—for information, for entertainment, for identity—whose fulfillment he seeks on the small screen. From this perspective, television is a kind of public utility, offering various kinds of gratification (Blumler and Katz, 1974). The viewer is a seeker. Certain theories suggest that television provokes the viewer to face personal, social, and aesthetic dilemmas, however sugarcoated, to discuss and to judge them (Newcomb and Hirsch, 1983; Liebes and Katz, 1990; Livingstone, 1990; Morley, 1980).

We know too little—even after forty years of television—to choose among these different theories of everyday viewing (Schudson, 1978; Katz, 1990). Perhaps they are all correct—for different sorts of viewers, or for the same viewers at different times. We simply do not know enough about the interaction between the role expectations of viewers and the roles offered by the "text." We still know too little about how people "read" routine television programs. To make matters even more complex, it seems likely that routine television viewing is changing, in the age of multiple sets, multiple channels, and videocassettes. It is moving in the direction of radio, that is, toward greater tailoring to differentiated audiences.

By contrast, consider a report on home viewing of the Gandhi funeral:

About an hour before the ceremony began, we were ready, washed and dressed, as if we were going to be physically present at the scene. My mother insisted that we wear long clothes and cover our heads as a mark of respect. A large group of people congregated at my house as they did around most television sets in the country. Both my servants, their entire families and my neighbours (who had their own TV) were squashed into my tiny living room. (Minwalla, 1990)

The major media events—the wedding, the funeral, the moon landing, the Olympics—follow the same pattern. We were invited, perhaps even commanded, to attend the wedding. We were urged for days in advance to prepare ourselves. The event was well advertised and well rehearsed, so that viewers would know what to anticipate on the day. Breakfast television programs in the United States sent their major teams to broadcast live from London a full week before the actual event. Throughout the English-speaking world, announcements were made of the timetable of the event, all aimed to engender a sense of holiday, of anticipation, of planning for festive viewing. We were addressed as if we would be asked—perhaps by our grandchildren—to retell the event, to report what it felt like. Most of all, we were told that the event was important, that it engaged some central value of the polity.

We came as mourners to the Kennedy funeral. The first news of the President's shooting was broadcast at 1:40 p.m. Eastern Standard Time on Friday, November 22, 1963. When the report was officially confirmed an hour later, most people in the United States had heard—more via word of mouth than from the media (Greenberg and Parker, 1965). "For three and a half days following first word of the assassination," says the normally businesslike Nielsen report, "all commercial television was suspended, not only as an expression of the nation's shock and grief but also in order to assure prompt and complete coverage of each succeeding development and to permit all who had access to a television set to share in such consolation as could be offered by the memorial events and funeral rites which marked the President's death." The networks, all broadcasting the same story, all without commercial interruption, were thus "constructing"—for three and a half days—a new viewer, one seeking neither commodities nor entertainment, hardly even information, but the opportunity to find in the television set a focus for expression of grief.[2]

We came in awe to the moon landings. By means of simulation techniques, viewers were briefed for days on the workings of rocket boosters, on the division of labor among astronauts and mission control, on the atmosphere of the moon, on the orbiting and the landing. The world was invited to set its alarm for the hour that the Eagle capsule would land on the moon. This was at 4:17 p.m. Eastern Daylight Time on Sunday, July 20, 1969, almost midnight in Europe and the Near East. All three United States networks were carrying the same pictures, signaling to viewers that this was by no means the evening news, but history.[3]

In such a situation the viewer takes note that the major channels are all carrying the same program. No choice here—except the residual one of choosing between channels. Not even the choice of switching off. No consumerism, because advertising would violate the sanctity of the occasion; no dozing, either, no using TV as moving wallpaper or chewing gum. No escapism, except the demand to shut out the concerns of everyday life in favor of single-minded attention to some shared value that is too often unsung. Indeed, if it were not for the motivation of viewers to receive the program, priestly television of the sort that occupies us here would be an authoritarian imposition, diametrically opposite to the ostensibly free choice of routine television.

Audiences for Festive Television

On an average evening in the mid-1980s, about 60 percent of American households had their TV sets on, for a net prime-time viewership of some 95 million adults or 100 million persons over the age of two.[4] Their viewing divided more or less equally among the three major networks, and the remainder were tuned to local or cable stations.

Among programs commercially sponsored and competitively broadcast, the all-time most popular single program in the history of American TV was the "MASH Special" of February 20, 1983, a commemorative program of two and a half hours' duration. Its average audience was 77 percent of all sets in use (what is called share). Next in all-time popularity was the Who Shot J.R.? episode of "Dallas," broadcast on November 21, 1980, which attracted 53 percent of TV households, or 76 percent of sets in use. "Roots," the annual Super Bowls, the Bob Hope Christmas specials, a 1976 two-part *Gone with the Wind*, and "The Day After" (a dramatized simulation of response in the United States to a nuclear bomb) were not far behind with percentages in the upper 40s.[5] It will be seen that these programs are "specials" of various kinds, just beyond the border of routine viewing: holiday programs, miniseries, highly dramatic or one-time or once-a-year shows. Their "special" character brings them to the brink of the genre of festive television. Indeed, the Super Bowl football games, which annually attract close to 100 million viewers on a Sunday afternoon in January for the live playoffs of American professional football, qualify as media events. The others, too, deserve serious attention, even if they do not qualify.

It is rare for any regularly broadcast series or serial to attract even one-quarter of households. The typical evening audience spreads itself across the wavelengths and comes together only for the extraordinary occasions illustrated above.

Media events, of course, have this special character. In the "ideal" case, they are broadcast by all national networks and thus automatically ensure the lion's share of sets in use. Sometimes they are also broadcast abroad. Many of them are political in character—and have to contend with the normally low level of political interest in the American population. Nevertheless, the number viewing the resignation of Richard Nixon is estimated at more than 100 million, and the audience at the moment of the landing on the moon reached 130 million (Lang and Lang, 1983). Viewers of the Kennedy burial probably numbered 190 million, or 80 percent of the American population of 240 million. Eighty-one percent were tuned in at 3:00 p.m. on the Monday of the funeral, and it is likely that most of the owners of the unwatched sets were watching in other people's homes. It is interesting to follow the growth of the TV audience from the 20 percent who were viewing on the Friday just before the shooting, to 45 percent within one hour of the first news, to the high vigil throughout the weekend, until the climax, then the immediate drop, on Monday afternoon.

For extended events such as Watergate or the Olympics, the numbers reached are even greater. It is estimated that more than 70 percent of Americans saw something of the live Watergate hearings (Lang and Lang, 1983),[6] and three-fourths saw something of the Olympics during the summer of 1984 (Rothenbuhler, 1985).[7] During this period, on a typical afternoon or evening a television set was turned on in two-thirds of households and the Olympics were on two-thirds of those screens. An average of 44 percent of households were tuned to the Olympics day and night, and this proportion was surely much higher for the major contests.

These figures are for the United States alone. Estimates of the world audience reach 500 million or more for the live broadcasts of the royal wedding, the Kennedy funeral, and the Apollo XI space missions, although nobody can certify these numbers. For balance, it is well to remember that the annual telecasts of the Academy Awards claim a worldwide audience (though not a simultaneous one) of 350 million or more (Real, 1982).[8] These Oscar awards qualify for the festive genre, too, but they are—as we shall note below—a very minor sort of high holiday. That these are the largest audiences in the history of the world goes without saying.

The Home as Public Space

Americans mobilize "indoors." Except for the occasional parade of commemoration or protest, not much is left outdoors as far as politics are concerned. Contrasting Italian and American television news, Hallin and Mancini (1984) note that Italians "take out" the information they receive from television news— to public discussions at local party headquarters, to the trade union hall, or to the coffeehouse. In Prague and in Bucharest, and at the Berlin wall, television followed the revolutionary assemblies "outside." Americans have allowed their public spaces to fall into disrepair.

They do not have much that is political inside, either. It is safe to say that Americans do not often discuss politics at home. Television news gives the illusion of political participation, as Lazarsfeld and Merton (1948) indicated long ago, and the decline in real participation may indeed have been influenced by this illusion.

The occasional media event transforms this domestic atomization. It transforms the home into a public space. It connects networks of interacting individuals, from house to house, across very large territories. While highly selective—and biased—in what is shown, television brings inside what cannot be seen otherwise. We refer not just to events that are physically inaccessible, but to events that take place primarily, sometimes exclusively, in the air. Most of the great political Conquests (Sadat, the moon, the Pope), or political Contests (Watergate, the presidential debates) are far out of sight of on-the-spot audiences but well within the reach of television homes.[9]

The Brazilian anthropologist Da Matta (1984) has written of "situations in which the house extends itself into the street and into the city in such a way that the social world is centralized by the domestic metaphor [and] on the other hand . . . when the street and its values tend to penetrate the private world of the residence, with the world of the house being integrated into the metaphor of public life." Unlike pilgrimages and military parades, for which one must leave home and city, religious processions bring the center, represented by the image of the saint held aloft, on a ceremonial tour of residential neighborhoods.

> As the saint passes and is seen, the faithful may transfer temporarily their group, class or social loyalties to this new focus . . . Group and other loyalties are dissolved in favor of an intimate, visual, penetrating and affective relationship . . . By means of the saint, a relationship develops that includes all of those who are following as well as those who are watching. Here the streets are transformed and the frontiers between street and house are weakened. In processions, no one refuses water to the participants, and the whole space is occupied by those who are related to the saint. The atmosphere is one of the transferring of loyalties and of opening oneself to the

sacred domain. Thus, windows and doors should remain open. Curtains and the best embroidered linen, as well as vases of flowers, are placed in the windows and on the verandas. All this is done so that the saint can "see" the house, in a dramatization of opening and of the relational domain that should pertain among men and their saint, even in their residences, where people have the strongest loyalties. We have, thus, the sacred, the saint entering and being received into the houses. (pp. 27–28)

A piquant example from the history of the transformation of private into public space is the royal Christmas message. On December 25, 1932, John (later Lord) Reith, who fashioned the BBC, finally succeeded in persuading George V "to make a national moral impression" by addressing the empire (Jack, 1982). The king said, "I speak now from my home and my heart to all of you. To men and women so cut off by the snows, the desert, or the sea, that only voices out of the air can reach. To all, to each, I wish a Happy Christmas. God bless you!" Radio listeners, in their homes, stood up as the king spoke. Some television viewers in England do so, even today. Waiting to sit down to their Christmas dinner, they pay homage to the crown.

Festive viewers do not always stand up for the playing of the national anthem at media events, but they often feel like doing so. They allow themselves great emotion: to cheer, to weep, to feel pride. They come prepared to be moved. Recall what we have been told about the Gandhi funeral: "About an hour before the ceremony began, we were ready, washed and dressed, as if we were going to be physically present at the scene. My mother insisted that we wear long clothes and cover our heads as a mark of respect" (Minwalla, 1990).

Americans and others gathered in one another's homes to follow the suspense-filled mission of Apollo XI and to cheer Neil Armstrong and Buzz Aldrin as they set foot on the moon. They knew from newspapers, magazines, classrooms, and offices what to expect, and what to pray for, as they seated themselves before their sets. The journey triggered all the excitement of an earlier age of exploration and the opening of new frontiers. Comparing the moon flight to voyages of the Vikings and Columbus, one observer (Eisele, 1979) notes the new dimension which was added by "the many spectators who vicariously traveled along as passengers with the space explorers. With the moon flight and landing, a society of voyagers took a voyage, a space odyssey, in which we enjoyed an unprecedented position, from which we entertained the explorers' risks without risk, experienced their discoveries without being there." The symbol of the eagle, continues Eisele, is both the national emblem and the emblem of conquest, but also a symbol of graceful settling down on "Tranquility Base" with its allusions to "home." This instant domestication of outward reality hints at another kind of echo that may have stirred viewers in their living-room chairs—that the world is, perhaps, a more secure place thanks to the American flag planted up there.

Evidence that people gather together to experience and celebrate media events in company is not just anecdotal. The first-ever presidential debates of 1960 were viewed in groups (Katz and Feldman, 1962). During the weekend of mourning for Kennedy, people sought out friends and relatives to grieve in front of their television sets (Barber, 1965). A national survey of the viewing of the 1984 Olympics (Rothenbuhler, 1985) found that those watching the games were more likely to be in the company of others than the minority who were viewing non-Olympic programs at the same time.[10] A third of the sample had invited someone over to view the games, a third had gone to someone else's home to watch, and 15 percent had gone to a public viewing place. Viewing with others was done repeatedly throughout the games. These others were "special," the people one spent holidays with, or went out with in the evening. Among those watching television with others, 80 percent of Olympics viewers talked about what they were viewing, compared with 38 percent of those viewing other programs.

In his study of the Super Bowl, Real (1982) reports that "the majority of viewers saw the game in a group setting, used it as a social occasion, talked and moved at prescribed times during the telecast, discussed the Super Bowl with acquaintances before and after the day of the game. Especially for the more than half of the adult males in America who watched the game it was a source of conversation at work, in the neighborhood, at shops, and wherever regular or accidental interaction occurs."

"By game time," Real continues, "the viewer-participants *know* they are joined with people in the room, in the stands— all over the country—in following this spectacle. As Ernst Cassirer and others point out, the essence of mythical belief lies in the feeling of collective participation and sharing of concerns and powers beyond the potential of the individual human."

The conversion of the home into a ceremonial place, focused on the center and aware of all the other homes in which the same thing is taking place at the same time, reminds one of festivals such as Christmas or Passover. These holidays place emphasis on home rites even more than those of church or synagogue. They are oriented to the extended family and are open to friends, even strangers. They purvey a sense that the whole world of Christendom or Judaism is celebrating simultaneously, diffusing a feeling of personal and communal fraternity and spirituality. These occasions link families to centers, past and present.

The Passover seder, especially, is quite explicit in assigning roles to the celebrants and in specifying the kinds of attitudes and information that should accompany these roles. The celebrant is commanded "to feel personally as if he had been liberated from Egypt." He is enjoined to invite the homeless and the needy. The children ask questions to which the elders must narrate a response. The saint, Elijah, hovers overhead and is expected at any moment, and the table is prepared for his entrance to partake in the feast. The house is altogether transformed—cleaned, polished, certified, and sanctified. The night is, indeed, different from all other nights.

Observers of ceremonial events—here it is difficult to separate the effects of television from the pervasive effects of the event itself—have often remarked on the expansive altruism and neighborliness that accompanies them. Shils and Young (1953) tell of the reconciliation among long-hostile neighbors at the time of the coronation. "Hospitality," says a writer on the funeral of Martin Luther King, Jr. (Pugh, 1968), "was everywhere in flowering Atlanta. You could get a lift just about anywhere and white people all over their part of town threw open their churches, and more important, their homes to Negroes and whites alike." The sense of fraternity was so great when the Pope visited Poland that our translator remarked, "We perceive our government not as a repressive force against the papal festival, but as participating in it, and thus endangering itself." It is characteristic of such events that they bring former antagonists to reconsider, or at least to suspend, their antagonism.

The communitas of good neighborliness and shared spirituality explains the open door of the seder as well as the open doors of the Kennedy and King mourners and of the wedding or Olympic celebrants. A participant in the King funeral said: "We can't find words to describe the way the funeral has brought black and white together. It's something else. I don't know if it is because the assassination made more of us wake to the reality that we are all brothers or whether we're afraid they'll burn the town down after they get him in the ground" (Pugh, 1968).[11]

Thus, the anxiety of the open door is evident too; celebrants of the seder regard the outside as potentially hostile.

The rhetoric of events very often spills over into the rhetoric of family: "He was our brother, not our uncle; he was the people's Pope."[12] Sadat spoke of the family of Abraham and chatted about grandchildren with Golda Meir. The funerals and the wedding are all about family. The reunions—the Iran and Entebbe hostages and the Korean refugees—are about family. Kate Smith was surrogate mother, sacrificing herself so that her boys in the army might be better supported (Merton, 1946). These references to family echo in the bosoms of the viewing families. The hosts serve refreshments. Olympic viewers shared food and drink with fellow viewers, more than did those viewing other programs (Rothenbuhler, 1985).

The viewers are focused, intent on what they are seeing. "When the station signed off," said a Minneapolis viewer of the Kennedy funeral, "we signed off . . . All day Saturday and Sunday I don't remember doing a thing. I didn't get dressed. I didn't make the beds. I didn't do anything. Monday we watched all day and cried all day." Another person said, "I walked around the block because I felt if I didn't I was going to scream. I thought I could get away from it for a while, but it was like a magnet." About 50 percent of viewers overtly mourned (Mindak and Hursch, 1965). The more they were with other people, this study found, the more they grieved. The more viewers experienced grief, the more they felt something to be seriously wrong with American society. And the more they grieved, the more they expressed a rededication to American institutions.

In the ethnography of media events, major importance must be assigned to the transformation of the home into a public space, at least for a moment. This transformation is accomplished by a parallel change in the personae of the viewers.

Festive Viewing Roles

Viewers seat different selves in front of their sets. Studies of the influence of television on children suggest that the circumstances under which a film is viewed will affect what is learned and remembered. Seen at school, a documentary about Eskimos will be remembered as a primer on igloo building; the same film seen at home will focus attention on the relations between Poppa and Momma Eskimo (McCormack, 1962). Seen with a parent, children will learn more from "Sesame Street" than when the same program is viewed alone. Children who expect entertainment from television will learn less than those who also expect to be informed (Salomon, 1979). Voters who have come to televised presidential debates for help in making up their minds will hear and see different things than those who seek arguments for use against the other side, and those who wish to place a bet on a horse race (Blumler and McQuail, 1968).

This choice of roles is not altogether under the viewer's control. Media technology and social definitions of media functions also play a part, as do the social and psychological characteristics of audience members. Radio, for example, has been redefined by society as an intimate medium in the era of television, and thanks to transistor technology it performs this job even better than before. Individuals switch on their ever-handy radios seeking music tailored to the taste of their age peers, or up-to-the-minute traffic bulletins, or advice on love or the stock market or car repair.

There is another source of constraint that contributes to the shaping of audience roles and expectations. This is the "text" itself—whether the text be book, film, TV program, or newspaper. Thus, the TV critic of the *New York Times* holds his nose as he reviews "Dallas," writing as if his readers have never heard of—surely never seen—J.R. He thereby proposes an identity to his readers, engaging in what some social psychologists have called altercasting. Texts (or films or programs) are produced with a reader in mind—one who comes prepared, or is enticed, to interact in a manner that has been preprogrammed, witting or not, by its authors or directors (Eco, 1989).

Often literary theorists, who have eyes only for texts, presume that the real readers coincide with the readers required by the texts. Critical theorists—those who have given attention to popular culture—also see the predominance of the text in shaping reader roles, but rather in the sense that the texts affect (or better, infect) their readers with a false consciousness of their social situations.

In contrast to scholars who infer readers from texts, there are others, oriented sociopsychologically, who infer texts from readers. They ascribe so much power to the selectivity of the audience—in exposure, perception, interpretation, and recall—that they assume that any text can be reshaped to fit audience needs. These are overstatements, of course, that correct the nearsightedness of the literati but ascribe too much sovereignty to the reader. The fact is that only recently has there been scholarly activity at the nexus of encoding and decoding. Certain literary and critical theorists are now asking how real readers deal with the constraints of the text (Hall, 1977; Morley, 1980; Radway, 1984). And certain media researchers are now interested in how texts limit the freedom of audience perceptions (Blumler et al., 1971; Liebes and Katz, 1990).

Media events provide a good opportunity to observe the interaction of real viewers with the constructed roles proposed by television texts. While there are only a few empirical studies of the roles and the "readings" performed by viewers of these historic broadcasts, all of us have our own experiences to draw upon. All of us—more precisely those of us who are thirty-five or older—remember vividly the weekend of mourning after John Kennedy, the moon landings, and the royal wedding. We have been in attendance, via television, at a number of the great events, and it is not by chance that we are able to recollect where we were at the time and how we "celebrated" them. We mourned Kennedy; we explored outer space; we reaffirmed our loyalty to, or admiration for, British tradition. We judged presidential debates, played jury at the Watergate hearings, witnessed Sadat's recognition of Israel, rooted for the Maccabi team at the World Cup, got up in the middle of the night for the Seoul Olympics.

Contests, Conquests, and Coronations each define different viewer roles, as was noted in Chapter 2. Contests—political and sporting events—invite viewers to desist from mere spectatorship and root for one of the sides. But even partisanship is more typical of Monday night football than of "historic" contests. It is more than mere partisanship when an African country defines its worth in the world through the achievements of its Olympic team. Partisanship is an understatement of the deep identification with a home team facing outsiders, whether it is at the World Cup, the Eurovision Song Contest, or the Olympics. The audience "on the home front" sends messages of undivided approval to its team, even if the efficient transmission of such messages must await the day of interactive television.

More typical of the historic contest, perhaps, is the judicial role. We are asked to decide, as a citizen jury and not only as partisans, who won the presidential debates. There is no other judge. In evaluating the presidential debates, even the experts try to second-guess the likely reaction of the audiences. Some events, of course, have their own judges: the World Series has umpires, the Democratic national convention has delegates, Miss USA has judges, the Eurovision Song Contest has a jury. Even here, however, public opinion is called upon to play the "verdictive" role of an arbiter (Austin, 1962): to judge together with the judges, even to judge the judges, to agree that the official verdict is fair. Although the Senate committee acted as a quasi-juridical body in the Watergate hearings, the President appealed to the public to judge these hearings as a contest between the executive and legislative branches, presumably because he saw more opportunity in the partisanship of Contest.

Reawakening to the meaning of the rules characterizes the subjunctive mood appropriate to liminality. In daily life, we are much more suspicious of the rules, wondering whom they benefit. We know that there are many who manage their way around them. In the liminal period of sacred Contests, the rules reaffirm their civilizing function. Contestants must be equal; viewers are present to warrant fairness.

Conquests propose another set of audience roles, although they overlap not a little with those of Contests. First, we are asked to attend the improbable deed. Sadat really threw away the rule book, got on his plane, and gave the de facto recognition Israel had been asking for. We saw the apprehension, then the smile, on his face as he shook hands with the Israelis. Recognition is a public act, and we TV viewers, not the few hundred Israeli officials who were at the airport, were the witnesses. We saw him offering himself as a sacrifice; we heard him talking of the sacrifice of Abraham's son; we listened to his demand for reciprocity. "Israel ought to do something big in return," we thought.

Sometimes it is the audience that is asked to reciprocate. We were shown Kate Smith, the all-American, giving of herself unsparingly, singing and talking through the day and night, appealing to us on the radio to support the war effort through the purchase of war bonds. To match her altruism, to repay her sacrifice for us, we telephoned our pledge (Merton, 1946).

We were shown our men on the moon, where John Kennedy

said they would go. We saw them defy the laws of gravity and of man's proper place. We marveled at the jeopardy in which they placed themselves, for our sake. We were asked to reaffirm our belief in American technological prowess; we were asked to renew our support for the National Aeronautics and Space Administration; we were asked to give the astronauts a hero's welcome for all they risked for us.

In his last gesture in office, overwhelmed by the display of power arrayed against him, President Nixon mentioned the theme of his sacrifice for the good of the nation six times in the fifty-seven sentences of his televised resignation speech (Lang and Lang, 1983, p. 191), "as if the president having chosen not to go to trial, was now appearing as his own character witness in a television defense." Still a Contest, it was already a Coronation, or its opposite. Nixon was contributing to the strengthening of national institutions while putting his head on the block. And it was also Conquest, a lone man staring down hostility. The network commentators warmed up. Dan Rather of CBS said, "Nixon went out with a touch of class, even nobility." Public and networks were relieved that the President did not lose control or mount a vicious attack, and the anxiety evaporated in a wave of sympathy and sadness.

Witness the sacrifice, witness the miracle of achievement, suspend disbelief, demand a just reward for the heroes, enter the potlatch of sacrifice and countersacrifice—these are the audience roles in the teledramas of Conquest. All these roles differ from that of mere spectator, because they involve a dimension of commitment.[13] In the early Christian definition of the term, witnesses are converts to a new definition of truth and instruments of its subsequent propagation. In Austin's (1962) sense, Conquests require their viewers to adopt a "commissive" role. They are converts, at least for a moment, to a new definition of the possible.

Coronations invite us to participate, initially as citizens and subjects, in the rites of passage of great men and women: their weddings, funerals, anniversaries, crownings, and decrownings. As in Contests and Conquests, there are separations and reentries, for both principals and audience. The space of liminality here, however, is occupied not by heroic trials or proposed redefinitions of the world, but by changes of status in the classic sense: from bachelorhood to wedlock, from life to death.

The barometers of audience size and enthusiasm are read as a reconfirmation of loyalty, as reiteration of the social contract between citizens and their leaders. The person is welcomed into office, or saluted in departure, heralded for achievement, or applauded for attaining adulthood (Blumler et al., 1971).

In the role of citizen, we shudder over the undoing of a leader who symbolized the values of an era and who succumbed to the forces of antiorder. Viewers are asked to share in the outrage, to resolve that disorder will not be allowed to triumph, and to accept the legitimacy of the succession. But beyond the civic role is the role of mourner or of member of the wedding participating expressively. Coronations call on us to attend, to share emotions, and to show that we care. Austin calls these "behabitives": greeting, well-wishing, condoling, saluting. The mourning is for the man, for order, and for the dream of the era he represented: the glory of Mountbatten's empire and the fraternity of war; the new look of the youthful Kennedys; the fiery blend of tradition and modernization in the Gandhi years. And, subjunctively, one allows oneself the hope that things may get better again.

Sometimes events speak directly to more than one country— to Egypt and Israel in the case of Sadat. Sometimes they embrace the world—as did the moon landings and Olympics. For those national events that have secondary audiences in other countries—Indira Gandhi's funeral, for example—festive viewing may be broadly defined as joining in an occasion intended for somebody else. Within the primary context of the event, however, the fact that it is not a spectacle but a concert of performances may be expressed in the language of Austin's (1962) "performatives." The organizers, of course, have an "exercitive" role; they have the power to declare public events. Television joins them in the "expositive" role of making clear what the organizers meant by proposing the event. The audience responds: "verdictively" in the case of Contests, "commissively" in the case of Conquests, "behabitively" in the case of Coronations.

Festive Readings

Festive roles imply festive readings that coincide with the "dominant" messages of the text. Festive viewers enter the preliminaries with a feeling of awe in the face of the heroic and the historic. They sense that the event is offered not just to set off the holiday from the everyday, but to mark a particular moment of transition for the society. The viewer is most likely to sense this in the case of events that are mounted in response to crisis: the live broadcasting of the Senate Watergate hearing, for example, or the funerals of martyred leaders. Other events are less immediately associated with acute crisis and offer new social arrangements for consideration. De Gaulle proposes liberation to Quebec; Sadat proposes a new deal in the Middle East; Khomeini unseats the shah and his modernization. The funeral of Enrico Berlinguer confirms the legitimacy of the Italian Communist party and signals a national front against the politics of terror and disorder (Hallin and Mancini, 1984).[14] Even the royal wedding—ostensibly the most trivial of our events—may have reminded Britain of its identity while economic and ethnic conflicts were raging. Ideally, political conventions, presidential debates, even sporting events, play this role—of putting the daily news into a different perspective, and calling attention to the essential (or potential) unity of the society.

A proper reading of the central message of the event involves the subjunctive mood. If successfully transmitted, the event evokes images of a better world, a more fraternal or equal society, a hint of the possibility of peace, a rededication to central institutions. Subjunctivity requires a suspension of disbelief, an intermission from reality.

Thus, listening to Sadat in the Knesset one might have thought that Egypt had always wished Israel well, that Egypt was on good terms with the other Arab states, indeed that the Arabs were a united people. The audiences in Israel and Egypt, and some of the secondary audiences in other countries as well, knew that such was not the case. Was Sadat lying? Or was he speaking of what might be? Only the subjunctive permits a benevolent reading by the festive viewer (Liebes-Plesner, 1984).

The Olympics, says MacAloon (1984), are deceptive in the same sense. They present a picture of a rule-abiding world at play, offering equal opportunity to blacks and whites, treating socialist and capitalist regimes as interchangeable, celebrating not ascription but achievement. Are the Olympics a collective masquerade? Only a subjunctive reading that translates the event in terms of what might be, or what ought to be, makes the "dominant" reading possible.

Alternative and Oppositional Readings

Of course it does not always work. Some people snub an event, in protest. Others view, but never abandon the distant role of spectator. They refuse to suspend disbelief. Some people enter the narrative, but with a different orientation, an alternative, even a hostile, role. Their interaction with the text and the roles proposed by the text may be quite different (Parkin, cited in Hall, 1977; also Morley, 1980). The Passover seder perceives this possibility clearly, even providing scripts for those who reject the "dominant" mode and choose "alternative" or "oppositional" readings. Thus, the seder service inscribed in the Haggadah distinguishes among four ideal readers, or "sons." There is the Wise Son, who abandons the spectator role to ask his question from "within," accepting the legitimacy of the occasion and its importance; and the answer he gets counts him a member of the group: "because of this God delivered us from Egypt." The Evil Son, the spectator, excludes himself. He asks, "What is all this to you?" and the textual retort offers him an answer in kind. The Naive Son asks, simply, "What's this?" and the answer invites him to abandon the spectator role and to join in. "He Who Does Not Know How to Ask"—the fourth son—gets help with both question and answer.

Far from the family ethos and paternalistic connotations of the seder, John MacAloon (1984) makes a related point in his discussion of the four facets of involvement he discerns in the Olympic Games: spectacle, festival, ritual, game. Spectacle is concerned with grandness, with overviewing the event as a whole, as a display of the combined forces of performers, people, and power. But spectacle is seen from a distance. Festival is total immersion where gamegoers, undirected from the center, contribute personally through picnics, cafes, promenades, and improvisations, adding color and affectivity to the scene. Ritual consists in invoking the continuity of the games with ancient tradition. In assigning ceremonial roles to the participants—at openings and closings and awards—it sets the games off, in parentheses, from the routine humdrum of everyday inequities and infelicities. Game, finally, is the contest itself from which the true spirit of the Olympics radiates the message of human striving, perseverance, and achievement in the face of enormous odds, and in the context of one world.

MacAloon tells us how the word "spectacle" became taboo in the official vocabulary of the International Olympics Committee, for fear that bigness and dazzle would further emphasize the show-business aspect of the games at the expense of the warmth, magic, and truth which are the reward of genuine involvement. Instead of entering the performance system through festival, ritual, or game, the distanced spectator poses questions. "Is this festival," he asks, if there is so much bureaucracy and politics? "Is this ritual" if the pageantry has replaced rededication? "Is this game" if commercialism and nationalism have distorted its truth?

Even these doubts, suggests MacAloon, may themselves lead to the conversion of the skeptical. He describes movingly the process whereby the games sometimes convert spectators who "merely came to look." They feel themselves caught up in the "flow" and abandon their suspiciousness. MacAloon writes, "The spectacle frame erected around ritual may serve as a recruiting device, disarming suspicion toward 'mere ritual' and luring the proudly uncommitted."

For MacAloon, television viewers are second-class spectators. Since "festival means being there, there is no festival at a distance." Television, he thinks, is capable only of spectacle—and a cheapened one at that. "There may be media festivals," he says, "but a festival by media is a doubtful proposition." Here we part company with MacAloon, arguing that the media-events spectator may also cross the liminal divide into festival, ritual, and game. True, he has access only to the re-presentation by television superimposed on the original; yet he also may create his own home festivals and rituals.

Certain media events, we grant MacAloon, never leave the realm of spectacle. Indeed, one wonders whether they qualify as more than that for the people who are there. Many contests are of this character. The annual Oscar ceremony is an example. Despite the huge size of its television audience—to repeat,

75 million domestic viewers and perhaps 350 million internationally (though not simultaneously)—two-thirds nevertheless expressed indifference when queried whether the event should be discontinued. Clearly, this is merely a spectacle about which viewers have doubts, and even that is a weak word. Viewers are well aware "that the Academy Awards are nothing more than a public relations event for the film industry" (Real, 1982).

Most serious events have their doubters, too. Some remained ambivalent about Sadat. In the national survey completed immediately after the 1984 Olympics (Rothenbuhler, 1985), roughly 30 percent insisted that the game had no message for anyone but the athletes. And some stayed away from the Watergate telecasts altogether: disproportionately more Republicans avoided the broadcasts, and more of the politically uninvolved. Those that remained did not all read the proceedings in the same way. As Lang and Lang (1983) say about the televised hearings, "Depending on the viewer's frame of mind, the proceedings could be seen as a unifying event, as a reaffirmation of due process before the law. Or they could be viewed oppositionally, as a degradation ceremony."[15]

Yet one can infer from viewers' statements about certain events that many do go beyond spectacle, to the heart of the matter. They recognized in Sadat not a deception but the possibility of true peace. They made a distinct choice between the two competing models of Watergate as "routine politics" and as "morality play." They partook of certain aspects of the Olympics festival at home, even if it was less exhilarating and seductive than MacAloon's festival. Among U.S. spectators, two-thirds connected the games to ideas about winning and losing that are "important to life" and not just to athletics (Rothenbuhler, 1989).

It is important to distinguish among intensity of involvement, scope of involvement, and type of involvement. Thus, Mac-

Aloon's spectator is (1) less intensely involved, (2) more narrowly involved, and (3) involved in a different role (observer) than his "festive" participant is. But these are quite different dimensions. One may become involved in the Olympics, in Watergate, or in a presidential election by placing a bet, by identifying with one side or the other, by taking interest in the rules, or by opposing the event itself. These are different types of involvement and are revealed in different types of "reading." The intensity of involvement, in each of these roles, may be superficial or strong; even opposition to an event may be intense. The scope of involvement may be defined as the number of different roles in which the participant joins the event. These dimensions apply to the experience of "not being there" as well as to the experience of "being there."

Diasporic Ceremonies

Can we still speak of a public event when it is celebrated at home? Is there a collective celebration when the collectivity is both atomized and scattered?

To say no would amount to denying the status of similarly scattered and home-based celebrations, often including essential tenets of religious traditions. The example of the Passover seder is illuminating because the occasion it constitutes is not only religious but political as well and might serve as a paradigm of Emile Durkheim's symmetrical theses on the social dimension of religion and on the religious dimension of sociality. The seder has served through the ages as a powerful means of unification, offering a ceremonial structure that takes account of geographic dispersion by translating a monumental occasion into a multiplicity of simultaneous, similarly programmed, home-bound microevents while focused, however, on a symbolic center. By proposing a collective ceremony "without a central cultic temple" (Bokser, 1984), by transferring public celebration to the home, the model of the seder—or, indeed, the home celebration of other holidays such as Christmas or Thanksgiving— seems to have solved a problem, mutatis mutandis, very similar to that now experienced by the dispersed mass of television viewers.

Media events differ from these holidays in that identical icons are delivered simultaneously to the homes of all celebrants. Media events, therefore, stand midway between the mass rally or pilgrimage and the subjectively conjured image of the center. Transforming the audience of mass ceremonies into the huge audience of media events has led to the reinvention, in a totally new context, of an ancient and domestic celebratory form— what might be called the diasporic ceremony. True, members of the audience are radically separated from the ceremonial locus of the event and are also isolated from each other; they no longer form masses or crowds except in an abstract, statistical sense.[16] Television celebrants cannot react directly to the ritual performance or to the reactions of other members of the participating public. The very hugeness of the television audience has paradoxically transposed the celebration into an intimate register. Attendance takes place in small groups congregated around the television set, concentrating on the symbolic center, keenly aware that myriad other groups are doing likewise, in similar manner and at the same time. Ceremonial space has been reconstituted, but in the home.

When there is no way of "being there," a ceremony is created to encapsulate the experience of "not being there." Rather than an impoverished and deviant experience, it is an altogether *different* experience.

6

Shamanizing Media Events

It is correct to regard most media events—no less than the traditional ceremonies studied by anthropologists—as "reinforcing" or "hegemonic," in the sense that they remind societies to renew their commitments to established values, offices, and persons. Occasional events, however, involve a discernible change in the realm of both the symbolic and the real. True, the proposed new values may be familiar, or revivals of ideals that had been despaired of, and the sponsors of change may be none other than the old elites themselves, albeit ambivalently or reluctantly. Willy-nilly, and however hegemonic in origin, certain media events serve as harbingers of change.

We will consider here the dynamics of interaction among the three contractual partners—organizers, broadcasters, and audiences—in a subset of events that may be described as "transformative." Our most prominent examples, of course, are the Conquests—Sadat in Jerusalem and the Pope in Poland. The Korean reunion event is equally important, while the Watergate hearings, the moon landings, and certain other occurrences also qualify in part. More recent and even more dramatic examples are provided by the live broadcast of the mass demand for political change in Eastern Europe in the fall of 1989.[1]

The magic of this process is the subject of the present chapter. We demonstrate how the ceremonial broadcast of a proposal for change can, under certain conditions, actually induce such

147

change. The process is reminiscent of what is called symbolic efficacy by anthropologists in their analyses of shamanic healings and transformations (Lévi-Strauss, 1963). Responding to the subjunctive moment when viewers of such events become converts, at least for the moment, to a new definition of the possible, the ceremonial leader, now endowed with the feedback of charisma, urges a next step.

We begin by putting these transformative events into context, proposing a typology for contextualizing media ceremonies with respect to antecedent and consequent events. Next, we discuss the dimensions in terms of which the anticipated change is foreseen. Finally, in the spirit of the anthropologists, we propose a sequence of stages or phases through which ceremonial action proceeds, as it emerges from its context, exemplifies its intent, mobilizes mass support, and translates into action. In other words, we consider context, "text," and process.

Contextualizing Media Events

Ceremonies can be read as a response to external events, whether cyclical and expected or unique and unexpected. They address routine events as well as grave crises. In their counterpoint to the attitudes of daily life they comment on the hopes and fears of the changing seasons, the undertaking of hazardous pursuits, the entry into new physiological conditions such as death or puberty, or the adoption of a new social condition such as marriage. But drastic changes of leadership, war and peace, natural catastrophes or social feuds, may also be attended by ceremonies which speak to the event so as to urge and smooth a desired—or imposed—transition. The same holds for media events: these are televised ceremonies that refer to events, and often address conflict or crisis. A typology of the relationships

between real-world events and crises and their ceremonial counterparts will help to clarify which ceremonies are merely reinforcing and which can be credited with introducing change.

As a start, let us distinguish between those ceremonies that
refer to preexisting events and those that do not (Table 3). Rather
than classifying the latter as ceremonies which do not refer to
events, however, we demonstrate that these are ceremonies
whose events are contained within themselves; they are ceremonies which themselves are events. Indeed, it will become
evident that these are the most powerful—the most transformative—of occasions.

Among the ceremonies that refer to independently existing
events, one set refers to events in the past and another to events
in the present. Ceremonies referring to past events can be
defined as "commemorative." The event has already been spoken for by history, but its fixity may vary considerably. Thus,
some events are past and dead; their meanings are somehow
"embalmed" and no longer negotiable. The Fourth of July fire-

Table 3   Events and ceremonies

A		B
Antecedent event is—	Antecedent event is recorded—	Referring to antecedent event, ceremonial event is—
Dead	In history	A commemoration
Alive	In news	A response Paying tribute Wishing well
Nonexistent	Nowhere	The event itself Restored Transformed

works carry only the faintest echo of the thunder of the American Revolution. The May Day parade, even in Eastern Europe before the revolution, has virtually lost sight of its foundations.

Some events, however past, may not be dead. Their specific outlines may no longer be salient, but their meanings are still negotiable. Such events do not require an abstraction—an unfreezing of their emotional import—because they are continually experienced as present and still malleable memories. Holocaust Day in Israel, for example, regularly reignites keenly felt emotions. The event returns with its full urgency, sweeping commemoration aside in a surge of feeling still demanding explanation and justification.

Other events, more remote, may sometimes be revived by the coincidence of a social situation and a ceremonial commemoration. New nations rediscover holidays that contribute to their need for identity. Certain holidays of the Jewish calendar have become more salient with the return to Zion, for example, while others have become less salient. Some holidays assume more importance as a response to "competing" holidays. Thus, in recent years, Hanukkah has assumed unexpected prominence in response to Christmas. Indeed, the career of holidays in any culture is not a stable one; there are ups and downs, eclipses and returns, freezings and rebirths. Paradigmatic Jewish holidays, for example, continually absorb newer events—triumphs and catastrophes—that resemble the founding event (Yerushalmi, 1982). Yet some events may be said to be born-again, when the present contains an echo of an earlier event or when a crisis of the present makes a past ceremonial form appropriate.

A second set of ceremonies refers to contemporary events. These may even be simultaneous, in the sense that the ceremony almost coincides with the event in time. Consider the funerals of Kennedy and Mountbatten, for example. These ceremonies are "responses." They mobilize popular reactions to trauma and rededicate a society to the values which were violated. They are first attempts to establish the meanings of events and institutionalize them in collective memory. Thus, the televised funeral of John Kennedy was an immediate attempt to give perspective, in ceremonial form, to the disparate mixture of shock, bewilderment, fragmentary information, and improvised protocol which flashed across the screen during those chaotic days. In a deliberate gesture, the funeral of Mountbatten snubbed all reference to the assassination that caused it. Phrased as requiem for the British Empire, its ritual message overlooked the immediate transgressions it was expected to address, dissolving the crime into a mere shadow of its larger significance. Usually, however, such ceremonies address corresponding events directly. When these are events in progress, the observances wish them well and launch them on their way.

So far we have described two sets of occasions which celebrate events that have taken place, or that are taking place, in the real world. In the one case, the event is only dimly recalled and not much discussed. In the other case, the event is fully present and requires attention and interpretation. If these events were not treated ceremonially, our access to the first type of event would be limited to the media of history, that is, to textbooks, monuments, and cultural memorabilia. History books, movies, and monuments are the custodians of the American Civil War, for example, which is not otherwise recalled ceremonially. Without ceremony, access to the still-salient event would be provided only by the news media. Imagine the Kennedy assassination as a major news event, without the Kennedy funeral.

Contrasting with these two is a third set of occasions. It relates to events which are neither dead nor alive, but are nowhere to be found "outside." Of course, there is a situation of malaise nagging for attention, but if it were not for the ceremony, no identifiable event would exist at all; the ceremony creates and constitutes the event. The major media events in our corpus—most of the Conquests—are of this third kind. Sadat in Jerusalem, the Pope in Poland, the Korean reunion event, the moon landing, are events in themselves. They seek to influence a future reality.

Not all would-be transformative events possess this power. We have already stressed the existence of events "manqué." But among those that do succeed, it is important to consider a further distinction: some events propose an innovative transformation of the existing order, while others, often playfully, offer no more than a suspension of this order, one which wishfully suggests the restoration of an earlier age.

These latter events might be called restorations. Some of them are no more than "recreations," with all the ambiguity inherent in the term. They interrupt daily life and offer a time-out from the complexities and animosities that characterize it. The change they propose is a return to another time, which may not even apply to any real past; they celebrate a golden age which, for a moment, is contrasted with the present. During this moment, spectators in situ and at home suspend disbelief in favor of a playful participation in the proposed utopia. "Inventing tradition" (Hobsbawm and Ranger, 1983), the pomp of the royal wedding, as redesigned for television (Dayan and Katz, 1982), allude to times when royal weddings were alliances between ruling families and actually played a decisive role in shaping the map of Europe. Similarly for the Olympic Greece invoked by Coubertin (MacAloon, 1984): while not an outright forgery, it is little more than a neoclassic utopia. Medieval chivalry in the versions of Sir Walter Scott or Richard Wagner might have served as well. Of course, these events are largely escapist in their reliance on nostalgia for a retouched past.

The ideological work of the restorative events must, nevertheless, be taken seriously. Through their idealization of some utopian past, models of behavior are offered and values are held high. By celebrating the attainments of champions in the abstracted realm of sports, or calling on the Cinderella tale, the myths of mobility and achievement are invoked. Cinderella's mobility is coupled with chance; that of the athletes with voluntarism and determination, also tinged by chance (Lowenthal, 1944). Far from being ideologically neutral, such "recreations" actively reinforce dominant paradigms, recalling the writings of the Frankfurt school, in which the media provide the status quo with an ideological buttress. In this sense, they are no less instrumental than those serious or tragic ceremonies which have been defined above as "responses" to trauma,[2] even if Boorstin (1964) would say that they are empty because they lack referents in the real world.

Among ceremonies that rely on no external event, there is also an "innovative" or "transformative" mode. Seeking neither to divest nor to restore, "transformative" ceremonies give full-dress treatment to a proposal for radical change, mobilizing an entire society to consider its acceptability.[3] These ceremonies contain their events within them: they are the event. The arrival of Sadat in Jerusalem or the Pope in Poland is not improvised in response to a crisis; it is the result of deliberate choice. There is, of course, a general context from which the event takes its meaning and a genre of ceremonial protocol that is called upon. But as far as specific events are concerned, the ceremony is the event and the event is the ceremony.

In spite of their advocacy of change, one should acknowledge that these events are sponsored by existing elites. Even if the Apollo mission to the moon, for example, was designed to bolster the military-industrial complex, both symbolic and real (McDougall, 1985), once the landing actually took place, other readings got the upper hand. Redrafting the map of the world, the ceremonial event transformed our perception of human space. Thus a hegemonic manipulation may also reveal—if only for a moment—that we become trapped in ways of thinking and acting that have alternatives: one gets a glimpse of the strictures that have been imposed on one's consciousness.

Sadat in Jerusalem and the Pope in Poland may be read as challenges to the belief of Israelis and Egyptians, Eastern and Western Europeans, that the existing order is unchangeable. Israel has an open door, it used to be said, but no Arab leader will accept the invitation to pass through it; this was the prevailing doctrine in Israel. Religion has no future in the Communist world, it used to be feared; nothing will ever restore its centrality. When circumstances conspired to bring Sadat and the Pope to launch their respective missions, the dominant doctrines were undermined.

Allowing for doctrinal reformulation is a remarkable example of hegemony at work. Official doctrines, like all social arrangements, require updating and refreshing, and it is a wise elite that takes the initiative of endorsing—thus co-opting and containing—inevitable change (Gouldner, 1976; Katz et al., 1963). In the case of both Sadat and the Pope, we know that secret meetings planned the events in advance and that, on arrival, the guests were equipped by their hosts with well-orchestrated scenarios. But we also argue that moments of challenge to official beliefs reveal willy-nilly (1) that alternatives to a present doctrine are available, thus relativizing the "only way," and (2) that the interruption offered by the ceremonial event induces a reflexive energy which cannot entirely be controlled, therefore leading to new perceptions of the possible. These relativizing or liberating moments are suspect if one sees them merely as tactical moves. Indeed, they may be intended as ideological face-lifts, begrudgingly conceded and involving only little substance. Notwithstanding their intent, they suspend the hegemonic rule of a given discourse by showing it in the embrace of an adversarial discourse, at least for a moment, or in the process of reformulating its own coherence. There are, in other words, ceremonial events whose interruptiveness affects not only daily life, but the rule of a dominant, not-to-be-questioned ideology.

To summarize what has been said so far, recall, in Table 3, that ceremonies relating to prior events, past or present, are commemorations or responses. Usually, these are limited to the A-B relationship shown in Table 4. Ceremonies that do not relate to any event outside themselves—that is, those which emerge from a problem situation which has not crystallized into a specific event—are often turned toward the production of consequent events (B-C in Table 4), whether restorative or transformative.

Thus, A and B in the second diagram speak of the relationship between antecedent events and the ceremonies that refer to them, while B and C speak of ceremonies that lead to subsequent events, such as the emergence and resurgence of the Polish solidarity movement after the Pope's visits,[4] or the Camp David talks in the wake of Sadat. Ceremonies that become the events they claim to be distinguish the most momentous of media events from the most trivial. In a sense, the most significant of media events are "pseudo-events" which work. Applying the famous formula of W. I. Thomas (1928), they become real because they are real in their consequences; they are responded to as such. Ceremonies of this type have a causative power.

Table 4   Relation of ceremonies to events

A	B	C
Antecedent event in the real world, often traumatic	Ceremony	Consequent event in the real world, resulting from the ceremony

They are not only expressive utterances but discrete and consequential actions.

Some events—Watergate, for example—run the gamut A-B-C. At first, the Watergate affair was no more than an A-B event. The congressional hearings might have been limited to a redressive ceremony, an attempt to restore the rules after the President's men had broken them. In this sense, the antecedent event would be the Watergate break-in as reported in the *Washington Post*, and the hearings a ceremonial conclusion to a case of deviance and its exposure, serving the Durkheimian (1915) function of reinforcing the norm by exposing deviance and illustrating Turner's notion of redressive ritual. Clearly, Watergate was more than that. The original event, in fact, was largely ignored at the time of its discovery, in spite of the persistence of investigative reporters. Not until the framing of the question by the Senate committee—the definition of the break-in as serious business, and the implication of the President—did the situation assume its historic proportions. Thus, the event in some sense was produced by the symbolic framing of the congressional procedure, as if the ceremony had constructed not only a subsequent event but its own antecedent event as well.

Live television showed the Congress solemnly examining the possible violation of a sacred norm, not just frowning upon a distasteful but insignificant political maneuver. This framing ultimately led to the resignation of the President, not because it directly required it, but because it initiated a process whereby that which had been unthinkable—to impeach a President, especially after a landslide victory—was gradually made thinkable (Alexander, 1988; Lang and Lang, 1983). Thus the ceremonial hearings (B) rewrote an ostensibly minor executive transgression (A), raising it to a new moral dimension and leading to the President's resignation (C).

The sequence event-ceremony-event in 1989 Czechoslovakia was even more dramatic. On November 17, police attacked a student-initiated protest of some tens of thousands of people assembled in Prague's Wenceslas Square. Fueled by outrage and sensing that Czechoslovakia's turn had come in the domino game, the newly formed Civic Forum activated all of the "alternative media" of revolution—graffiti, posters, pamphlets, illegal books and newspapers, church rallies and pilgrimages, agitation at factories, and word-of-mouth in the streets—to mobilize hundreds of thousands of people for the now-nightly rallies and to build toward the two-hour general strike scheduled for November 27. Television—an organ of the state—ignored the immense activity until November 22, when broadcast-journalists decided to respond to the protesters' call for coverage of the demonstrations and were forcibly prevented from doing so. There were intermittent broadcasts nevertheless, and continued police restraint, when suddenly, without explanation, television went live to the demonstrators. On Saturday, November 25, says Ash (1990, p. 100):

> At two p.m., in freezing snow, there is the biggest demonstration of all; over half a million people, in the park near the Letna football stadium . . . with the flags and banners and upturned faces vivid against the white snow . . . whole sections of the crowd jump up and down together to keep warm. The essential fact is that they are there, at the Forum's invitation . . . Television is opening up to report on the revolution.

Apple (1989) picks up the story on Sunday:

> From one end of Czechoslovakia to the other, people sat riveted to their television sets as the national network carried a skillfully produced live broadcast from the Letenske Gardens,

an open assembly ground in Prague that is used for circuses and other public events. There were speeches by dissident leaders like Vaclav Havel, who only a few days ago had to disseminate their views through pitifully tiny samisdat newspapers. The cameras, supposedly at the service of the party, captured all of the powerful emotions of opposition to it— close-ups of ordinary people, bundled against the cold in parkas and ski caps, chanting anti-regime slogans, making the V-for-victory sign of Winston Churchill and Lech Walesa, rattling keys to symbolize escape from the prison of conformity, swaying and singing and sometimes crying. Opposition speeches were transmitted without belittling commentary. It was powerful political theater, the raw drama of protest, sponsored by the target of protest.

Here, then, was political ceremony (B) in response to the violent events of ten days before. Whether this was a last and desperate effort to vent the steam or to co-opt the opposition by offering free access to the national network, or whether it was simply a collapse of authority, still needs clarification. But this was more than protest; it was the first ceremony of orderly change; for the prime minister himself appeared, live on television, to face the opposition. As Apple says, "The climax came in the appearance of Prime Minister Ladislav Adamec who discovered today how hard it is to be the man in the middle, the man trying to hold things together, when the contagion of change is in the air." Alexander Dubcek, the old hero of 1968, said he was proud to share the platform with Mr. Adamec and tried to explain the prime minister's plight, without much success. The confrontation with the old guard turned the rally into a debate, "as if," says Apple, "there were a liberal democracy already." Thus, within the ceremony (B), mass protest (A) was transformed into a rehearsal for the reinstatement of the parliamentary democracy (C) that would soon follow.[5] Obviously, television did not cause the revolution; rather, it framed revolutionary actions as symbolic gestures that, together, had results in the real world.[6]

Two days after the strike (A) there was another ceremony (B), the special session of the parliament that unanimously repealed the constitutional clause granting a "leading role" to the Communist party and calling for elections.[7] One month later, Havel was chosen president of the republic and Dubcek president of the parliament. Elections were held the following June, resulting in an absolute majority for the Civic Forum.

Yet a different sequence of event-ceremony-event can be discerned in the prelude and aftermath of the funeral of Martin Luther King in April 1968. Urban rioting was at its worst, and television newspeople were at a loss over how to report it without seeming to exacerbate it (Russo, 1983). Word of King's assassination made matters much worse, until the funeral and the worldwide attention it aroused created an island of calm, shifting attention, Russo surmises, away from the underlying causes. With the funeral of John Kennedy as a reference mark, television followed the casket, on a mule-drawn farm wagon, past the headquarters of the Southern Christian Leadership Conference in which King had his office, through black Atlanta to the Georgia state house. Walter Cronkite singled out distinguished guests from among the hundred thousand participants: Hubert Humphrey, the vice president, Senator Robert Kennedy (two months before his own assassination), Andrew Young, Rosa Parks (the black woman who had refused to give up her seat to a white person on the bus in Montgomery, Alabama), Mahalia Jackson, and many others. On Thursday, April 11, two days later, President Lyndon Johnson signed into law the Civil Rights Act of 1968, noting that it signified a lasting memorial to the slain leader of the civil rights movement.

The B-C relationship in "transformative" events demonstrates the power of ceremonies to beget and give meaning to new historical realities. The process involved is one of replacement, inside the ceremonial frame, of a given paradigm by a new one, and presentation of the new paradigm to the world. Transformative ceremonies provide a new basis for action in the translation or remodeling of areas of reality previously structured by dominant languages and familiar models. These new models have latent roots in the culture, of course; they are not invented *ex nihilo.*

The Text of Transformative Events

The ceremonial launching of change begins with the unveiling of some new way of thinking about a long-smoldering, ostensibly incurable problem. We shall soon consider the process of this unveiling in detail, but first we wish to address the question of what precisely is unveiled. The answer, we believe, is a changed frame of reference, a paradigm that proposes a new sense of time and a new sense of space, one that strives to fend off the traces of other, conflicting memories. Thus, we are proposing that transformative media ceremonies (1) address a latent conflict, (2) by enacting, within themselves, a reorganization of time and space—that is, of history and geography, (3) thus making formerly unthinkable solutions thinkable. If the ceremony (B) can be viewed as a miniature of the new era, then the events in its wake (C) demonstrate that the now-thinkable is also feasible.[8]

A New Era Is Proclaimed

A transformative ceremony, then, is a turning point, organizing time retrospectively up to the ceremonial moment, and prospectively from the ceremony forward. The liminal moment of the ceremony itself—the moment of interruption of routinized social time—stops history in its tracks. It invites society to consider alternative routes and, in so doing, to reexperience some of the chaos, anguish, and exhilaration of its genesis. New projects are born, in the light of which the past is reinvented and collective memory is reorganized.

Consider how the clock of history was rewound for the Korean, Israeli, and Polish events. In each case, the media ceremony symbolized the onset of a more open "postwar" period.

In the Korean case, the ceremony may be read as the somehow heretical announcement that a society cannot stay mobilized forever. The family reunion demonstrated the legitimacy of individual concerns and aspirations in a huge collective experience. Family division might have been North Korea's fault, but it was perpetuated largely through South Korean neglect, through an indifference to individual need that characterizes this and other cold wars. Arising from the domestic sphere, the family reunion was an indirect "answer" to the military coup that had preceded it by some three years. In a way, it marked the end of the postwar period. Since then, South Koreans have proven their distrust of "providential" authority and their consequent ability to challenge it, to take fate into their own hands, even when what was involved was no longer in the domestic realm but in the public sphere.

The visit of Sadat to Jerusalem was also perceived as the end of a postwar period. It concluded the phase of Israeli history that began with the Yom Kippur War, perhaps even the war of independence. The foreign policy of the Labor-led government until its fall in 1977 had been based on the axiom of "the impossibility of a stable peace among the nations of the Middle East." The strategy was "to maximize military advantage" while expressing a willingness to enter direct and unconditional peace talks that would presumably lead to the yielding of occupied territory in exchange for peace agreements (Lewis, 1978). With Sadat's coming, Israeli leaders could act on their word.

Dating from Sadat's visit, Middle Eastern crises and hostilities were no longer perceived or reported exclusively in terms of conflict between the Arabs and the Israelis. The framing of news about Israel split between the ongoing story of hostility as usual, and the new story of the progress of peace. During the visit, the focus shifted to the common past of Jews and Arabs: the kinship between them as descendants of Abraham; the Sephardi component of the Israeli heritage; the Judeo-Arab civilizations of Moslem Spain; the large numbers of "Arab Jews" in Israel; the common past of Sadat and Begin as freedom fighters against colonialism and inmates of British jails.[9] Of course, Sadat's former Nazi sympathies were forgotten.

The visit of John Paul II to Poland was also an example of a postwar period reaching its end. The ceremony of the visit marked the end of a hiatus during which Poland had come to be identified with its godless neighbors. It began in 1948 under the Soviet-backed United Polish Workers party and culminated in 1953 when Cardinal Wyszynski was placed under house arrest, while eight bishops and nine hundred priests were imprisoned. Of course the period of brutal repression had not lasted more than a few years, and since Gomulka the Polish church had steadily reinforced power. Despite its remarkable expansion, in 1979 it was still without legal existence or guaranteed rights, a situation which the former Bishop Wojtyla had protested by saying, "Being such a large community, a community almost as large as the nation, we cannot be outside the law."[10] John Paul II's visit reenacted the interlocking origins of faith and nation.

In his famous exhortation "Courage, don't be frightened!" John Paul II also reoriented collective memory by reminding the Poles that Christianity is based on the paradoxical compatibility of triumph and oppression. He urged Poland to adopt a historical project reminiscent of early Christendom, to find in oppression the opportunity of asserting itself. He posed the example of Christ to show that powerlessness may lead not to passivity but to Passion.[11]

The paradigm of martyrdom thus appears as a link between the future of Poland and a past symbolically represented by the holy figure of Bishop Stanislaw, beheaded for challenging the temporal power of King Boleslaw II. Interestingly, the myth of Saint Stanislaw will be reenacted in a fashion reminiscent of passion plays, in the brutal episode of the assassination and drowning of Father Popieluszko in 1984. Both martyrs are now merged in a common cult that illustrates the continuity between societal project and symbolically congruent elements of collective memory.

Persecution and oppression are not only essential to the history of Christianity, leading to the ideal of martyrdom, but they are also "root metaphors" (Turner, 1974) for Polish identity. Through a history of maintaining faith in the face of invasions and occupations, Poland sees itself historically as the martyr of Europe, the agent of its eventual salvation, and as a "chosen people," the "collective prophet of a new era," a "Christ among nations" (Jeanneney, 1987).

And, indeed, the Polish initiative did prove prophetic. "If I was forced to name a single date for the beginning of the end in this inner story of Eastern Europe, it would be June 1979 . . . I do believe that the Pope's first great pilgrimage to Poland was that turning point. Here, for the first time, we saw that massive, sustained, yet supremely peaceful and self-disciplined manifestation of social unity; the gentle crowd against the Party-state" (Ash, 1990, p. 133).

Ten years after the Pope's visit, nine years after the beginnings of Polish revolt, Poland seated its first non-Communist prime minister, the Berlin wall was breached, and Vaclav Havel was installed as president of Czechoslovakia—in what Dahrendorf (1990) calls *annus mirabilis*, 1989. "And talking about images, for it was a year of television too," says Dahrendorf, "anyone who watched the slipping countenance of the Romanian dictator Nicolae Ceausescu during the mass meeting organized by his agents on 21 December, which turned into an angry demonstration against him as he was speaking, will forever know what it means that rulers lose their nerve before the people get their way."[12] This was the end, continues Dahrendorf, of "over four decades which began in 1946 when George Kennan sent his 'long telegram' from Moscow about the limits of Soviet interest in a common order for the world, and Winston Churchill made his 'Iron Curtain' speech in Fulton, Missouri. They were the decades of the Cold War."

Something similar can be said about Watergate and symbolic time. The congressional hearings not only offered a societal response to a scandal, but marked the perceived end of the "imperial presidency" and suggested a return to a concerned America. Thus Alexander (1988) ascribes to Watergate the latent function of mending the cleavage between the "silent majority" and the radical movements of the sixties which opted out of the mainstream values, protested unequal rights, and opposed the Vietnam War. In his analysis, Watergate was a ritual of national reconciliation. Thus another postwar period was ceremonially ended.

Ushering in a new paradigm, the ceremonial event induces a reflexive perception of what came before it. The immediate past is suddenly objectified as an era or a period and given a name. The hours just before the ceremony are now echoes of another era. The past appears as prehistory, and the present is reconnected to an earlier moment when history stopped. In each case, the event seems to mark a return to a society's true vocation, and history now begins (Alberoni, 1983). These events can be compared to wars, both as "moral equivalents" (James, 1917) and markers of historical time. Couched in the often hyperbolic idioms of folk historiography, transformative events convey the perception that "if this much is possible, then we are already in a new era."

A New Sense of Place

Media events of a transformative nature also affect a society's sense of place. The society's members are as if reborn to a different world. Of course they remain just where they were, but the world has remodeled itself around them. Transformative media events affect symbolic geography.

The transformations induced by these events resemble one another. Each one remodels symbolic space, challenging the immutability of the relationship between physical geography and social identity. All are dramatic variations on the theme of insularity.

The moon landings are an obvious example. While in some distant way everybody—or almost everybody—knew the earth not to be the whole of the universe, the Apollo missions translated the concept into an experience.[13]

Consider the Korean example. Prior to the family reunion broadcasts, North and South Korea seemed irremediably separate and discontinuous. The reunion broadcast showed that the geography of partition did not always account for the problem of divided families, and led to the thought that partition was often used as a scapegoat or a lame justification. This suggested a continuity between the two Koreas, running much deeper than the official stance of ideological hostility. The number of frontier incidents occurring shortly thereafter can be read as a nervousness over the threatening perception that borders might now be opening to exchanges. Indeed, steps were actually taken toward such exchanges (and they were largely facilitated by the impending occurrence of another, still hopeful media event: the Seoul Olympic Games).

Poland, too, resituated itself geographically in the wake of the Pope's first visit. By exhibiting—live on television—the centrality of Catholicism to the identity of the Polish people, the European dimension of that identity superseded its Slavic component. Memories were reactivated of the time when Poland was not part of an "Eastern bloc," but entertained close links with daughters of the church such as France (the Leczynski dynasty) and Italy (whose architectural influence is still visible in many Polish cities). The fact that the visiting Pope was a Pole further suggested that the Vatican was in some way an extension of Poland, a perception which John Paul II unambiguously encouraged in his mass at Jasna-Gora: "Our lady of the bright mountain, I consecrate to you Europe and all the continents. I consecrate to you Rome and Poland, united through your servant." In a change of geographic perception, the Poles—with the aid of the Pope—saw their country as an outpost of Western Europe. They were no longer an extension of the Soviet Union, but the somehow decentered heart of Catholic Europe.

This change in perception is a mirror image of the one experienced by the Israelis after Sadat's visit. If the Poles felt they were no longer part of Eastern Europe—that they had become a Catholic island—the Israelis felt they were no longer an island, a Western outpost or besieged fortress in the Middle East. Sadat's visit had underlined the elementary fact that the thirty minutes it takes to fly from Cairo to Tel Aviv are not just an invitation to enemy bombers, but an encouragement of neighborly relations. Discovering this proximity, Israelis actually began to book reservations for tourist travel to Egypt, suddenly aware that there was an exciting new world at their very doorstep. A proposal was made to give Tel Aviv and Alexandria the status of sister cities. Another urged that Arabic be the first foreign language taught in Israeli schools. Israel was back in the Middle East, at least for a while.

The same thing happened to the East Central European states when the Iron Curtain fell. No longer an island, they had rejoined the continent. Ash (1990) says it extremely well: "Travelling to and fro between the two halves of the divided continent, I have sometimes thought that the real divide is between those (in the West) who have Europe and those (in the East) who believe in it. And everywhere, in all the lands, the phrase people use to sum up what is happening is the 'return to Europe.'"[14]

Unraveling Transformative Events

Transformative events can be shown to share a typical sequential structure. They follow a recognizable scenario of progress through a succession of identifiable phases. Even though this sequence is not always present in its entirety, it can be identified in all of our major examples. It echoes the phase theories that anthropologists have applied to change processes such as rites of passage (Wallace, 1966, cited in Myerhoff, 1982; Turner and Turner, 1978).[15]

In each case, the following steps occur.

(1) The ceremony is mounted in the midst of a long-standing problem that is considered crippling and incurable, one that has become accepted as part of the order of things and survives in a state of latency.

(2) The announcement of an impending ceremonial event that will openly address the problems suggests the possibility of change. This signaling reawakens silenced aspirations. A wave of expectation and public excitement is thus created, culminating in the ceremonial event itself.

(3) The event starts in the form of a gesture that is presented as an instrumental step toward solving the problem. Simultaneously, it is an expressive dramatization, a modeling or an illustrating of the desirable state of affairs. This is where the visual medium of television enters the shamanic process.

(4) Ceremonial performers not only enact gestures, they also deliver straightforward messages. Of all the phases, that of framing comes closest to embodying a standard view of mass communication. Yet speeches can be seen not only as culminations of a corresponding event, but also as interpretations aimed at commenting on the preceding gestures and guiding audiences in their reading. Guidance of this type involves a manipulation of cultural repertoires which often amounts to an original elaboration of mythical contents. In this regard, we propose that ceremonial leaders of the events themselves engage in a modern form of shamanizing.

(5) The last phase concerns the aftermath of the event and the role of the public in modulating its consequences and, above all, in evaluating its effects.

Latency

A latent crisis prevails. This situation is well encrusted in our examples, in contrast, say, to the open scandal of Watergate. The crisis is encased in a time-worn frame of reference: the rift in Korea will never be repaired; Catholicism in Poland must remain underground; the two superpowers will never be reconciled; the conflicting nations in the Middle East will never trust each other. The crisis is part of a reality within which people have learned to live.

Thus transformative media events do not respond to situations of urgency. They respond to silenced aspirations, which explains how in some cases—Korea, for example, or Eastern

Europe—they erupt without clear-cut leadership. Their power comes largely from answering long-standing expectations; from catalyzing a consensus through the resurrection of values that bind the elite no less than the common people. Transformative events reiterate a promise once made and forgotten. They reactualize an overlooked dimension of the social contract. They are events that fulfill.

In ordinary circumstances, those who call for such radical solutions may hold to their opinions; they may even speak up, but they are heard only by one another. Often the alternatives they propose drop out of sight because the majority media ignore them, or the establishment media suppress them, and consequently their adherents are marginalized, caught in what Noelle-Neumann (1984) calls a spiral of silence.

Signaling

For one reason or another, a new paradigm—one which may be familiar but dormant—comes into view and is embraced, sometimes reluctantly, by the elite. Thus Begin endorses Sadat's self-invitation, assuring Walter Cronkite that, indeed, Israel has always promised to welcome any Arab leader who wishes to talk peace. The Polish authorities similarly confirm that the Pope, of course, is welcome to his homeland. The Czechoslovak government makes clear that it will tolerate public rallies of the opposition and restrain the police. The White House cannot but confirm that illegal entry into the offices of a rival political party deserves to be taken seriously.

In ideological terms, these are hegemonic efforts to co-opt a challenge (Gouldner, 1976). The leadership may wish to broaden its appeal; it may be challenged to do so by the compelling character of a manifestly popular countervailing model, or by the pressure of other factions within the elite, or, as in

Eastern Europe, by the retreat or defeat of a "big brother." In terms of leadership theory, such a move illustrates a well-known strategy: leaders who have previously been identified as champions of a prevailing norm may nevertheless succeed in proposing the adoption of a new norm when the earlier one proves inappropriate or insufficient, thereby mitigating revolutionary action and bolstering their own political survival (Homans, 1961).

Notice that transformative media events are more likely to be conceded than initiated by the elites who stand out as their putative organizers. The people want these events; leaders sometimes exert their leadership by following (Merei, 1949). Potentially threatened, they avoid or abandon any direct expression of dissent. Their attitude, rather, suggests ambivalence. When they object to the aspirations conveyed by the event, they do so on practical grounds, stressing matters of feasibility. Of course, they can hardly repudiate events which embody principles to which they are officially committed.

The announcement of the impending ceremony—Sadat will be welcomed; the Pope will celebrate a mass in Warsaw; the Senate will hold hearings; KBS will extend interactive search broadcasts indefinitely; the Czechoslovak rallies will be broadcast live—is a signal to the public that the old, heretofore dominant paradigm is officially open for reexamination. And a promise is implied, again reluctantly, that television will document the proceedings. Excepting the case of Czechoslovakia and Romania—where revolutionary action intervened between latency and signaling—the period of latency ends with the signal that a position until now deemed totally utopian is to be given serious attention. Indeed, the television spotlights in Wenceslas Square were the signal in Prague that revolutionary change was thinkable.

Signaling breaks the spiral of silence. It reverses the movement which ended in the silencing of feelings and aspirations. Individuals and groups who had reluctantly accommodated themselves to the status quo feel called upon to openly denounce it. The "small," "alternate," and "underground" media—the ones that had kept the opposing paradigm alive— suddenly emerge above ground. New opinion leaders emerge: Polish Catholics rally in their churches; parents of Israeli soldiers speak their anguish; Koreans obtain massive means to search for their lost relatives; Eastern Europeans crowd the protest rallies. In a mood close to that which Alberoni ascribes to the "statu nascendi" (Alberoni, 1983), signaling acts as a ferment, reorganizing everything around the announced change.

This reorganization does not happen in an instant. Triggering a liminal period, the phase of signaling parallels the moment when pilgrims abandon their daily concerns as they prepare to set out for the shrine. The routines of daily life are distanced and reconsidered in the light of the impending event.[16]

Suspension of the dominant paradigm clears the public's mind of existing agendas. It also conjures up a full array of questions on society's future and past. Thus, on the eve of Sadat's visit, Israeli opinion is occupied with assessing whether previous opportunities for peace had been missed; whether the Yom Kippur War could have been avoided, or, alternatively, whether that costly episode was not the very basis for the emergence of a partner willing to negotiate. Meanwhile, the daily news keeps fueling explanations and possibilities. Various scenarios are imagined, to anticipate the consequences of the event. By now the old paradigm has been moved from the taken-for-granted to the explicit. It has been relativized as one possibility among others. As to the new paradigm, its nature is still the subject of speculation. What will Sadat ask in exchange? Will Israel return the whole of the Sinai peninsula? Will Israel demand Sadat's tacit recognition of its right to the occupied west bank of the Jordan? Is peace with Israel what Sadat wants? Is he merely engaged in public relations in view of an American loan? Does he represent the rest of the Arab world?

Thus, before the television event even starts, changes are already occurring. Signaling has set off a wave of reflexivity. Various possibilities are envisaged by the media, by the population at large, and by all those who share the dominant skepticism. This intensely speculative mood suggests a cognitive shift. The usual down-to-earth, "indicative" approach to political reality has given way to an exceptional interest in the realm of the possible. This shift might be characterized as a "suspension of disbelief" (Freud, 1939).[17] Let us stress that suspension of disbelief takes place within a specific frame. It is self-conscious and conditional, an exercise in subjunctive imagination. At this stage, there is neither spectacle nor ceremonial broadcast nor mass meetings—except in the Eastern European revolutions where the protest rallies have begun.

Sperber's (1975) work on contradiction applies here; it provides insight into the process which leads to the transformation of symbolic time.[18] When the announcement of the impending event takes place, audience members are confronted by a paradox. Israel sees itself as besieged, surrounded by Arab hatred and rejection, yet the very man who started the Yom Kippur War has come to propose peace. Poland sees its leadership bent on eradicating Catholicism, yet this same leadership has extended an invitation to the Pope. North Korea is held responsible for the war that tore families apart, yet thousands of these lost persons were found by their unknowing relatives living near them in South Korea. Russian tanks are expected at just such a moment, yet hundreds of thousands are assembled in Wenceslas

Square to protest the Communist regime.[19] In each case, the new perception contradicts established knowledge but seems too crucial to be dismissed. Two contradictory propositions cannot coexist; one or the other must give way.

If the new proposition contradicts existing knowledge, one might solve the contradiction by defining this knowledge as time bound, and thus no longer relevant. The new and the old can be equally relevant, but to different periods; their contradiction can be avoided by insisting that the new proposition belongs to a new era. For example, to the question "How can an offer of peace emanate from our worst enemy?" one answer might be that things have changed, that this is a new era. The restructuring of time is one kind of symbolic response to a cognitive problem.

Modeling

In his famous essay on the efficacy of symbols, Lévi-Strauss (1963) emphasizes that both shaman and psychoanalyst use language to promote healing. But while the psychoanalyst helps the patient to construct a personal myth in order to give meaning to his experience, the shaman relies on a cultural myth that incorporates an analogue to the situation addressed. Like the analyst, the shaman does not need to manipulate the patient's body. His tactic, rather, is to simulate the patient's condition by symbolic analogy. The healing transformation results from submitting the patient's ailments to a directive, cultural interpretation. These ailments are translated in terms that make them intelligible. Yet healing does not simply result from mythic diagnosis. Translation into myth has an additional role, which is to allow the shaman access to the ailments via symbolic manipulation of the corresponding concepts. Once the ailments are structured in terms of a crisis, that is, of a clash or contradiction between conflicting notions or entities, the invocation of myth will offer a "narrative solution" to the crisis.

While the situations that interest us are collective rather than individual, and the corresponding ceremonies are often innovative rather than merely repetitive, Lévi-Strauss's view of the shamanic procedure as some sort of task-oriented algebra seems quite relevant. The situations addressed in our events, being ideological constructs, are symbolic throughout; thus, they are even more susceptible than physical illness to the evocation of a collective myth. And indeed, Sadat or John Paul II do perform in the style of Lévi-Strauss's shaman, translating the reality of the societies they address into paradigms consistent with their respective ends. They rely on analogies strategically excerpted from the myths of those societies themselves.

The performance of the ceremonial leaders is a complex one, better thought of as two distinct performances. The first is a gestural performance which, following Handelman (1990),[20] we call illustrating or modeling. The second is a discursive performance made up of addresses and speeches which, following Goffman (1974), we call framing. Speech and gesture may in some cases be simultaneous but there is generally a time lag. Usually the gesture comes first; speeches come later. Typically the arrival ceremony—live on television—condenses the whole situation in a visual style reminiscent of celebratory painting. In these tableaux, television presents the principals' gesture as a metaphor of the new paradigm. From the semantic point of view, this visualization and the earlier stage of signaling have the same content. Pragmatically, though, they have a different weight: modeling actualizes what the announcement had made thinkable. Modeling relies on the powers of ceremony, enlisting a larger audience than the one mobilized by signaling. It encapsulates the event in dramatic form, proposing a reduced-scale model of what the event strives to achieve. Clearly, television is the main protagonist at this stage.

As the public takes its seats in front of the television set, it is immersed in an extraordinary state of anticipation. Viewers are plunged into an intellectual and affective turmoil from which the ceremony itself seems almost a release. What happens then is a symbolic enactment of the newly proposed paradigm. Sadat is greeted with a twenty-one-gun salute, as befits an ally, not an enemy. The Pope kisses the ground of Poland and shakes the hands of its leaders. Czech and Romanian television transmit a revolutionary rally in real time. "Incredibly," said the *New York Times* about the Czechoslovakian case, "the Communist Party has made its most potent weapon, state television, available to the opposition, as if this were a liberal democracy already" (Apple, 1989).

Statements at this point are still brief and formalistic. The new paradigm is displayed, but not much spoken. It is eloquently heralded by the situation, brought to collective attention in one sweeping gesture.

The televised ceremonies from Prague—the protest rally in the gardens when the prime minister appeared on the scene, and the special session of parliament on November 29—are particularly good examples of modeling as a foretaste of the situation-to-be. For the Czechoslovakian people, the availability to the opposition of live cameras fulfilled the promise of the signaling phase. But even more, the fact that what was shown took the form of a Contest between the feared party leadership and the opposition enacted the promise of the open society whose emblem is the public debate.

The Korean event seems to be an exception to this pattern. First, its drama involves no great men or women performing for the world, but a myriad of figures who would remain anonymous but for the brief appearance of placards bearing their names. Second, the family reunions do not seem to involve a major riveting gesture. This last point, however, deserves further scrutiny.

The family reunions began as a commemorative broadcast fatalistically recalling the anguish and suffering for which the south holds the north responsible. Unlike previous years, this broadcast was not a dramatic reconstitution of some heroic event of the war; instead, the 1983 commemoration took the form of cinema-verité interviews, followed by an interactive broadcast.[21]

What is striking to the observer is the surprise of the Koreans themselves over the unexpected significance of audience response. At a first level one might describe what happened here as the transformation of a symbolic gesture—a commemorative broadcast—into a pragmatic campaign: television was used instrumentally to reunite families. This instrumental activity itself reached such a high pitch of collective fervor that it became a gesture again. Yet its meaning was now totally different. The event was no longer a retrospective commemoration of the pains inflicted by war. It conveyed the potential for the reunion of all dispersed families in South Korea, thus generating a tidal wave of live broadcasting dedicated to this purpose. These broadcasts and the thousands of reunions they effected served in turn as metaphor for a project that reached beyond the private domain and into the political. The reunion of broken families was turned into a national ritual of healing. Pent up for thirty years, the demand for a search for lost relatives was the almost spontaneous affirmation of a turning point in the history of Korea. The civil war was over.

Thus, in line with our other examples, the meaning of the Korean event was also offered in gestural form. It was not a stately gesture, nor a definitive tableau, but a succession and accumulation of smaller gestures which collectively amounted to an acting-out of popular feelings. The broadcasts made explicit an aspiration that resided in latent form in people's minds, almost revealing it to the Koreans themselves. Family reunions set the ground for the more daring utopia of doing away with the strictures of the cold war. Such a project was never clearly formulated. There was no ceremonial leader in charge of glossing the gesture, no rhetoric to do the work of shamanizing and guiding. Yet, as the event proceeded, it led to an unspiraling of the fatalistic silence that had prevailed and began to influence the real world, not only in further broadcast-reunions but in a variety of subsequent events that have made some headway in thawing relations between the two Koreas.[22]

On the basis of these examples, we can define the modeling phase of transformative events as an anticipated echo of a desired state of things, an enactment of utopia. Had the gestures been less lofty and less immediately consequential, one could speak of a play situation: an acting "as if" the problem addressed by the event had already been solved. Sadat is shown behaving as if peace had already taken place; the Poles rejoice in their faith as if they were no longer under surveillance; Koreans seem to have crossed an invisible threshold into a new era; the propaganda arm of the Czech Communist party goes live to an opposition rally.

Particularly conspicuous in all but the Korean case, "as if" is endowed with authority because it emanates from individuals associated with society's center, and in situations of utmost seriousness. Thus play—in this case, Huizinga's category of mimicry—turns into "deep play" as opposed to what it would be, were it performed by lesser figures (Geertz, 1973) or by actors on a stage. Television translates "as-if-ness" into a collective reality. It offers the "not-happened-yet" as an experience to its dispersed audience. Sensing themselves part of a reorientation of history, spectators wish not to witness it alone. Collective viewing reinforces a shared perception of reality. It permits viewers to confirm that the gestures they are watching on the screen are actually taking place.

This distortion of time is a major aesthetic feature of such events; they are time machines, trips into the future. Their paradox resides in the opposing claims that the desired future is at hand and that such a future needs to be brought about. A similar paradox is underlined by Alberoni (1983), when he points out that "on the symbolic level, the nascent state is fully realized, and, at the same time, it is yet to be realized in practice." Modeling demonstrates that a transformation has taken place on the symbolic level; on the practical level, nothing has happened except the televised gesture.[23] The modeling gesture has now provided a metaphor. Whether the event becomes more than that will depend on the public's response and on what happens in the following stages.

Framing

In a Turnerian perspective, the ceremonial climax should come at the moment when the protagonists address their public in speech, delivering the transformative message of the event directly in an equivalent of the mass which concludes pilgrimages. In the news coverage of the event as well, this is usually the high point. Yet sometimes this moment is altogether absent—as is the case in the Korean event—and sometimes the event's climax is already over. We are suggesting, therefore, that modeling is the key moment, not simply a prelude, and that framing serves, rather, as a caption for the gesture.

Undoubtedly the rhetoric takes place in an already polemical context. Tensions which were played down in the modeling phase manifest themselves anew. Transformative media events are utopian, yet also, as we know, somehow subversive. On the world stage, transformative events are often gestures of reconciliation. In the smaller arena of national politics, they are more likely to take the form of challenges.

These events get the consent of the powers in charge, often reluctantly. When they are not spontaneous happenings, bursting out unexpectedly with no identifiable leadership—as in the Korean reunions or in recent events in Eastern Europe—they are "conceded" events. In the case of Sadat and the Pope, perhaps in Czechoslovakia, too, those events are led by a "guest." Ceremonial leadership thus acquires a complex dimension. We could suggest that under the pressure of national expectations and international opinion, the familiar leader of "structure"— uneasily and of course temporarily—bows to the leader of "antistructure" (Turner, 1969). This cosponsorship leads to events that serve two masters. As Apple (1989) says about the confrontation of the old guard and the opposition at the Letenske Garden event in Prague, "It was powerful political theater, the raw drama of protest, sponsored by the target of protest"—except that Havel and Dubcek are not quite guests, but oppositional leaders.[24]

Ceremonies are often seen as paradigmatic examples of univocality, models for those authoritative discourses which Bakhtin (1981) defines as "monologic." Transformative media events, on the contrary, are characteristically "dialogic." To the "host," ceremoniality is meant to contain the event, to set its boundaries, to assert its discrete and temporary nature, to isolate it from the mainstream of social reality. To the "guest" leader, ceremoniality is meant to help the event overcome, to infiltrate the world of "structure," to ultimately remap social reality. Blended into one gesture at the modeling phase, these two attitudes tend to polarize in two symmetrical strategies: a defensive one, in the case of the host-leaders, and an offensive one, on the part of their guests.

Being part of the event, host-leaders have the opportunity of connecting their own program with the spontaneous aspirations of the public. Challenge is blunted when its formulation seems to emanate from the challenged party. Being part of the cast allows establishment rhetoric to influence the event from inside and to tie the call for change to the values of the political center. Yet even the most Machiavellian of hosts may succumb.[25] Like the sorcerer's apprentice, they themselves may be co-opted to legitimate the changes heralded in the event; to let the contents of the event, no matter how hegemonically glossed, become a collective experience; to allow the spiral of silence to unwind and deliver its message. Of course, all these unwanted outcomes are actively encouraged by the guest-leader's "offensive" performance.

Lacking any formal power over the society they are addressing, or any institutional means of acting on it, the guests—the leaders of "antistructure"—have to achieve effects by relying on the charisma they bring with them, or that which is conferred on them by the occasion. Their performance consists in translating the situations they are facing into a symbolic frame consistent with their ends. Their effort is to reshape social reality through the imposition of meaning.

The ceremonial performance has two main tasks: (1) to show that the utopia as modeled has always been a driving force in the life of the society, such that collective memory exhibits traces of a continuous aspiration toward it, and (2) to confirm the feasibility of the proposed transformation by investing the wealth of aspirations in a popular program of action.

The guest-leader has to maintain the mood he has created by the gesture of his appearance, to keep fueling expectations, but also to translate them into a program compatible with reality and to do so without directly antagonizing the hosts. All this amounts to walking on a tightrope. De Gaulle's event manqué—"Vive le Québec libre"—is a good example of a failure.

Gorbachev's performances at the Washington summit ended rather better. If Havel and Dubcek may be considered "guests" of the Czech Communist party, their performance was a marked success—during the broadcast event, and after.

The guest-leader is in no position to put forth a full and detailed program. Too much of what he proposes has to remain unspecified or ambiguous, since any actual implementation depends not on him alone but also on his negotiating partners. Thus he, too, preaches patience, warns audiences that the dream cannot be realized at once, proposes minor but realizable steps to confirm that the remote-seeming utopia is attainable. Instead of the full-blown program that an opposition leader might propose, a guest-leader suggests a major but largely undefined project congruent with the new paradigm of time and space, and calls upon the audience to be its main protagonist. Through gesture he has enacted utopia. Through speech he attempts to mediate between its urgency and its feasibility. Avoiding the realm of direct action, he calls for its prerequisite, urging his audiences to undergo a "conversion." In Czechoslovakia, by contrast, this is where the opposition leadership calls for real action—the general strike. [26]

Thus, the guest-leader acts as myth maker. In Lévi-Straussian fashion, his statements weave a middle way between the possible and the impossible. He is a messiah figure, a mediator of extreme oppositions, a realistic dreamer, both utopian and practical, shrewd and imaginative. To use Alberoni's (1983) description, his performance is "an exploration of the possible from the point of view of the impossible; an effort to impose the imaginary on existence."

Besides calling for the public's conversion and turning the present moment into a *statu nascendi*—a beginning, not of the utopian age itself, but at least of the path that leads to it—the guest-leader shows that the utopian alternative has always been

present. While minimizing the immediate future and its prac-
ticalities, he draws a line symbolically connecting past history
and proposed future, leading not only to the reorganization of
time but to a new perception of space. As we have seen in signaling, the notion of a new era allows the public to solve a
cognitive problem. The new era exists only as a blank page. Its
contents are not specifiable. What is meant by "triumph of
Catholicism" or "return to Europe" or "peace in the Middle
East" is largely unknown.

The proposition "This is a new era" cannot be accepted cognitively for lack of content; such content can be provided by the
continuity assumed to exist between the new era and that of
which the departing era is now constructed to have been an
interruption. Rather than a move toward the unknown, the new
era can be seen as a coming-home of sorts. It continues a tradition once stopped in its tracks. This tradition or golden age,
of course, is chosen by the guest-leader on the basis of perceptions supportive of the new paradigm. The ending era always
involves the immediate yesterday, but at this stage it can extend
back in time until one reaches any moment or age whose
remembered image seems to validate the content of the new
proposition. Focusing on such an age results in a restructurali-
zation of collective memory, in a change of geographical perceptions. Thus in the case of Sadat, the question "What is the
new era like?" calls for situations in which Arabs are no longer
seen as enemies but as neighbors. The Andalusian golden age
offers such images of Moslem-Jewish cohabitation. John Paul II
reinvokes a Poland that belonged to Catholic Europe rather
than the "Eastern bloc." Korea learns that blood ties are stronger
than iron curtains. Democracy in Czechoslovakia is restored.
These examples suggest that transformative events also include
a restorative dimension.

Reorganizing collective memory in the light of the proposed project, the guest-leader uses his performance as a form of agenda setting, reaching into the future but also projected into the past. He does not mean to offer a scientific description of the era which has reached its supposed end, nor to obey existing historiographic conventions, but to produce a new vantage point on the time and space of the society he addresses. We must stress, however, that the success of this performance requires public sympathy for the new proposal. If it does not elicit enthusiasm, this proposal would be too problematic, too cumbersome, and too costly not to be discarded. This means not only that the announced event is contradictory to existing beliefs, but that the contradiction is welcome. The announced changes are desirable. They correspond to powerful—if hitherto silenced— aspirations. They presuppose a public that is already more than willing to embark on the adventure. The guest-leader's performance presupposes what we have called latency.

Evaluating

The evaluating phase may be said to extend the process of interpretation which began while the event was still in progress. Its origin is in the reactions of individuals or small groups to the signaling and modeling stages. It continues through the framing of the ceremonial leaders, which constitutes a first major attempt at interpreting the event from within. These interpretations concentrate, at the stage of framing, on what we have described as the "offensive" myth making of the guest-leaders. Yet this is only a moment in a long process, and the time lag between thrust and content explains the recourse to media events in deadlocked political or diplomatic situations. Host-leaders whose policies seem threatened by a transformative event believe that they can limit the risks inherent in an event by relying on their power to gloss that event. They know that the content of the event does not inhere in the event but depends ultimately on the treatment it receives within the public sphere—which the host-leader will seek to influence.

Now that the event is over, this process acquires a formal dimension through public debate involving political leaders, parties, and the media. These debates are meant to assess the event's impact but, as recent studies of public opinion suggest, their role is not simply one of assessing, but also one of constructing the event's significance. They modulate the consequences of the event, selectively choosing some but not others of the themes of the controversies surrounding the event (Missika and Bregman, 1987), and calling upon certain values but not others to frame these controversies (Rokeach and Ball-Rokeach, 1989).

The phase of evaluating is essential to a determination of the impact of transformative events both in historical terms and in political terms. No longer dominated by the event itself, nor by the transformative power of ceremonies, the routine functioning of the public sphere has now set in. The evaluating phase thus fits better with the problems of opinion research than with ceremonial anthropology.

Transformative events have a specific career born of their intrinsic ambiguity, the polysemy of their gestures. In fact, their power depends on the combination of a strong thrust in a given direction and of a multivocal content. Both thrust and content are elements of their meaning. But while the thrust of a media event—the values it advocates—is unmistakably identified, its long-term content depends on the interpretations constructed by the various concerned parties.

The host-leader's influence is less than certain when the public sphere itself has been qualitatively transformed by an event;

such, for example, was the case of Sadat's journey to Jerusalem.[27] In the wake of the visit, new actors entered the political scene, often recruited from groups traditionally expected to remain silent. High school students and reserve officers organized sit-ins, singing rallies, petitions, and open letters. Noninstitutional forms of political communication were used to demand implementation of the new norms.

The chanting students and workers of Prague were new political actors, too. With no previous experience of mutual commonality or trust, they achieved major historical change in Wenceslas Square in November 1989. But the further progress of the Czechoslovak affair was quite different. Here was a truly revolutionary event where the public sphere, through a combination of real and symbolic means, was not only shaken up but institutionally transformed.

Collaborative Shamanizing

Looking back at the different phases, we wish to stress several points. Note, first of all, that the phases that begin and end the transformative process stand outside the ceremonial realm. *Latency* is the precondition, and *evaluation* resituates the event in the normal political process.

Second, it should be emphasized that the three intermediate stages—those inside the ceremonial event—echo and reinforce one another. The cognitive processes mobilized by *signaling* reactivate a glimpse of the promised land, and the gestures of *modeling* enact it. The rhetoric of the *framing* replicates the cognitive remapping triggered by modeling, in the words of guidance offered by the principals of the event. Unlike modeling, framing relies on speech. The principals now try to dispel the ambiguity of the gestures they have enacted, and attempt to gain control of the process that has been set in motion. It should be clear from our discussion that we consider signaling and modeling more consequential than framing.

Third, we wish to stress that although there is interaction among the three partners to the event—principals, broadcasters, and audiences—at every stage, a major protagonist emerges in each. The public, trapped in a hegemonic paradigm, is at the center of the latency stage, just as the institutions of public debate, and the collective behavior that seeks to influence the debate, constitute the cast of the evaluation stage. Since signaling may be said to begin with the announcement made by organizers of the event, the establishment—the host-leader's initiative—is at the center of this phase. Reporting and interpreting the announcement, the media provoke, frame, and display domestic and international reactions to the initiative. But obviously, at this stage as well, the public's processing of the announcement makes the subsequent stages possible. The announcement challenges the symbolic process into action, triggering what Sperber (1975) calls evocation.

Modeling, like signaling, addresses the paradox of the event: How can the lamb live alongside the lion? But this paradox is submitted to a major transformation. By being presented live on screen, the paradoxical information is reframed as a declarative rather than an interrogative. Look! The lion and the lamb *are* living side by side, thus moving us from the improbable to the documented. Acting as a shaman, television is inviting us to consider in vitro what the next stage will invite us to enact in vivo. Clearly, television is the principal protagonist in the modeling stage. Its very presence results in "deepening the play."

The guest or opposition leader is the central figure of the rhetorical framing phase. Taking his turn as shaman, he offers the words that direct us to achieve the full-scale version of the model. He explores collective memory and draws attention to the root paradigms that are meant to point the way. The guest-leader must be aware of the paradoxical problems encountered by the public in view of the new proposal. Publicly and explicitly, he guides his followers while also retracing the steps of the cognitive process which the audience has undergone. In so doing, he is not only a shaman but a bard.

7

Reviewing Media Events

From the argument of the previous chapters—that the experience of media events is different from the experience of everyday television—it follows that the concepts and methods that have been applied to the study of everyday media effects may be insufficient to the task of assessing the effects of media events. In an effort to find these effects a theoretical home, this chapter attempts to recall and generalize the main effects of media events, gathering them together from all over the book. That traditional effects research will be found wanting is already evident. The reader will have noted how frequently we invoke the anthropology of ceremony to augment propositions derived from functional, critical, and technological theorists. The Appendix elaborates on this orchestration in an attempt to "fit" our findings to the predominant conceptualizations of communications research.

First of all, then, we wish to recapitulate some of the propositions about the effects of the live broadcasting of public ceremonies that are sprinkled throughout the preceding pages. The reader will find them familiar because they tend to appear in more than one place, in the several contexts in which they were found relevant. It is important, however, to beware confusing familiarity with proof. As we have said, only very few events have been studied empirically from the point of view of their effects. Although we draw as much as possible on events which have been studied—by ourselves and others—it is best to think of our catalogue of effects as contributions to a set of interlocking hypotheses.

The review is organized in terms of two dimensions. A first distinction is between effects that take place "inside" the event and those that take place "outside." This distinction may sound paradoxical inasmuch as the mutual influence of organizers, broadcasters, and audiences—the inside effects—are incorporated into the very definition of events. But these are among the most interesting of effects. From the moment the lights are lit—indeed, even as the lights are lit in the minds of the three partners in anticipation of the event—effects begin to take place. The anticipated size of an expectant audience, for example, may affect the work and rhetoric of organizers and broadcasters.

Inside effects take place "during" the event, of course, while outside effects usually occur "after" the event—but may, in fact, take place "before" or "during" as well. Thus, during an event, the pressure for the event to succeed is classified as an inside effect, whereas the cessation of hostilities following a summit meeting is surely an outside effect. Think of a wedding: the guests who cry at the sight of the bride are emotionally affected within the ceremony; but whether the ceremony strengthens or weakens interethnic relations in the community or attitudes toward the institution of marriage is an aftereffect of the ceremony.

A second dimension concerns the object of effect. We wish to distinguish between effects on the participants themselves—organizers, principals, broadcasting organizations, journalists, spectators—and effects on institutions, such as those of politics, religion, leisure, and collective memory. The institutional effects are as likely to result from the expectations engendered by a succession of events—that is, from the existence of the genre—as from individual events. Thus, while an occasional event may affect the political system, for example, it is not specific instances of such events which are of institutional interest but rather the genre of live political broadcasts of press conference, party conventions, presidential debates, election night returns, and the like.

In the review that follows, the discussion is divided roughly between "inside effects" (that take place "during," affect participants, and result from the specifics of a particular ceremony) and "outside effects" (that take place "after," affect institutions, and result from the existence of the genre rather than from a specific instance of the genre).[1]

Inside Effects on Participants

We begin with the moment at which the decision is made to give "media-events treatment" to a particular ceremony. To examine such effects, we must dissolve the partnership of organizers, broadcasters, and viewers in order to examine the effects of an event, separately, on each.

Effects on Organizers and Principals

1. *The public commitment to mount an event makes the organizers politically vulnerable even before the event takes place.* In the days or weeks preceding an event, policy changes are demanded, in keeping with the openness of the occasion and/or its consensual claims. On the international scene, for example, participants in summit meetings have to make themselves available to one another and to the press—for more questions than they care to answer. Similarly, the countries hosting Olympic Games have repeatedly been pressured by other nations to live up to the spirit of the event or be boycotted and denounced, as were the Nazis in the case of a black athlete, Jesse Owens, in

the Berlin Olympics of 1936. More recently, the Carter administration tried unsuccessfully to pressure the Soviets to relent in Afghanistan, under threat of a boycott of the Moscow Olympics of 1980. Protests against British refusal to denounce South African apartheid prompted twenty-seven of the forty-nine nations to withdraw from the Commonwealth Games of 1986, to the considerable displeasure of the British organizers and their political leaders, including the queen.[2]

2. *During an event, principals are cast in mythic roles,* often by the media. Thus, John Kennedy at his funeral is cast as Lincoln, and Lady Di as Cinderella. The principals may also use the spotlight to recast themselves: Sadat and the Pope both enveloped themselves in primordial roles: the one offered himself as a sacrifice in Jerusalem, and the other visited lepers and delivered sermons from hilltop favelas in Brazil.[3]

3. *The live broadcasting of an event creates pressure on the event to succeed.* Broadcasters can bring pressure on the principals by brandishing the evidence of public response, which they command. Depicting Sadat's journey as a sacrifice, for example, evoked the norm of reciprocity—the idea that he was owed something in return—which was fed back to the principals as "public opinion" and used to pressure the Israeli organizers. There is, apparently, a strong fear of failing with the whole world watching. Thus the Reagan-Gorbachev summit in Geneva may well have been embarrassed into "succeeding" by television and public opinion.[4] The criteria for success are formulated by negotiations between principals and broadcasters, and audiences watch for the signs.[5] The pressure is not only moral but aesthetic. The event must succeed, but it must succeed within a foreseeable time, that is, in full sight of the cameras. The emotion generated by the event can only be sustained if the ceremonial progress culminates in a cathartic conclusion.

The pressure to succeed while on stage and within ceremonial time leads to an imperative which we perceive as showmanship, but which, in Sadat's declaration, acquired the mythical status of a natural law: the success of media events depends on their sustained momentum. The primary effect of momentum is to propel the events beyond their projected boundaries.

4. *Live broadcasting enhances the status of the principals, conferring both legitimacy and charisma during the event and after.* The fact of addressing a world constituency places a new set of aims and responsibilities on the leader's shoulders. Once validated by public response, what might have been a shrewdly projected image may envelop the actor himself. Media events make "celebrities" of the supporting cast as well, whether they are astronauts, journalists, assassins such as Jack Ruby, or philanthropist-entrepreneurs such as Bob Geldof of Live Aid.

5. *Media events liberate leaders to act more or differently than they otherwise might.* Live broadcasting unties the hands of the principals. Capitalizing on their charisma, they feel free to make larger gestures than usual. Reagan felt free to change his rhetoric about the Soviet adversary after the Geneva summit; John Paul II ignored safeguards and cautions while on stage; Sadat and Begin exceeded what their advisors and political parties might otherwise have permitted them; the congressmen of the Watergate hearings abandoned partisanship and assumed a statesmanlike stance. The conferral of charisma may lead the political actor to the experience of a new self, as in a process of conversion.

Effect on Journalists and Broadcasting Organizations

1. *Media events redefine the rules of journalism.* Journalists become priests, as we have shown, and full members of the

wedding, equals of the principal actors. (Indeed, journalists come to be praised for their statesmanship and politicians for their communications skills.) Yet journalists and broadcasters tend to be neutralized by their ceremonial role, trapped in the rhetoric of reverential lubrication. They are then torn by role conflict (Levy, 1981). Some journalists avoid this conflict by refusing to participate; others who overspecialize in the reporting of such events sometimes turn into establishment panegyrists.[6]

2. Nevertheless, *broadcasters are rewarded with status and legitimacy for abandoning their "adversarial" stance in favor of an integrative role*. The suspending of commercial advertising, together with the reverence with which the event is presented, gives broadcasters and broadcasting organizations the opportunity of repledging their allegiance to the central values of the commonwealth. Media events are thus occasions for media organizations to demonstrate that their role is not exclusively adversarial but can be consensual as well; that they are capable of alliance with authorities; that they can espouse the variations in public mood and stand as a vox populi. Whenever the event is accepted as both consequential and consensual, broadcasters are seen to rise above partisanship, thus to gain in credibility and respectability.

3. *Broadcasters also gain status as "donors" of an event*. Recall those paintings of the late Middle Ages or early Renaissance in which powerful noblemen or rich merchants are depicted on their knees, hands joined in prayer, bowing to a nativity scene, attending the Holy Infant's circumcision, or his presentation to the synagogue. Portrayed in devotion, these worldly patrons of the arts are incorporated into the sanctity of the represented occasion. Similarly, the recurring "logos" of the broadcasting organizations and the omnipresence of their representatives in

the midst of the principals remind us of the effort and sacrifice invested by the networks as participants in, and patrons of, the sacred.

4. *Media events provide media organizations with an opportunity to test new formats and to embark on technical experimentation.* Media events also provide a showcase for broadcasters to display the talents of their journalists and producers, thus inviting advertisers and viewers to support their regular programs when normalcy resumes. Indeed, media events play an important role in the spread of the electronic media. The first ceremonial transmission of any magnitude took place from the Berlin Olympic Games of 1936, and we know the role played by the coronation of Queen Elizabeth II in the grand reopening of television in the 1950s after the war. The Olympics gave a big push to the introduction of television in the Third World. Altogether, the diffusion of television in particular countries is intimately associated with major political events and international sports.

5. For media organizations, *the challenge of the event reactivates the often forgotten enthusiasm of the beginnings of television.* Mobilizing for the coverage of a historic event, media organizations undergo the born-again experience that Alberoni (1983) calls *statu nascendi.* For old-timers the event provides a new "honeymoon," a sense of challenge, excitement, and risk. They repeatedly invoke the term "miracle" to describe their accomplishment. For newcomers used to an already institutionalized television, the event provides a demanding *rite de passage* and a taste of the old days when TV was all live. Even within long-established broadcasting organizations, unusual cooperation among the units is required, straining the ability to deploy personnel, equipment, advice, encouragement, and practical recipes on a very large scale. Such events also require pooling and other forms of cooperation among normally competing net-

works. Reinstated is the sense of professional achievement in the service of the national or international community.[7]

Effects on Viewers

1. *Media events interrupt the rhythm and focus of people's lives.* The momentous occasion commands attention to the exclusion of all else. The interruption is defined not just as "time out" but as "sacred time."

2. *The live broadcast transforms the ordinary roles of viewers, causing them to assume the roles proposed by the script* of the ceremony. Even if the set is turned on initially by escapists or entertainment seekers, media events invite more active participation. They call for mourners, pilgrims, philanthropists, and the like. Viewers thereby join principals and journalists in being "constructed" by the script of the event. Some terminally ill people manage to postpone their deaths for the sake of a media event as if it were a celebration of a more personal kind (Phillips, 1983). In a stunning reversal of the notion of "social death," they feed on collective life; their role keeps them alive.

3. *Media events give new status to the living room.* By declaring an event sacred, and appointing the television set as its medium, the homely setting takes on a new luster. Television is revived as the family focus, commanding attention and interest and bringing family members and friends together again.

4. Such festive viewing leads to that alternative model of social life in which the usual down-to-earth, "indicative" approach to social reality gives way to a *"subjunctive" and utopian openness to alternative possibilities.* In the cognitive domain, the interruption of social time calls for a frame awareness, a reflexive evaluation of what is serious and what is not. Or does it give access to a higher reality? The public may reject the event's claims by eventually ignoring it, or by amusing

themselves at its pretentious expense. Yet its interruptiveness may create a heightened attention to the situation it interrupts, exposing the norms of daily life as superficial, arbitrary, or unfounded. Audiences are aware of the constructed character of the event, but the construction may reveal that their own reality is also relative, a construction in its own right.

5. *The event creates an upsurge of fellow feeling*, an epidemic of communitas. Family ties and friendships are reactivated. People telephone and visit each other to comment on the event; they make plans to view together. As in religious celebrations (or quasi-religious celebrations such as Thanksgiving), parties are organized, reuniting families, friends, and neighbors. The event serves as a pretext for putting an end to long-standing rivalries and feuds. Often, and despite the usual presence of crowds on the site of the event, there is a decrease in criminality. Customary forms of entertainment are neglected or shunned.

6. Thus, the *event connects center and periphery*, not only through the experience of communitas, but through direct communion with central symbols and values, through the assumption of ritual roles in a ceremony conducted by establishment leaders, and through the presence of small groups of known and valued others. Linked by networks of long-reaching affinity, the mass audiences of television events partially overcome their dispersion and atomization.

7. *Media events offer moments of "mechanical solidarity."* A consequence of the new model of public ceremony is that the whole of a population is allowed—and expected—to attend. As opposed to many tribal ceremonies, or to royal progresses, or even to the relatively recent example of Lincoln's funeral in nineteenth-century America, the event can neither be declared off limits to any willing participants nor made up of different presentations to different segments of the public.[8] The event

offers, and affirms, shared membership in a national or international community.

The ceremoniality of media events embraces entire societies, and sometimes the globe. All those within reach of a television set are simultaneously and equally exposed, and they share the knowledge that everybody else is too. Technology here allows the spirit of communitas to overcome the divisions inherent in "organic solidarity." Durkheimians would agree that the one is prerequisite to the other.

8. *Media events have the power to redefine the boundaries of societies.* They can determine with which others we will share an experience. One of the strongest effects of media events is immanent to their performance: it consists in the mapping of new constituencies (by linking the TV networks of Israel and Egypt for Sadat's visit, for example) or in the reactivating of obsolete constituencies (as when the broadcast of the royal wedding momentarily revived the British Empire, just as the Pope's televised visit revived dreams of a European Poland. Indeed, the social formations integrated by media events often are their own creations. Such ceremonies are fragments of the civil religion of polities that may exist only for the duration of the broadcast. More than retrospective celebrations of the symbols that are central to the identity of an extant society, some events are bets on the advent of some future society.[9]

9. *The success of an event is a cathartic experience for viewers.* Media events respond to needs that are fulfilled by the viewers' consciousness of the sheer size of the audience and by the "oceanic" feeling of being immersed in it. These needs are also fulfilled by the ceremonial progression of a scenario which takes viewers through the many steps that lead from a crisis, actual or abreacted, to a proposed solution—or as Lévi-Strauss would put it, the "aesthetic resolution" of myth. Documented by a whole

array of studies, the cathartic effectiveness of John Kennedy's funeral owed much to its symbolism, staging, and timing. The funeral was able to provide an aesthetic sense of completion, offering a response to many days of turmoil.

10. The attitudes engendered in secondary audiences reach beyond the cognitive, sometimes triggering sympathetic interest in the ways in which other people rejoice, mourn, play, or pray. *The empathic experiences which media events engender—sharing another nation's inner feelings*, as in the Kennedy funeral or the royal wedding—may be counted strong effects. Until now, only direct personal contact of the sort that characterizes war, colonialism, and tourism induced this kind of intimacy.

Outside Effects on Institutions

To assess the impact of the genre, we ask how the punctuation of our lives by an irregular set of momentous ceremonies, broadcast live and in real time, might affect not the immediate context in which each event takes place but societal institutions more generally. For example, it is said of the novel that it changed the composition of the reading public, created new forms of book distribution, portrayed a certain picture of the social classes, gave voice to suppressed emotions, and contributed to the emergence of individualism and the liberation of women. This is different, of course, from saying that Harriet Beecher Stowe's novel was a contributing cause of the Civil War and the liberation of black slaves in the American South. Both of these are outside effects—one generic, the other specific.

We shall proceed telegraphically, as before, to outline a variety of effects of the media-events genre as documented in earlier parts of this book. Widening the spectrum, we examine generic as well as specific effects on public opinion and on the institutional realms of politics, diplomacy, family, leisure, religion, collective memory. We conclude at our own doorstep, so to speak, with a consideration of how the genre has affected the aesthetics of public ceremonies.

Effects on Public Opinion

1. In the eye of public opinion, *media events confer status on the institutions with which they deal.* Thus sports and athletes are reinforced by the Olympic Games; the royal wedding gave a new luster to monarchy; the Watergate hearings gave new prominence to the legislative branch of government. NASA and the advocates of technological innovations were strengthened by the success of the Apollo program and severely weakened by the live coverage of the Challenger accident.[10] Functioning as an official "calling card," the event led to reconsidered attitudes. The Apollo moon landings were accepted by world opinion as renewed proof of American technological superiority.

2. *Media events focus public opinion* and activate debate on a given issue or set of issues, although not all sides benefit from equal attention. Media events seek to enroll support but they also attract opposition. Their agenda-setting power acts like a magnet, gathering protests and demonstrations. The attention lavished on them makes them ideal targets for terrorists.

3. Thus, *media events may affect public opinion by encouraging or inhibiting the expression of preferences, values, or beliefs.* On the one hand, media events tend to inhibit manifestations perceived as hostile to the values conveyed by the event. Typically, potential dissenters are ostracized. Sometimes, however, an event may also unwind the "spiral of silence," freeing the expression of previously unpopular attitudes on given issues. The papal visits to Latin America, for example, stimulated a flurry of proclamations by theologians of liberation.

4. *Media events may result in attitude changes of major mag-*

nitude, as evidenced in Sadat's reversal of the Israeli appraisal of Egypt's warlike intentions. Less dramatic but no less pervasive was the influence of the Watergate hearings on American opinion toward Richard Nixon. The impact was such that it legitimized the use of judicial procedure against a recently reelected president and made impeachment conceivable.

5. *Certain events crystallize latent trends in public opinion, giving voice to formerly inarticulate or dormant proposals.* Thus, Sadat's visit to Jerusalem reactivated a long-silenced Israeli wish for peaceful integration in the Middle East and almost succeeded in achieving it; John Paul II's trip to Poland reaffirmed the centrality of a Catholicism which had been speaking in whispers. Similarly, the funeral of Enrico Berlinguer confirmed the degree of recognition and widespread legitimacy attained by the Italian Communist party within the national consensus, while the Watergate hearings revealed a convergence between radical movements on the one hand and the silent majority on the other. Media events thus legitimize groups whose goals are aligned with the occasion, even though in the case of "transformative" events these groups may previously have been little known or heard.

6. Besides coalescing subterranean trends and allowing the emergence of latent consensus, *media events may sometimes serve as catalysts to unexpected social movements.* Something like this took place in Eastern Europe, when television confirmed the legitimacy of opposition in Czechoslovakia and Romania. And it took place in the family reunion event in South Korea: starting as a broadcast commemoration of the war between the Koreas, the event was rapidly taken over by its audience, who rescripted it into a huge campaign aimed at reuniting families whose members had been dispersed by the war. Through a spontaneous collective agreement, the commemoration of wounds was turned into a healing ritual.[11]

7. *Media events affect the international image of the society in which they take place.* Such events increasingly seek an international audience, and are designed to be seen beyond the national boundaries as well. For a given society, an event of this type is a "cultural performance," in Milton Singer's sense, offering the opportunity of a solemn "presentation of self" to other societies. Major media events thus picture societies at those moments when their actual practice and explicit ideals coincide.

Effects on Political Institutions

1. *Media events socialize citizens to the political structure of society.* Olympic Games, Miss America contests, political conventions, and the urban marathon races[12] say something about the structure of the societies that engendered them, no less than Memorial Day in Yankee City displayed the town's class and fraternal composition, the reviewing stand in Moscow on May Day displayed the hierarchy of Soviet power, and the *palio* displays the boroughs of medieval Siena. As "cultural performances," these happenings may symbolically omit social elements that stand outside the consensus, as Lukes (1975) has noted. But they are nonetheless instructive of the order of society—including omissions—and sometimes they give genuine insight into the workings of the system, as did the Watergate hearings, the Iran-contra hearings, election night vigils, or the Indira Gandhi funeral.[13] The live broadcasts of political debate in Prague, in the very midst of revolution, foretold the change that was in fact already in progress.

2. *Media events reinforce the status of leaders.* Presidents and prime ministers are to be seen and heard not only in political conventions or summit meetings, but at Olympic Games, during moon landings, and so on. The result, on the whole, is to

enhance the personalization of politics and to associate leadership with consensual causes.[14] Sometimes, as in 1989 Czechoslovakia and Romania, new leaders are put on display.

3. *Media events displace intermediaries.*[15] The cumulative effect of such events is to downplay the roles of intermediaries and subordinates—even those instrumental in organizing the event—but especially to weaken parliaments. Charles de Gaulle, with his flare for events and his fondness for referendum-style consultations, often stretched French democracy into a dialogue between himself and a public whom he addressed directly, and from whom he expected equally unmediated response. Institutionalized representation is short-circuited thereby, leading to a potentially dangerous concentration of power and to an inflated image of unanimous followership. Indeed, the dangers of the "imperial presidency" are what the Watergate hearings were about. In that case at least, Congress used the genre itself to stage its own event in reassertion of its mediating role.

4. *Direct access to top leaders tends to reduce the operation of selectivity in exposure to political communications.* Before the era of live political broadcasting, citizens exposed themselves much more selectively to their "own" side. We have said that media events promote consensual politics, but when the event is a contest—such as a presidential debate or a political party convention—the citizen is likely to give equal attention to both contestants, as an ideal democratic polity would hope. Some scholars believe, however, that such balanced presentation— indeed, the political balance of television news altogether— works to turn citizens into apolitical spectators.[16]

5. *The organizational forms of politics are affected by media events.* Political campaigning, of course, has moved into the television studio, but little of it takes the form of live events— with the major exception of presidential debates and political

conventions. The live reporting of a political convention abolishes the architecture of the convention hall; it gives at least as much attention, perhaps more, to what is happening in the wings and on the floor as to what is happening on the rostrum. Television journalists also anticipate dramatic disclosures and act as provocateurs. The highlight of the Republican convention of 1980 was a live bargaining session between candidate Ronald Reagan and former president Gerald Ford, who was given the opportunity of publicly deliberating—before the television audience, not the plenum of the convention—the conditions under which he would agree to accept a copresidency arrangement. The 1988 campaign featured a spontaneous debate between newscaster Dan Rather and the Republican candidate for the vice presidency. Similar bargaining sometimes characterizes the live broadcasts of election returns. Responding to televised projections of the vote long before they are officially validated, party representatives in Israel, for example, have sometimes entered into "as if" coalitions before the mass election-night audience (Levin, 1982).[17]

6. *Some media events lead directly to social and political change.* Ultimately, one can credit the Camp David peace talks (although they almost failed) and the reinvigoration of the peace movement to the impact of Sadat's visit to Jerusalem; one can trace the rise of the Polish worker's movement Solidarity to the Pope's visit. The demand for the liberalization of Korea, and for progress toward its reunification, may be connected to the family reunion marathon.[18] Television contributed to the velvetization of the Czech revolution.

7. *Media events breed the expectation of openness* in politics and diplomacy. Even if their continuation was delayed for sixteen years, the first television debates which opposed Kennedy to Nixon in 1960 put steady pressure on the political system to arrange for similar confrontations between the major candi-

dates. Moreover, the institution of live televised debates has been exported to other countries—even reluctantly democratic ones—as if the confrontation between candidates in an election campaign were an intrinsic part of the television itself. The most "open" events in our corpus are the live broadcasts from the Eastern European revolutions of 1989.

8. *The live broadcasting of media events can integrate nations.* As media entertainment becomes increasingly segmented—as cable, satellite, and computer technologies multiply the number of channels and diversify choice—the integrative role of the electronic media will tend to wane. The desire to give expression to national belongingness, however, and a desire for some shared experience of the "center" will be felt at various levels of the polity. Radio played this role until it was superseded by television. As television goes the way of radio, media events will, from time to time, sound a call for undivided attention.

Effects on Diplomacy

1. *Media events abet summitry* and, like national and local politics, diplomacy is thereby infected by the personalization of power. Media events—as Abba Eban says—short-circuit existing diplomatic channels. Ambassadors are made redundant, their role trivialized. Nowadays they may often be reduced to warning visiting statesmen against breaches of local etiquette and cultural faux pas.

2. *The pressure of media events on diplomacy is to go public.* However public, the misapplied "parliamentarianism" of international assemblies prevents the exercise of diplomacy by replacing dialogue or negotiation with harangues aimed at constituents back home and assured majorities. But what takes place in media events seems a far cry from international exercises in

name-calling. Public exhortations pressure negotiators into not slamming doors. Losing face consists in failing to emerge with a positive statement. The drama of diplomatic media events is one of overcoming differences. When all else has failed, media events may succeed in breaking diplomatic deadlocks or in surmounting stalemates by creating a climate conducive to negotiation, one in which the public signals its anticipation of reconciliation.

3. *Media events create a new resource for diplomacy.* The diplomacy of gesture may have the power to create a favorable climate for a contract or to seal a bargain. Gestures cannot replace negotiation; indeed, they themselves are often the result of arduous negotiation. An "open" negotiator is confronted with the impossible task of addressing his own constituency back home, his partner's constituency, and, last but not least, world public opinion—all at the same time. And yet it can be done; the fact is that media events manage to deliver different messages simultaneously. Their power in difficult or blocked situations derives from what diplomats call constructive ambiguity; that is, from the paradoxical framing of elusive content in strong declarations of intent.

Effects on the Family

1. For a moment, therefore, *media events reverse the trend toward the individualization and segmentation of family viewing patterns.* The event takes on the character of a family holiday. Family members experience the event together, thus strengthening group memory and generational ties. If everyday television viewing is becoming increasingly lonely—what with the multiplication of sets, the dwindling number of household members, and the differences in working schedules—media events reunite families and friends as in the days of yore. People

invite others—families, friends, and neighbors—to share the experience. People do not wish to view these events by themselves.

2. When friends and neighbors come together to view a media event, the involvement and *interaction with the set and with other viewers transform the home into a "public space."* A public space is where unfettered conversation generates rational public opinion. While the home hardly qualifies for Jürgen Habermas' ideal communication situation, the fact is that we have little access nowadays to political salons or cafés. Television proposes a substitute "forum." The vast network of similar and simultaneous miniforums in the millions of households attending an event calls attention to the communicative potential of home and family.

Effects on Leisure

1. *Media events affect the structure of leisure activities.* Sports is the best example. The high holidays of football, soccer, and baseball—the Super Bowl, the World Cup,[19] the World Series, and so forth—are among the mainstays of media use. Living-room celebrations of these games, and of the Olympics, involve rituals of conviviality, knowledgeable exchange, and a level of attention and sociability far exceeding that of everyday television. This sociability can reach disastrous heights, as in the parody of communitas which has marred recent European soccer matches and in the explosions of enthusiasm which may now be seen in the streets of cities whose teams have just won a televised game; television spectators pour out of their homes and jam the streets in frenzied cavorting and motor carnivals.

2. *Certain sports events create new forms of sociability.* Although television privileges team sports that have constituencies such as cities or nations, certain solitary sports have also

been converted into media events. The most surprising example, that of municipal marathons, is based on the loneliest of experiences—the earnest, ear-plugged practice of jogging. In marathons, runners jog with (not away from) their fellow citizens. The spectators are not knowledgeable fans, and the participants are not champions, except for the international stars of the "contest" which is superimposed on the folk festival. They all participate in the experience that transforms a dangerous city—Los Angeles, New York, or Paris—into an amiable stadium. They also participate in the interactive experience that permits ordinary spectators to step collectively into a media event, to bask in its aura. Home viewers of these events rediscover their cities.

Effects on Religion

1. *Media events mark holidays of the civil religion* on the secular calendar, and perform some of the same functions as religious holidays.[20] Indeed, religion is often involved in these civic ceremonies. This is obvious in the case of weddings and funerals and the Pope's pilgrimages, and less obvious but no less true in the case of Sadat, the moon landings, coronations, inaugurations, and other events. The church lends aura to the state, and is given a part to play in the great events.

2. *Media events blur the boundary between the sacred and the profane.* In spite of their religious character, the trips of the Pope cannot be defined as strictly Catholic events. Loaded with diplomatic implications, they reach diverse audiences where Catholics are often no more than a significant minority. They take place in profane surroundings, in sites which—though consecrated—tend to maintain meanings of their own. The performance may thereby lose its sacred character, and the event may be marred by embarrassing clashes of symbols.[21]

There is the opposite problem as well: the profane may be sacralized by religious events. From television coverage of the Pope's itinerary, viewers begin to equate its festival and spectacle with the moments of traditional ritual. As a result, the Pope's celebration of mass for the television audience "lacks the impact it had on those who waited hours for his arrival" at the cathedral, stadium, or open-air liturgical space (Reynolds, 1985). The televised mass seems to blend into the whole of the event—motorcades and all—which becomes a new liturgy in itself.

3. *Media events blur the limits between religions*, promoting an ecumenism of their own. Even if one does not take account of events staged for specifically ecumenical purposes, the thrust of religious media events is to stress shared features, to disregard irreducible differences between religions. Media events tend to recast specific religions as "religion" in general, to invite their blending into one another.

True, their distinctiveness may also be highlighted. Media events dispense fragments of religious knowledge both directly (the Bible quiz in Israel) and indirectly (every trip of the Pope involves a pilgrimage to a saintly figure). We also acquire a familiarity with competing liturgical styles, from Anglican sacraments (royal family events) to Moslem worship (Sadat praying at the dome of the Rock). But the message conveyed by the genre of media events, underneath hagiographic exercises and scriptural variation, stresses the interchangeability of liturgies. With the help of television commentary, media events allow moments of sympathetic identification, of real intimacy, with the symbols of another creed.

4. *Media events sharpen religious hierarchies and personalize power*. The history of religion is replete with examples of vaulting over established authority in order to institute or restore "true" religion. Protestantism used print to neutralize the intermediacy of the priest, and broadcast evangelists use television to

talk over the heads of the local church, and in doing so, aggran-
dize themselves. Tightly controlling his image—there is a Vat-
ican-based agency in charge of papal trips—the Pope also uses
television to vault over would-be mediators between himself and
his flock. No longer a mysterious presence in the recesses of the
Vatican, this Pope uses his televised trips to turn virtual power
into effective authority. By talking over the heads of bishops and
local dignitaries, he robs them of their splendor.

5. At the same time, *media events may publicize tension and
struggles within the church.* By reaching unusually large audiences, media events naturally magnify internal differences—
personal and doctrinal—for all to see.

Effects on Public Ceremony

1. At a very elementary level, the *genre of media events may
be said to cause the reorganization of the great civic ceremonies.*
The demands of live broadcasting that an event be framed in
time, and that its parts cohere, constrain organizers to give new
thought to the production of public events. Thus, the expectation that an occasion may be accorded media-events treatment
means that an event must be telescoped in time, introducing a
story line to guide the narrative. Lincoln's funeral procession
lasted twenty-one days, moving by railroad, heralded by newspaper and telegraph, greeted by mourning multitudes in city
after city. Television and its audience mourned Kennedy for
four days, of which only a few hours were devoted to the ceremony itself. The royal wedding of television is a model of pre-
cision and storytelling compared with the wedding, say, of
Queen Victoria. Hobsbawm and Ranger (1973) credit radio and
television with having engendered the British flare for ceremoniality that is mistakenly attributed to long-ingrained tradition.

2. *Media events push ceremonial forms in the direction of fic-*

tion spectacles. Proposing a civic event to a diversified public that is in attendance from beginning to end leads to a new discursive approach. The event is no longer a string of ritual interactions with different subgroups of the population; it is now a unified spectacle. It acquires a story line, a dramatic progression, that raises questions about the effects of fiction forms on real performances. Transformed into a show, the ritual focuses not only on the performances of the ceremonial personae, but also on the tension between symbolic figures and the individuals who "impersonate" them. In a characteristic shift, the new congregants switch to an attitude familiar to moviegoers. They identify with the performer's plight.

3. *Media events institutionalize a cinematographic model of "publicness."* Public events may be said to have moved from a theatrical model—where performance and reaction are joined in the same space—to a cinematographic model which dissociates performers not only from their public but sometimes from each other as well. Of course, television has transformed the model inherited from cinema. With electronic communication, the reconstituted performance can be simultaneous, within a temporal frame shared by all protagonists and by the audience. These are "live" broadcasts, which means that simulation of a performance has reached a state of near-perfection: it has become temporally indistinguishable from the performance itself. This live dimension of the broadcast ostensibly returns us to theater and church. But shared time conceals another dimension of the cinematographic model: that public reaction is no longer a reaction to the original performance, but to its simultaneous substitute.

4. *The event as represented is the one that is experienced and remembered.* The status of the original—and indeed the invidious distinction between original and copy—is further demoted. The reproduction is now *more* important than the original, and

sometimes there is no original at all. Even when an original exists—as in most media events so far—it is offered to the broadcasters with full knowledge that the reproduction will have the greater social weight. Both broadcasters and organizers are careful, of course; that is what the "negotiations" (Chapter 3) are about, and an overall "loyalty" to the event (Chapter 4) is the result. Nevertheless, the copy is different from the original and generally even the organizers want it so. Media events are not televised events. They are television events. "Being there," attending on the spot, in person, is still an enjoyable experience. However enjoyable, it is no longer the sole route to ceremonial participation. The reality of the event—that which will be retold—is not what happened "there."

5. *Media events have shifted the locus of ceremoniality* from the piazza and the stadium to the living room. Instead of the expressive crowd, society is mobilized in small groups to participate in an event through attention and discussion—but also affective expression—aware that everybody else is doing likewise.

Effects on Collective Memory

1. *Media events are electronic monuments.* They are meant to live in collective memory through association with either the traumas to which they are responses or the exceptional nature of the gratifications they provide. The memory of President Kennedy will forever evoke the image of the funeral as seen on television. One of the most important effects of "response ceremonies" is that they become so firmly sutured to the situations in which they arise that they ultimately come to represent them, retrospectively mediating or even displacing our experience of them.

2. *Media events endow collective memory not only with a sub-*

stance but with a frame: they are mnemonics for organizing personal and historical time. To members of the same generation, media events provide shared reference points, the sense of a common past, bridges between personal and collective history. People who watched the moon landing can still tell you where they were and what they were doing when the broadcast took place. Olympics viewers associate events in their lives with different Olympic Games. [22]

3. *Media events are interruptions marking breaks in time, sometimes signaling the beginnings and ends of an "era."* Like wars, they disrupt existing calendars. Thus, presidential inaugurations may or may not succeed as media events, depending on the transitions they mark; the end of the Carter presidency and the beginning of Reagan's *was* a media event. [23] Media events may be counted as "catastrophic time"—a decisive and meaningful intervention in history—rather than as the regularized progression from minor crisis to minor crisis which Braudy (1982) calls "soap opera time." The "end of an era" was the immediate meaning assigned to the intervention of state-run television on the side of the revolutionaries in Czechoslovakia and Romania. The disruptive nature of such events, it should be noted, enhances their mnemonic function.

4. *Media events edit and reedit collective memory.* Often serving the same functions as religious holidays, they "quote" from earlier events. Thus Nixon's resignation echoed other tragic partings, such as Kennedy's (Lang and Lang, 1983). By the same token, Kennedy's funeral recalled Lincoln's, but not Garfield's or McKinley's—who had also died at the hands of assassins. Media events also refer and give meaning to current events; the moon landing of Christmas 1968 was experienced as solace for the traumas (Vietnam, the assassinations, the riots) of the year then ending. Each serves as a discursive center which gives perspective to ongoing history.

5. *Thus media events and their narration are in competition with the writing of history* in defining the contents of collective memory. Their disruptive and heroic character is indeed what is remembered, upstaging the efforts of historians and social scientists to perceive continuities and to reach beyond the personal. Moreover, ceremonial events are constantly quoted in edited or fictionalized form within television itself, finding their way into films, historical miniseries, or contemporary serials. One thinks of films such as *All the President's Men* (Watergate), *Chariots of Fire* (Olympics), *The Right Stuff* (moon landing). The coronation was quoted in the televised version of the "Forsyte Saga"; the royal wedding in "Coronation Street"; Kennedy's death and King's "I had a dream" speech in "Kennedy." A series was devoted to Sadat; one to Jesse Owens. This alliance of ritualization and fictionalization makes it even more evident that the professional recording of history is not synonymous with what is remembered.

A Thematic Overview of Effects

Five major themes underlie this list of propositions. These themes may be different facets of a single, overarching phenomenon.

First is the theme of *conferring status* on persons and issues. It has to do with the effectiveness of media events in agenda setting and calling attention to the values that they celebrate. We have seen the workings of this process in the context of politics, sports, religion, and other areas where the principals of media events are boosted to heroic status and the concerns they address made the center of public attention. We have seen how unheeded minorities or silent majorities may be catapulted into the "center." We have also seen nations become the object of international empathy for hosting media events, just as the institutions that organize them are given new prestige, credibility, and resources.

A second theme that underlies these propositions has to do with the *personalization of power*. The heroic status bestowed by media events gives leaders an increased freedom of decision and action, a sense of liberation from everyday dependence on their advisors, parties, bureaucracies—even from the policies— to which they are normally committed. Thus, media events sharpen hierarchies and represent moments of high concentration of power.

A countervailing third theme, however, mitigates the abuse of this power. It is the theme we have called the *expectation of openness*. Media events turn the lights on social structures that are not always visible, and dramatize processes that typically take place offstage. Recall the workings of these mechanisms in the live broadcasts of shuttle diplomacy, political summitry, legislative inquiry, and religious dissent. The expectation that is exported with the technology of television brings openness.

A fourth theme has to do with the influence of media events on the structure of social relations. With almost every event, we have seen *communitas and camaraderie* emerge from normally atomized—and sometimes deeply divided—societies. We have paid rather less attention, perhaps, to the further atomization of societies that might result from the charismatic concentration of power.

A final theme—the one that may encompass all the others— is the process whereby media events allow their principals to *talk over the heads of* the middlemen who normally mediate between leaders and their public. This may be a key to the entire phenomenon of mass-mediated communication, beginning with the Protestant Reformation when direct access to printed translations of the Bible allowed God's message to be read "over the heads of" the clergy who claimed to be its official custodian.

Media events offer powerful condensations of this process. [24] Thus, Sadat talks to the Israelis over the heads of their leaders; the Pope reaches over the heads of communist dignitaries and local prelates; national leaders, in summit meetings, gesture over the heads of their own diplomats and, in direct address to their people, appeal over the heads of legislators. In similar manner, the broadcasting of primaries and political conventions allows candidates to address the voters directly, winking over the heads of seated delegates and political parties, and television itself flies over the heads of historians in proposing its own version of what should be entered in collective memory.

Consider the model implicit in these exercises of short-circuiting. We call it *disintermediation*, borrowing a term from the world of finance. In schematic form (see Figure 1), it might be represented as a principal (A) talking to a public (C) over the head of traditional intermediaries (B) by means of a new medium (D). Recall Franklin Roosevelt (A), whose fireside chats spoke directly to the American people (C) over the heads of Congress (B) by means of the new medium of radio (D). Or

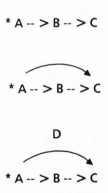

Figure 1   Schematic of disintermediation. A = principal, B = traditional intermediaries, C = public, D = new medium.

think of the evangelists (A) who employ television (D) to reach the faithful (C) over the heads of the parish priests (B). Or consider the manufacturers (A) who wished to neutralize the influence of the retailers (B) by creating brand loyalty in consumers (C) through the invention of national advertising (D). In each of these examples, the actor (A) is attempting to establish more exclusive control over a public (C), rather than share his power with intermediaries (B) who are both social institution (parliament, local church, retailer) and channel of communication—and, often, a source of protection to C against A.

This model can be used to illuminate all our other themes. Disintermediation affects leaders and organizers (A) by giving them enhanced status and increased freedom from the pressure of traditional intermediaries (B). It gives them direct (and potentially threatening) access to the public (C). The media (D) facilitate this access by undercutting the power of former intermediaries (B) and fostering a communal and egalitarian experience. However liberating this type of communitas may seem to be, disintermediation may be an ominous step toward enactment of the mass-society scenario, insofar as it may involve the weakening of representative and grass-roots institutions (B).

Thus, the model illustrates the tension between the traditional intermediaries (B) and the new media (D). In radical cases, D succeeds in eliminating B. In most cases, however, the process is more subtle and involves a redefinition of the role of B in view of the ascendance of D. As a result, historians are obliged to take account of the competing historiography of events as televised and often turn into its commentators or critics; diplomacy is forced to divert its efforts from privacy to publicity, from words to gestures, and from whispered duplicities to broadcast ambiguities; new liturgical formats are invented for the era of television, blurring the limits between the sacred and the profane.

More generally, the model suggests that the powers-to-be or the powers-that-want-to-be are continually striving to establish ever more direct contact with ever larger constituencies. From the introduction of print to the CNN satellite, the technologies of mass communication have been harnessed to achieve this goal. The contemporary political campaign, for example, uses television for this purpose, bypassing the party apparatus as a first step, and neutralizing the professional intermediacy of journalists as a second.

It would be wrong, however, to cast television so exclusively in the role of disintermediator. In democratic societies, as we have repeatedly said, it is also true that the media are not automatic allies of establishments, even if they have an ostensibly shared interest in the short-circuiting of traditional go-betweens. Media organizations and professionals benefit from exerting their independence vis-à-vis establishments, acting in the name of the presumed public demand for openness and the right to know. Even in nondemocratic systems it is important to remember that the media are not merely phatic channels; they are social institutions with values and interests of their own. Unlike the powers that try to control the media, media organizations wish not so much to disintermediate as to *reintermediate*.

These concepts serve us well because they illustrate—in the case of public ceremony—how the introduction of a new medium may transform not only a "message," not only the nature of response, but an entire structure of social relations. Indeed, the live broadcasting of media events has redefined the relative power of organizers, intermediaries, broadcasters, and viewers, and the very essence of a public event.

APPENDIX
NOTES
REFERENCES
INDEX

APPENDIX

Five Frames for Assessing the Effects of Media Events

One would expect the empirical generalizations reviewed in Chapter 7 to find their place in one or more of the traditions of research on media effects. The fact is, however, that the fit is not easy. In what follows, we try to show why—by examining the media-events propositions in the light of each of four current schools of media effects. To improve the fit, we call attention again to the value we have found in the work of cultural anthropologists, and the usefulness of comparing the "symbolic efficacy" of the shamanic ceremony and that of the media ceremony. Mass communication, like mass production, is thought to be a quintessentially modern institution, whereas anthropology usually deals with small systems of interacting individuals anchored in "tradition." The present proposal to reconcile the two recalls an earlier period in which media research stumbled on the relevance of interpersonal communication at a time when such informal interaction was considered anachronistic, and therefore irrelevant, a priori, to an understanding of media effects.

Keeping the list of propositions in mind, we first turn to conventional "persuasion research" to examine the extent to which theories in this realm offer a place to the hypothesized effects of media events. We then explore the traditions of "critical theory," "gratifications research," and "technological theory" from the same vantage point, concluding with a last glance at symbolic anthropology.

221

Persuasion research. What might be called persuasion research encompasses several different traditions of work (Katz, 1980a). Thus, campaign studies assess the success of purposive attempts by the media to influence "what we think"; agenda-setting studies postulate that the media tell us "what to think about"; diffusion studies trace the flow of an innovation through society as if to tell us "when to think." The common concern of these studies is with (1) change (2) in the cognitions (3) of individuals (4) in the short run, (5) resulting from media messages. On the whole, the history of this research tends to prove how difficult it is to achieve change in the opinions, attitudes, and behaviors of individuals (McGuire, 1986).

There are, of course, certain obvious points of contact between these traditions of work and the effects of media events. For one thing, we have noted striking examples of attitude change in response to media events; recall the change of Israeli attitudes toward Egypt following the live broadcast of Sadat's visit. What is particularly interesting is that this change, although not a lasting one, was of a magnitude rarely encountered in media studies.

The same thing is true for agenda-setting: "what to think about." Media events, we have noted, clear the air of competing issues. They demand rapt attention to the only legitimate event on society's agenda. They make the everyday pale or tarnish by contrast, in the way that the royal wedding blinded us to Brixton and Toxteth, Northern Ireland, the value of the pound sterling, and the controversies around Mrs. Thatcher. Thus, media events find a ready place in everyday effects research in the area of attitude and behavior change and agenda-setting.

The study of media events provides certain clues, therefore, to the conditions under which the media may be effective. The monopolistic character of media events is surely one such clue; indeed, it has long been hypothesized in effects research that monopoly enhances the likelihood of successful persuasion (Lazarsfeld and Merton, 1948). The attentiveness to media events is another clue; people are far more likely to get the message when they are prepared to receive it than when they assume their casual everyday viewing positions. Lazarsfeld's (1948) typology of persuasive effects, which includes not just "conversion" but "crystallization" and "activation," is of obvious relevance.

A related clue is that media events catapult the viewer out of his usual role as consumer and entertainment seeker. He is addressed in the role of citizen or sports fan, and given a message that befits his role. All of these—monopoly, attentiveness, identity—suggest why media events are more powerful sources of influence on attitudes and agenda than everyday television: festive television creates more receptive viewers.

But paradigms of cognitive change take us only a short distance toward finding a conceptual home for the effects of media events. Events influence feelings and the sense of belonging, not just cognitions; they affect institutions, not just individuals; they feed back on organizers and broadcasters and do not just proceed linearly to affect audiences; and they are no less—probably more—explicitly concerned with reinforcement and the stability of society than with change.

The critical paradigm. By taking short-run change as its centerpiece, persuasion research fails to treat reinforcement seriously, even if it is an everyday finding that prior opinions and attitudes are more likely to be strengthened than to be changed as a result of exposure to mass communications. Thus, prejudiced viewers do not see the prejudice in Archie Bunker, nor do they find it funny; rather, they find support for their prior opinions (Ball-Rokeach, 1985). Staunch Republicans had no doubt that Nixon outdebated Kennedy in 1960, even if less committed or undecided voters felt otherwise (Katz and Feldman, 1962).

Persuasion research has always regarded reinforcement as a residual matter, far less interesting than change. The "critical" theorists, on the other hand, early spoke of the role of the media in maintaining the status quo (Horkheimer and Adorno, 1972). It did not occur to them, or to the "persuasion" theorists, that the reinforcement of campaign research might be connected with the status quo of the critical paradigm. Yet the two themes are obviously connected, for reinforcement in the short run maintains the status quo in the long run.

Reproduction of the social system is the primary concern of the critical school. Early theorists implied that the media were agents of a social elite charged with promulgating a reassuring false consciousness. The illusion of a common culture, and thus common class membership, was achieved by the media mix of high culture with working-class culture, which Adorno and Horkheimer (1973) decry. More recent theories shift the emphasis away from a dominant elite guiding the cameras in favor of the more subtle process of hegemony, whereby the media act as keepers of the consensus, allowing debates within agreed limits, even co-opting deviance if necessary (Gouldner, 1976). Addressing the audience as consumers, as voters and pleasure seekers, rather than as workers and members of a class, is regarded as one of the most effective strategies for repressing the interests that inhere in capitalist society.

The notions of reinforcement and reproduction, obviously, are of great relevance for conceptualizing the effects of media events. While the most dramatic of our events deal with radical change, the theme of reinforcement of values and the sense of communitas permeate all of them. Indeed, most of the central events are salutes to the status quo, legitimations of elites, and reiterations of the national well-being. The messages of the royal wedding, for example, reinforce the traditional values of courtship, family, mobility, stratification, religion, monarchy, loyalty. The events we have dubbed Coronations all have this quality, but—as in the Kennedy and Mountbatten funerals— they also have a reflexive dimension, inviting us to consider where we have gone wrong, to reflect on needed changes and better ways. Similarly, Contests remind us of the rules, and even Conquests that propose change do so under the aegis of an existing elite. It is worth reiterating that situational change—as social psychologists know (Katz et al., 1957; Homans, 1961)—is always risky business for the stability of leaders.

The entire genre of media events deals with the relationships among elites, broadcasters, and audience. As we have tried to show throughout, this is not simply a linear relationship, but one which is circular and systemic, as much contractual as hegemonic. Nevertheless, the reverence with which media events are presented, the moments of equality and communitas which they propose, are undoubtedly reinforcing of the existing power structure, even if they open delicate, potentially subversive questions concerning alternative arrangements for the operation of power and the nature of stratification.

Everyday persuasion research can hardly help us with these, but the critical paradigm obviously can.

Summarizing the differences between the critical paradigm and persuasion research, one might say that the former conceptualizes media effects in terms of (1) reinforcement, or non-change, (2) of power arrangements, (3) in society (4) over the long run. Ostensibly this is the polar opposite of (1) change (2) in the cognitions (3) of individuals (4) in the short run. But the two traditions are not as far apart as they seem. Both originate in assumptions about the vulnerability of individuals in the mass society to the power of the media (even if persuasion research has moved away from some of these assumptions). Both see the media as operating on the cognitions of individuals through the display of choice—of ways of life, consumer goods, and presidential candidates. For critical theory, apart from the objection to grouping politics and marketing, this is the mere illusion of choice—no genuine difference is being offered—leading to false consciousness and the consequent reproduction of the status quo. For persuasion research, the choice—however circumscribed—makes for social participation in a system of evolutionary and consensual change. For both sets of theorists, the mass media serve as agents of remote social control guiding the scope of change.

In spite of these latent similarities, however, it is evident that critical research offers a much more comprehensive frame for encompassing the effects of media events. In this view, media events are establishment exercises in which the media are enlisted in sham ceremonies designed to mobilize affirmation (see Adorno and Horkheimer, 1973; Edelman, 1989) and reconfirmation. The illusion of equality engendered by such events is more of the same. In short, critical theory would propose an "oppositional reading" (Hall, 1977; Morley, 1980) of media events.

True, these are establishment-sponsored events, yet some of them propose change. The Pope's first visit to Poland is a reluctant co-optation by an establishment of a revolutionary gesture embraced by the populace. In fact, all of these events—even the most reverent of them—invoke subjunctive thoughts of alternative social order, and these are threatening, at least potentially, to leadership. Critical theory would have a hard time explaining the role of the media in the Eastern European revolutions of 1989, or in the overthrow of the shah in Iran, given his control over the media.

Critical theory underestimates the power of audiences. We have argued repeatedly that both audience and media have veto power and may cause an event to fail or to be misread. In a word, critical theory understates the extent to which media events are mutual accommodations. It invests the media with too much power to influence the masses and the elite with too much power to rule over the media.

Gratifications research. In sharp contrast, gratifications research accords power to the viewer, perhaps too much of it. Reacting against the image of the vulnerable viewer of persuasion (and critical) paradigms, the viewer is now seen to possess defenses against the imposition of the media, by virtue of the mechanism of selectivity, and to be less lonely, by virtue of membership in networks of interpersonal communication. Gratifications research asks not "What do the media do to people?" but rather "What do people do with the media?" Proceeding from the notion of selectivity, this approach rests not only on cognitive defensiveness but on interest. In other words, the media offer a cafeteria of resources, and the individual, as seeker, chooses what he needs. Critical theory condemns the interests and needs themselves as media inspired and the choices as illusory or trivial. Undaunted, gratifications theory proceeds to argue that needs and interests arise from institutional roles and from the social and psychological circumstances in which the viewer finds himself. The need for belonging, for example, would come readily to the mind of a gratifications researcher studying the functions of media events.

Gratifications research thus offers students of media events the idea that individuals come to the media in particular roles and that "gratifications obtained" are a function of "gratifications sought" (Rosengren, Wenner, and Palmgreen, 1985; Blumler, Gurevitch, and Katz, 1985). It shows how the roles in which viewers approach everyday television—as seekers of information, of entertainment, of identity—may influence not only different sorts of short-run gratifications, but also different kinds of long-run outcomes. In sum, gratifications may be defined as (1) reinforcement (2) of cognitive, affective, and integrative needs (3) of individuals in their roles (4) in the short run.

Research on the effects of media events finds this emphasis on role congenial. The festive viewer assumes very different roles from the everyday viewer, as we have shown. Even if the viewer is sometimes positioned by the media, effect is nevertheless a function of whether the altercasting "took." Here is the point where revisionist critical theories join gratifications research in the empirical study of "readings." Clearly, the empirical study of media events must proceed in this way.

Gratifications research also sees the individual as more than an opinion-and-attitude machine. Because of their interest in the process of "using" the media, gratificationists place emphasis on the affective functions of mass communication as well as on its function of forging identity, of achieving status and social integration. These functions are as important for the study of media events as are cognitive functions.

But gratifications research falls short for several reasons. First of all, its focus—at least to date—is very individualistic; it has little to say about the uses of media at the societal level, even though there is much that ought to be said. There is some connection to the institutional level, however, via the concept of role. Second, it is limited for our purposes because it has invested the viewer with so much power that the text is virtually forgotten. While this aspect of the theory is being reconsidered (Blumler, Gurevitch, and Katz, 1985), a theory of media events cannot possibly treat the text as if it were simply a product of the viewer's projections. Third, gratifications research is flawed by its emphasis, willy-nilly, on the overall stability of a system in which individuals in their roles use the media to gratify needs and advance toward goals. Of course, it includes the functionalist notion of unanticipated consequences of media use—and in this sense makes more room for change than does critical theory—but it does not go very far in explaining the apparent power of media events to introduce social change.

Technological theory. Finally, there is a strand of theory that might be called technological. It has even less interest in the text than gratifications research. Like persuasion and critical studies, it attributes higher power to the media per se. In other words, it has little interest in either the power of audiences or the power of messages.

Technological theory proposes that the media teach us "how to think" by causing our brains to learn to process information in the manner dictated by the medium that predominates in any given era. The media also tell us "where we belong" in the sense of organizing and connecting us with others who have access. It is in this latter sense that technological theory has bearing on the study of media events.

Theorists of media technology have proposed truly powerful media effects: for example, that writing has created the role of historian (Goody and Watt, 1968); that reading has undermined the authority of elders (Riesman, Denny, and Glazer, 1950); that print contributed to the Protestant Reformation and to the rise of science (Eisenstein, 1979); that the newspaper was an important ingredient in European nationalism; that the abundance of paper and the high-speed press have created a demand for ideology and interpretation (Gouldner, 1976); that photography and cinema have demoted the museum (Benjamin, 1968a); that television has abolished privacy (Meyrowitz, 1985). These theories all deal with the effects of media technology on social organization. They bear resemblance to those of our propositions which suggest that media events influence the forms of social and ceremonial order; that they define their own boundaries of community and polity; that they affect the organization of political campaigning or of diplomacy; that a "reproduction" may be more valuable than its "original." These ideas lead to what we have called short-circuiting or disintermediation, whereby a mass medium displaces or replaces an established intermediary in both organizational and topographic terms. Schematically, technological theory may be defined as (1) change (2) of social arrangements (3) of societies (4) in the long run.

Technological theory has an important bearing on the understanding of media events; it is guilty, however, of too much determinism. In focusing so positivistically on the ways in which technology shapes society, it ignores the simple fact that society shapes the definitions and uses of technology. The study of media events makes this omission particularly salient inasmuch as media events employ the very technology of everyday television to accomplish something altogether different. Nevertheless, a sociologically tempered technological theory has much to contribute to media-events research.

Each of these four traditions of research offers shelter to certain component elements of a theory of the effects of media events. Students of the short-run effects of media persuasion will find the cognitive effects familiar, albeit more powerful than what is normal for everyday viewing. Critical research offers support for the reinforcing functions of media events, but the possibility that media may cause change is essentially denied. Gratifications research anticipates the centrality of the roles assumed by viewers as prerequisite to an understanding of cognitive decodings and effects, but also addresses the affective, identity-oriented, and integrative needs gratified by media events. Technological theory, more than the other three, focuses on change without flinching, and does so at the level of social organization.

A composite of these four theories may perhaps help to conceptualize the major effects of media events. Two of the theories direct us to observe change (persuasion/technology) and two to observe reinforcement (critical/gratifications); two direct attention to cognitions (persuasion/critical) and two to affective and organizational dimensions (gratifications/technology); two highlight effects on the individual in the short run (persuasion/gratifications) and two on society in the long run (critical/technology).

But the result is still deficient; there is a lack. First of all, festive events deserve a theory which takes specific account of their festive dimension; that is what Victor Turner has taught us. Second, the theories we have reviewed are too linear. With the possible exception of critical theory, they do not allow for the kind of systemic thinking in which effects on one part of the system are transformed into stimuli for the other parts (as when organizers and broadcasters are affected by the response—even the imagined response—of the audience), causing the event to fan itself into a whirlwind. Third, communications theories come packaged in a big black box which is too rarely opened; we are concerned here as much with what goes on inside these events as with their direct effects on the outside. That is why we have made reference to Austin's typology of speech acts. Finally, our attempt to speak of media events in terms of generic effects leads to propositions which are abstracted from the flow of societies whose history they interrupt. Our propositions are disjointed and need to be connected to each other more dynamically, moving from one kind of effect to the next; from the individual level to the societal level; from momentary metaphors to full-scale social processes; from reinforcement to change; from the affective to the cognitive to the integrative.

Ceremonial anthropology. Anthropologists of ceremony help us complete the conceptual framework for which we are searching. They approach ceremony (1) as systems of performers, performances, functions, and consequences; (2) phased over time; (3) in the context of a community and its problems (cyclical and episodic). They favor a narrative approach that may help us put the pieces together in a manner which will complement traditional effects research in the field of communication.

We have introduced anthropological concepts throughout this book. Ostensibly, the shared interest in the ways societies represent themselves and in the effects of such representations and their rhetoric should have led to a greater mutual awareness between students of mass communication and cultural anthropologists. At least one reason for the existing gap may be the concentration of media research on the daily routines of broadcasting to abstracted individuals in a mass, while the anthropology of ceremony is concerned, rather, with the functions of special events in organized social systems.

Of course, ceremonies have functions other than effecting change. Writing on the subject of cultural performances in India, Milton Singer (in MacAloon, 1984), for example, says that "perhaps all people think of their culture as encapsulated in such discrete performances which they can exhibit to outsiders as well as to themselves. For the outsider they can conveniently be taken as the most concrete observable units of the cultural structure, for each performance has a definitely limited time span, a beginning and an end . . . displaying persisting relations among media, texts, themes and cultural centers." The roots of this anthropological interest in the relationship between the social level of concrete relations and the cultural level of performance is to be found, of course, in Durkheim (1915; see Alexander, 1988) who argued that ceremonies are a form of symbolic representation of the social structure. We have noted how Warner (1962), MacAloon (1984), Handelman (1990), and others have illustrated the modernity of these insights.

Also relevant is the concept of rites of passage, which usher individuals through the life cycle and whole societies through the culturally defined seasons. The notion of a collective ceremonial response to a traumatic event (such as drought, plague, earthquake, or war), however recurrent, is no less useful to the understanding of many television events.

Media-events research obviously is interested in ceremonies that represent society, but even more in those that act upon it. From this point of view, Victor Turner's work (1974, 1977) is essential, particularly his theory that "social dramas" are a response to moments of high tension in social relations. They follow a flagrant breach of some norm that polarizes society, says Turner, each faction calling for total mobilization. At such moments, an effort is made to organize a "redressive assembly," which may take the form of a legal trial, religious convocation, or some other type of public ceremony. If the event succeeds, the effect is a reiteration of loyalty to the values of the commonwealth, says Turner, and if it fails, there may be a schism and secession—what Hirschman (1970) calls "exit." Ceremonies mounted in response to crisis may have a one-time, ad hoc character, or may follow institutional patterns.

Certain symbolic anthropologists have taken a further step and proposed that there are cultural performances that are primarily devoted to change. An example is Peacock's (1968) study of *ludruk*, a Javanese dramatic genre utilized to encourage the modernization of society by means of symbolic action.

The anthropological interest in ceremony parallels the concern of communications research both with messages and with media, and recalls the questions raised by philosophers of language about "how to do things with words" (Austin, 1962). The problems of how symbols and ceremonies are "applied" to heal psychological and somatic disease, to affect the tides and climate, to induce victory in war, to change the status of individuals, and, of course, to effect social integration and sometimes change, are no less the concern of communication studies. That ceremonies may not only celebrate tradition but seek to enlist support for change is an important counterweight to the argument that ceremony and conservatism come packaged together.

NOTES

1. Defining Media Events

1. The typologies of relationship among storyteller, camera, actors, and audience have all been carefully dissected. And the ideological implications of changes within and among film genres—for continuity and change in values and social structure—have been the subject of continuous speculation. Somehow cinema studies have fallen to the humanist and broadcasting to the social scientist. The rich theorizing of the humanist and the careful empiricism of the social scientist are only now being combined in the analysis of television. The humanists have found interest (and at last legitimacy) in the study of television, and certain social scientists have responded by building conceptual bridges and methods to facilitate joint work (for example, Schudson, 1978). It was in the aftermath of the antiestablishmentarianism of the 1960s that this began to happen, with the politicization of media studies. It led to a renewal of the dialogue between humanists and social scientists that characterized the early days of the study of mass communication, and to renewed interest in critical schools of media studies such as the German-American Frankfurt School, American "cultural studies," and the work of the semiologists in France.

2. The earliest postwar examples include the American presidential conventions of 1948 and 1952, the return of General Douglas MacArthur from the Pacific in 1951, Senator Estes Kefauver's hearings on crime the same year, the inaugurations of Harry Truman and Dwight Eisenhower, Truman's guided tour of the White House in 1952, and, most memorable of all, the coronation of Elizabeth II on June 22, 1953. For details on the broadcasts of these events, see Russo (1983). The analysis by Lang and Lang (1953) of the MacArthur Day procession is the pioneering classic of media-events research.

235

3. We observed and collected relevant material on the occasion of the first presidential debates (Katz and Feldman, 1962), Sadat's journey to Jerusalem (Katz, Dayan, and Motyl, 1983), and the royal wedding (Dayan and Katz, 1982). We went to Poland to examine materials on the Pope's first visit (Dayan, Katz, and Kerns, 1984). One of our colleagues made an empirical study of the television audience of the 1984 Olympics (Rothenbuhler, 1985, 1988, 1989).

4. Russo's (1983) dissertation sketches the organizational and technological solutions to the problems of the live broadcasting of special events from remote locations. He shows, for example, how the series of space shots stimulated important developments in video technology that were subsequently employed in quite different contexts, such as coverage of the Kennedy assassination and funeral. We shall repeatedly draw on Russo's work.

5. Huizinga (1950) and Caillois (1961) face the same sort of problem with their multifaceted definition of play. Their definition is an overview of the different types of games. Thus, play is an activity (1) entered voluntarily (except when ceremonial roles or social pressures force participation); (2) situated "outside" ordinary life and accompanied by an awareness of its "unreality"; (3) intensely absorbing to the participants; (4) bounded in time and space; (5) governed by rules of order; (6) uncertain of outcome; and (7) promoting the formation of social groupings. Some of these elements also define media events; others are characteristics of ordinary television viewing (Stephenson, 1967). The problems of specifying the social conditions that give rise to play, the types of play, and the function of play for individual and society are closely related to the problems that confront the present project.

6. Russo (1983, p. 42) distinguishes three genres of television news—regular news, documentaries, and special events—but does not make the distinction between major news events and major ceremonial events that is central to our argument. "Special events broadcasting," Russo's subject, "refers to a genre or type of news coverage which deals with live origination of a major news story."

7. The Appendix to this volume attempts to compare the effects of

media events with those highlighted in the various traditions of research on media effects.

8. President Sadat's visit to Jerusalem was covered by an unprecedented number of newspapers and broadcasting organizations, mobilizing about 1,500 newsmen—580 from the United States alone. The live broadcast began at Ben Gurion Airport on Saturday night, November 19, 1977. Television followed the visitor and his hosts almost continually for most of the forty-four hours of his visit, to sites such as the Al Aqsa mosque, the Yad Vashem memorial, the Church of the Holy Sepulchre, and, most important, to his address before the Knesset. The live pictures provided by Israeli television were relayed to Egypt and to Western broadcasting organizations, which supplied their own commentaries and experts including Abba Eban (ABC) and John Kissinger (NBC). American television journalists played catalytic roles, beginning with Walter Cronkite's parallel interviews with Menachem Begin and Anwar el-Sadat on the eve of the visit. While the visit was in progress, exclusive joint interviews of the two protagonists were broadcast by CBS (Walter Cronkite), NBC (John Chancellor), and ABC (Barbara Walters). Egyptian television produced a live broadcast of Sadat's triumphant return to Cairo, which was relayed to Israel over the microwave link, with a commentary in Hebrew by an Egyptian broadcaster. Audiences for the broadcasts included almost all Israelis; only 3 percent recalled that they did not view the arrival ceremony (Israel Institute of Applied Social Research, 1979). It is estimated that perhaps 3 million Arab viewers saw Israeli television from across the border, and Israeli radio claimed 50 million Arab listeners. In the United States, the Knesset speech attracted an estimated 30 million viewers (Nasser, 1978), and in France, 58 percent of a 1978 viewing panel reported having seen at least part of the trip (Centre d'Etudes d'Opinion, 1981). Two years later, 87 percent of Israelis thought that it was "important" for them to have seen the live broadcast, and 94 percent of them thought it a "historic moment" (Peled, 1979).

9. In anticipation of the Pope's visit in 1979, Irish television (Radio Telefis Eirann) consulted the prior experience of Poland and Mex-

ico. Equipment valued at 12 million pounds and including forty-four cameras was assembled for the occasion, in the biggest collective effort RTE had ever made (Sorohan, 1979; Gleeson, 1979). Russo (1983, p. 320) estimated that the Kennedy assassination and funeral involved virtually all of the 2,000 employees of the three U.S. network news organizations, at a cost of perhaps $32 million. The BBC's royal wedding required some sixty television cameras in the largest outside-broadcasting operation in its history (Griffin-Beale, 1981). Media events involve a huge amount of sharing and pooling of equipment among broadcasters. A great sense of pride in the "miracle" of accomplishment typically follows these events (Sorohan, 1979; Todorovic, 1980).

10. The trial of Adolf Eichmann, recorded on film by Alan Rosenthal, was later transferred to videotape but was not broadcast during the period of the trial.

11. Compare Martin's (1969, p. 93) discussion of the checks on divinely validated temporal power when the church—like the media, in the case of media events—has "the capacity both to compound and challenge . . . temporal authority." Martin points to "institutional checks," "symbolic checks," and, rather in despair, to the conclusion that restraint "is realized less in those who perform the acts of temporal and spiritual union than by those suffering and excluded groups who recognize that an ideal has been violated. It is the poor and meek of the earth who realize that crucial limiting concepts are available whereby they can assert the crown rights of the Redeemer against the rights of the crown." For a conclusion opposite to the one drawn here, see Zelizer (in press).

12. The Live Aid event was broadcast on July 13, 1985. It originated from multiple locations, including Wembley in the United Kingdom, Philadelphia, and Moscow. The event lasted sixteen hours and was diffused via thirteen satellites to 150 countries, including India and China. The international audience was estimated at 650 million (presumably based on some percentage of the 2 billion potential in the countries reached). The U.S. figure was 180 million. The event cost 3.7 million dollars and 4 million pounds,

which was obtained through sale of TV rights and corporate donations. Estimates of money raised vary from $70 million to $147 million (Hickey, 1987).

13. Only in the fall of 1989 did Czech television openly defy the already crippled communist government by presenting live broadcasts of the mass rallies in Wenceslas Square. "If he [Jiri Hrabovsky, new anchor of Czech television] and a few hundred colleagues hadn't stuck their necks out earlier and broadcast the people's protests, Czechoslovakia's rout of communism might not have gone so far. People made this revolution. Television has spread it" (Newman, 1989). Observations on the mass uprisings in Czechoslovakia and Romania are given at several points in this volume, especially in Chapter 6.

14. Yet there was a discussion over whether to risk publicizing failure in the live broadcasting of American space shots (Russo, 1983). Note also that, subsequent to the Challenger disaster, the Soviets offered a live broadcast of a space shot. We return to this issue in Chapter 3.

2. Scripting Media Events

1. The televising of the political conventions and election returns of 1948 and 1952 mark the debut of the genre. While radio was still the predominant medium in 1948, the choice of Philadelphia as the site of the party conventions was influenced by the experimental cable hookup between Washington and New York (Russo, 1983). Chicago was chosen for the 1952 convention because it was thought to be optimally compatible with the time-zone differences in the United States (Lang and Lang, 1968). Michael Russo and Gladys and Kurt Lang note that the 1952 conventions set the style for coverage of subsequent conventions, with pooled camera work, star presenters, and so on. Eighteen stations carried the 1948 convention to an estimated 10 million viewers, at a time when only about 300,000 sets were in use (Russo, 1983). Coverage of the

1952 conventions extended beyond seventy hours each and reached some 65–70 million viewers, according to network sources.

2. The coronation of Elizabeth II took place on June 2, 1952. Although television was not yet generally available at the time, Briggs (1979, citing *BBC Audience Research*) reports that more than 56 percent of the British population viewed the BBC broadcast either at home (7.8 million people), in the homes of friends (10.4 million), or in public places (1.5 million). The broadcast began at 10:15 a.m. and lasted more than eight hours. Since videotape was not yet available, a film of the program was flown to Canada for rebroadcast in North America by CBC, NBC, CBS, and (in part) ABC. The American television audience at the time was estimated at 85 million viewers. Sound coverage was transmitted by thirty-two broadcasting organizations, sixteen of them European.

3. Chicago is one of the cities—including San Francisco, Milwaukee, New York, and Washington—that welcomed General MacArthur on his return from the Pacific, President Truman having recalled him in April 1951. His visit on April 26, 1951, was covered from his arrival at Midway Airport until the evening rally at Soldier's Field. Since there were relatively few television sets in 1951, many people watched in public places, such as bars (Russo, 1983, also citing *Broadcasting*, April 16 and April 30, 1951). This event also marks the beginning of research on television events (Lang and Lang, 1953).

4. Anything that offered the bare possibility of competition was arranged by the Greeks into contests "ranging from beauty contests for men, to the sacred games at Olympia" (Huizinga, 1950).

5. Huizinga cites a typical Chinese legend, where "the founding of a kingdom shows the hero-prince vanquishing his opponents by miraculous proofs of strength or amazing feats, thus demonstrating his superiority" (1950, p. 55).

6. Stephenson's theory draws on Huizinga (1950), but also on certain students of media audiences who have given more than the usual attention to the obvious fact that mass communication is also

entertainment! Hyman (1974) and Davison (1983) are prominent examples. Considerably more thought is now being devoted to the psychology and sociology of popular entertainment, of which Mendelsohn (1964) should be cited as pioneer and Tannenbaum (1980) as an important later effort. See also Bogart (1956), Steiner (1963), and Goodhardt, Ehrenberg, and Collins (1987).

7. Schramm's (1965) early distinction between fantasy and reality genres in television can hardly withstand the current narrativistic approach to analysis of news and, a fortiori, to media ceremonies of the sort reported here.

8. Attention to the rhetorics of science, not just social science, has sharply increased in recent years. See for example Silverstone (1981), Gusfield and Michalowicz (1984), and the review by Becker (1987). Some story forms of journalism are discussed in Darnton (1975), Tuchman (1978), Hallin (1987), and Gamson and Modigliani (1989).

9. Television adopted the Israeli government's name for its invasion of Lebanon, "Peace of the Galilee."

10. "In 1954, the televising of the Army-McCarthy hearings appeared to be the Senator's undoing. These hearings, in which the Wisconsin Republican attempted to bulldoze with reckless charges several members of the establishment, certainly coincided with the turn in the controversial Senator's political fortunes . . . [Although] no study substantiates any massive shift in attitude in response to the Senator's antics, the hearings did make an impression on his fellow legislators" (Lang and Lang, 1983, p. 67). This is a good example of the "third-person effect" (Davison, 1983).

11. The presidential debate between François Mitterrand and Valéry Giscard d'Estaing on May 5, 1981, was preceded by a bitter polemic over the rules and format of the debate. Giscard preferred a one-on-one contest, without journalists; Mitterrand, who insisted that the questions should be put by journalists, finally won the procedural contest (and the election).

12. Ninety percent of TV households viewed at least one of the four Kennedy-Nixon debates, the first of which took place on September 26, 1960. Seventy million viewers—half of the adult population—watched some part of the first debate, which was broadcast

at 8:30 p.m. Eastern Daylight Time (Kraus, 1962; Nielsen, cited in Russo, 1983).

13. Kantorowicz's classic, *The King's Two Bodies* (1957), and more recent studies (Giesey, 1960; Marin, 1981; Boureau, 1989) emphasize the role of the dead monarch's image in ensuring the continuity of the state.

14. Lord Mountbatten's funeral took place on September 5, 1979, following his assassination on August 27. According to John Grist, then of BBC, the live broadcast was seen by 5 million viewers, and the evening reprise by an estimated 15 million. The two-hour live broadcast was augmented by a one-hour film produced in part by Mountbatten himself, in anticipation of his death.

15. During an investigation of the Sadat visit two years later, Israelis were asked, "When you saw or heard the live broadcast of Sadat's visit, did you feel that the process and events that you were seeing or hearing were all preplanned, or did you feel that 'anything could happen'?" Seventy-eight percent were convinced that the broadcast was spontaneous enough to leave room for surprises (Peled, 1979).

16. Like the funerals of Martin Luther King, Jr., of John Kennedy, of Lord Mountbatten, or, in a highly dissonant style, the funeral-without-a-body of Aldo Moro in 1978, Indira Gandhi's cremation ceremony was meant as a response to a crisis: she had been assassinated by her bodyguards on October 31, 1984.

17. De Gaulle's speech was delivered during a state visit to Canada on Monday, July 24, 1967, from the balcony of the Montreal City Hall. His exhortation, "Vive le Québec libre, vive le Canada français, vive la France," provoked a scandal. Protesting this interference in Canadian affairs, Prime Minister Pearson pronounced the statement unacceptable. De Gaulle left Canada on July 26, omitting his planned visit to Ottawa.

18. Kate Smith's radio marathon on September 21, 1943, consisted of sixty-five interventions of one to two minutes each, over a period of eighteen hours from 8:00 a.m. until 2:00 a.m. the next morning. It was broadcast from New York over the CBS network.

19. For Lang and Lang (1983) the role of the audience is a key element in the classification of events. They distinguish between events which would take place even in the absence of an audience—where the audience is just a group of witnesses or bystanders—and events which are specifically staged for an audience. A presidential inauguration or the signing of a peace treaty is an example of the first; MacArthur's homecoming parade (Lang and Lang, 1953) is an example of the second.

   Further classifying these events by whether they are "unifying" (such as a presidential inauguration) or "controversy" (such as a presidential debate) yields four types of events which are labeled *Ceremony* (unifying/audience as witness); *Spectacle* (unifying/audience as necessary); *Esoteric Debate* (controversy/audience as witness); *Adversary Proceeding* (controversy/audience as necessary). Lang and Lang argue that the televised House Judiciary Committee that debated the impeachment of President Nixon moved the proceedings from an Esoteric Debate to an Adversary Proceeding "by evoking symbols of national unity" such as the Constitution, the office of the President, the sacred nature of the legislature's role, and so on. There is a resemblance between our Coronation and the Spectacle and Ceremony of the Langs, and between our Contest and their Esoteric Debate and Adversary Proceeding. But we are uneasy—as are the Langs—with the idea that the audience is "just" a witness in Ceremony and Esoteric Debate. A wedding, any wedding, *requires* witnesses; they are necessary role players. A fortiori, the royal wedding would be unthinkable without its worldwide audience.

20. In listing these attributes of the charismatic leader, Schwartz (1983) proposes that Weber shows no awareness of a competing form of democratic leadership—such as that of George Washington. This kind of person is reluctantly drafted into leadership, betrays self-doubt, administers power and justice according to "universalistic" standards, exhibits no extraordinary talent or political feat, is dedicated to institution building, and derives prestige almost from the relinquishing of power, thus demonstrating "vir-

tue." Curiously, Schwartz shows us that Washington was looked upon "as the most extraordinary moral hero of his time . . . [because] in late eighteenth century America . . . the refusal to accept power and haste in giving it up, were the ingredients that went into political spectacles."

21. The control of news stories by their sources is discussed by Molotch and Lester (1974) and by Sigal (1986). Unlike Kissinger, George Shultz is said to have shuttled into crisis by announcing that (1) the problem seemed quite capable of solution, and (2) he would give it all the time that might be needed. This would explain why reporters are said to have questioned aloud whether Secretary Shultz did not miscast himself in the role of the hero. We are grateful to Ambassador Simha Dinitz for this example.

22. The Korean family reunion campaign began on June 30, 1983, at 10:00 p.m. and continued beyond its scheduled two hours until 2:30 a.m., before being extended for the next eight days, then turned into a regular program. Nine local stations cooperated with KBS headquarters in Seoul to make the programs interactive, and international hookups were arranged via Los Angeles, New York, and Frankfurt. This event reached 78 percent of the viewing audience, the highest rating ever on Korean television.

23. These televised events differ profoundly from the festivals described by Ozouf (1976) in the context of the French Revolution.

24. The Romanian revolution which followed seemed to replay the Czechoslovakian script but did not quite succeed—either in the revolution itself or in the televising. Unlike the Czechs, the Romanian revolutionaries encamped inside the television station, which served as both party headquarters and loudspeaker. The staff was willingly commandeered by the rebels, and the station itself became a target of the counterrevolution. The broadcasting of liberation and the introduction of the new/old leadership were interspersed with shooting, calls for help, and rumors of massacre. Television recounted the evils of the old regime and displayed its sordid demise. While Czechoslovakian television quickly took distance and displayed its independence of the sides, Romanian television simply changed sides (Katz, Dayan, and Hauser, 1990). Here and at later points in the book we draw on the reports from

Eastern Europe published in the *New York Times* (Apple, 1989; copyright © 1989 by the New York Times Company; reprinted by permission), the *Wall Street Journal* (Newman, 1989), and *Le Monde* (Kaufmann, 1989). We utilize also the analysis of Shinar (1990) and discussion with G. Bar Haim. For overall reportage and analysis we have consulted Ash (1990; copyright © 1990 by Timothy Garton Ash; reprinted by permission of Random House, Inc.) and Dahrendorf (1990).

3. Negotiating Media Events

1. The manpower (often in thousands), the logistics, the security, the equipment, the costs (in millions of dollars) of mounting such events are prodigious. For details of particular events see Griffin-Beale (1981), Sorohan (1979), Pearce (1979), de Montclos (1990), *Newsweek* (1985), Todorovic (1988), Hickey (1987), and Russo (1983). The successful production of these events is regularly dubbed a miracle by the professionals involved. See also note 9 to Chapter 1 and note 7 to Chapter 7.

2. Writing of the forms of popular culture, Cawelti (1976) discusses the nature of the "contract" between producers and audiences. In this case, the producers enlist the loyalty of their audiences by adapting narrative conventions to their taste. By producers, however, Cawelti implies a coalition of publishers and writers, thus limiting the contract to two actual parties.

3. In this connection Mosse (1980, p. 108) cites a Protestant theologian and church historian writing during the French republic, who explained that "festivals meant emphasis on the national cohesion, not only because of the growth of national spirit but also because of the fear of political anarchy . . . They must cement the national spirit in a republic troubled by a weak executive."

4. Ozouf (1976) does not agree with the extent of this failure. She points out that, however contrived, the "fêtes révolutionnaires" nonetheless provided a direct experience of the ethos of revolution.

5. The Pope's first visit to Poland (there were two subsequent visits, in 1983 and 1987) took place June 2–10, 1979. More than twenty of the thirty hours of broadcasting were live. The national broad-

casts (coverage was not always national) were of the meetings with Polish officials in the Belvedere Palace and the ceremonies in Warsaw, Czestochowa, Wadowice, Auschwitz, Nowitarsk, and Cracow. Thirty percent of all broadcast time devoted to news was spent on the Pope's visit. Huge audiences followed the Pope everywhere. Despite the effort of authorities to prevent crossing of people from one zone of the country to another, and their reluctance to allow the size of the audience to exceed that of the earlier Brezhnev visit, 4 million individuals attended the open-air mass at Auschwitz-Birkenau. Security arrangements included 40,000 church volunteers and 85,000 state policemen. Television coverage of the event was assigned to the news department (first channel, studio two) of Telewisja Polska (Poltel), with the collaboration of religious experts. Cities were deserted: people were either at home watching or on the spot attending the events (*Time*, June 11, 1979; "CBS Special," June 7, 1979; interviews in Warsaw conducted by the authors and Pierre Motyl in July 1980).

6. The American experience, of course, has been different. Barber (1980) argues that "at least since Ben Franklin, there has been a market in America for politics as fun—a theme that sets us apart." The blend of politics and fun, morality and entertainment, was conceived by private enterprise, says Barber, and came to be institutionalized in the Chautauqua movement, whose "literary and scientific circles sprang up all over the country. For nearly three decades, traveling-tent Chautauquas spread culture, fun, and knowledge." It brought politicians and political debate into the context of entertainment. "No other popular medium could match it in engaging and extending mass sentiment in America," continues Barber. "Chautauqua refined an approach to public enlightenment and titillation that would be broadcasting's inheritance, television's teacher" (p. 221). The role of the impresario in Chautauqua—as he asks the political speaker waiting in the wings, "Shall I put you on now, or let them enjoy themselves awhile longer?" (p. 222)—surely recalls the role of television, not only in the mix of politics and showmanship but in the independence of the producer from the politician. Expressing an either/or attitude

in the live broadcast of the 1987 election results, the anchorman of Germany's ARD network kept prodding the politicians, and seemingly tempting the audience, with the need to conclude the proceedings in order to reinstate the "very good" programs that had been preempted for the election special.

7. Anyone who thinks that television does this easily or routinely is mistaken. And Paddy Chayefsky, who should know better, is wrong in his 1975 film *Network* if he believes that a maddened television news presenter, even with management support, can rally disenchanted people sitting in their armchairs; so is Daniel Schorr (1976), who thinks Chayefsky may be right.

8. This is not to say that broadcasters necessarily behave in this way; we repeat that this is a question yet to be explored. Daniel Boorstin (1964) thinks they do not. We are merely arguing that, in principle, they have the "right" to so behave, as well as the power to do so. And the extent to which this right is recognized—and to be sure, the extent to which it is exercised—transforms the process of negotiating and producing events. Russo (1983) provides a number of examples where broadcasters have said no, absolutely or contingently.

9. According to Kornhauser's highly useful definition, "mass society is a social system in which elites are readily accessible to influence by non-elites and non-elites are readily available for mobilization by elites" (1959, p. 37).

10. We note repeatedly (see especially Chapter 6) that these are, nevertheless, establishment-sponsored events, even when the organizers may be divided among themselves over the televising (for example, the Watergate hearings). That hegemony is complex and incomplete, and that the press may act against the interest of its owners or their class, is discussed in Gouldner (1976).

11. "Most people when they read that the Queen walked on the slopes of Windsor—that the Prince of Wales went to the Derby—have imagined that too much thought and prominence were given to little things. But they have been in error; and it is nice to trace how the actions of a retired widow and an unemployed youth become of such importance" (Bagehot, 1927, p. 30).

12. Geertz (1980) tells us that there are striking differences among the

"royal progresses" of the kings of Morocco, England, and Bali. Hassan's script reestablishes authority through the symbolic reenactment of Conquest; Elizabeth I sought an exchange of reciprocal pledges and contracts at each stop of her tour; Balinese monarchs display the traditional basis of kingly authority through the professed homology between the hierarchy of their court and the structure of the cosmos. While the three progresses are properly scripted as Coronations, they subdivide in emphasis on the personal charisma of Conquest, the legalism and mutuality that anticipate Contest, and the traditional symbolism of Coronation. All of this demonstrates that the fit between the announced label and the actual script is far from obvious, raising the question of how the latter is decided upon and implemented with regard to the specifics of the situation and of the aims that determine the protagonists' involvement.

13. President Reagan used much the same rhetoric at the end of 1988, in trying to extricate his administration from the uproar over the arms-for-hostages deals with Khomeini's Iran and the Nicaraguan rebels.

14. Lang and Lang (1983, p. 73) report this information.

15. Eighty-nine percent of households tuned in to at least some portion of the first debate between Jimmy Carter and Gerald Ford. This debate was broadcast from Philadelphia on September 23, 1976.

16. The 1960 debates between Kennedy and Nixon were made legally possible by special legislation suspending section 315 of the broadcast regulations (Kraus, 1962). Debates in subsequent campaigns were organized under private auspices.

17. As is true of the Olympics organizers, the sanctimoniousness of the organizers of political conventions must be carefully scrutinized. No less than the impresarios of sports, political impresarios know where the drama is.

18. Live coverage of the six-day visit of President Nixon to China (February 21–27, 1972) was produced by a pool team of Chinese and Americans. It was provided intermittently by the three American

networks, averaging ten to seventeen hours each, and NBC relayed its broadcasts overseas (*EBU Review*, 1972, p. 43). Citing NBC figures, *Broadcasting* (February 28, 1972) estimated that 100 million Americans saw some portion of the visit. Although the audience figure is high, it is widely thought that the event did not arouse much enthusiasm because it was variously interpreted as spelling the abandonment of Taiwan, as a confession of error by U.S. imperialism, or simply as an elaborate show of Chinese hospitality.

19. Reagan's day of solidarity with Poland was proclaimed on January 30, 1981. The political nature of the gesture required the approval of the Senate, which it obtained, but the major networks nevertheless shunned it. The day was marked by a program of entertainment and interviews with heads of state offered in thirty-nine languages and relayed by satellite to some fifty countries. It was fully transmitted, however, in only five countries, and was given just one minute on the BBC. The cast consisted of volunteers from Hollywood, headed by Charlton Heston, Glenda Jackson, Henry Fonda, Orson Welles, Bob Hope, and Frank Sinatra, who sang in Polish (*Le Monde*, February 2, 1981).

20. The Ayatollah Khomeini returned to Iran from France on February 1, 1979, and was greeted by 5 million people, amassed at Tehran Airport, in the streets of Tehran, and at the Beheshte Zahra cemetery. The whole of the event, including the ride through the city and the visit to the cemetery, was shown on the news in the United States but was "denied" to Iranian viewers. The announcement that the arrival broadcast would be rescheduled for February 9 is said to have triggered the revolution (Davidian, 1983; Sreberny-Mohammadi, 1990).

21. Some of the Iranian viewers were so upset, it is claimed, that they began throwing TV sets from the windows (Sreberny-Mohammadi, 1990).

22. The Catholic Church did not take much note of printing, either. The church apparently did not anticipate the role of the Bible, translated and printed, in the Protestant Reformation.

23. The funeral of Anwar el-Sadat took place on Saturday morning, October 10, 1981, near the spot where he was assassinated during a military parade four days earlier. Broadcast by Egyptian television, the stark and disorganized funeral, which lasted one hour, stood in sharp contrast to the grandiose event of 1977 and to the funeral of Gamal Abdul Nasser in 1970. Leaders of the Western powers were in attendance, and the live broadcast was seen on TFI in France and on the American networks.

24. The tragedy of the Munich Olympics, held between August 25 and September 10, 1972, calls to mind how frequently the Olympics have served as a political arena—from the Berlin games of 1936, supervised by Dr. Goebbels, to the Moscow games of 1980, which were played despite a boycott and against the background of the Russian invasion of Afghanistan.

25. Ninety million people (more than half of the adult population) viewed some portion of the twenty hours broadcast from the Democratic national convention in Chicago by the three major networks, according to *Broadcasting* (September 2, 1968).

26. The Egyptian-Israeli peace treaty was signed in Washington, D.C., on March 26, 1979. Ceremonies began at 2:00 p.m., Eastern Standard Time. They included a press conference at the White House and appearances at the Senate by President Carter, President Sadat, and Prime Minister Begin.

27. Broadcast by both BBC and ITV on July 29, 1981, the royal wedding of Prince Charles and Lady Diana attracted the largest audience in the history of British broadcasting: three-quarters of the population. Of these viewers, according to the BBC, two-thirds tuned to BBC-1. The event was broadcast live in seventy-nine countries. Five years later the wedding of Prince Andrew and Lady Sarah on July 23, 1986, attracted a smaller audience worldwide, estimated by *Le Monde* (July 25, 1986) at "only" 400 million in forty-two countries.

28. A high officer of the Church, invited to sit on the dais in Washington during the Pope's first American visit, elected to watch the live proceedings on television.

4. Performing Media Events

1. Eco (1989) addresses this point and other aspects of the aesthetics of live broadcasting in a 1964 essay, recently translated into English.
2. We have elaborated on this point in Dayan, Katz, and Kerns (1984), basing ourselves on Brown (1981). See also Dupront (1973).
3. Both broadcasting organizations inadvertently missed the cue.
4. The glance of journalists may be characterized by distance and, within distance, by mobility. It is typically concerned with recontextualizing the event by situating it in larger frames. It is always alert to possible departures from the announced script, since such departures constitute information. With respect to the royal wedding, for example, the British trade magazine *Broadcast* notes: "There is another, less happy purpose in the dual feed, about which our sources are naturally circumspect. If anything untoward were to happen anywhere, it would be possible to continue transmitting the planned picture while also feeding back the unexpected event to Television Centre for recording and assessment there by Philip Lewis and if circumstances develop that require a journalistic decision, by Dick Francis" (Griffin-Beale, 1981). The security glance, by contrast, is little interested in context. Now a familiar feature of media events, the perpetually shifting eyes of unidentified characters surrounding the principals reveal security people scanning the event for possible sources of disruption.
5. This example illustrates the limits of what Newcomb (1974) has described as television "dialogism," whereby TV programs are thought to comment on each other and to reframe each other. The present instance is less a mutual commentary than it is a mutual annihilation.
6. For this reason in part, media events are often made the responsibility of sports units or "special-events" units (Russo, 1983). Still, how can one avoid bringing in journalists, when the event has news value and political or diplomatic implications? Why should

a network deprive itself of its experts, precisely when they are most needed? And yet the problem remains that this is not quite journalism. Unlike the news, media events are not descriptive of a state of affairs, but symbolically instrumental in bringing about that state of affairs. They do have some of the qualities inherent in primitive rituals with which they share, in particular, a pragmatically oriented reliance on magical evocation: media events display symbolically what they wish to achieve.

7. "Aura," according to Benjamin (1968b), is a function of distance. It is lost as a consequence of equal and intimate access.

8. This was the case for Peter Jennings, covering the event for ABC from Ben Gurion Airport's tarmac. The situation was similar for the CBS team. Bob Simon: "Of course I cannot see from here, but President Katzir will be greeting President Sadat . . ." Also, from CBS's studio: "And here is the handshake! If only we had a microphone in that small gathering . . ."

9. President Mitterrand's inauguration took place on Thursday, May 21, 1981. The focal ceremony was the visit to the Panthéon, where the new president placed red roses—an emblem of the French Socialist party—on the graves of Jean Jaurès, Jean Moulin, and Victor Schoelcher. Directed by Antenne 2's Serge Moati, the two-hour ceremony was broadcast live.

10. Lang and Lang were first to point to the unique perspective of media events, although they attributed it—rather too hastily—to the medium of television in general.

11. Boorstin might grant that promotional events transmitted by the media but originating outside are less "pseudo" than those initiated by the media themselves. Technically, however, both types of events qualify for Boorstin's derision.

12. Compare: "Television and the press had decided that the cremation [of Indira Gandhi] was the all-important event of the day. No mention was made of the gruesome riots just a few miles away in which thousands of Sikhs were being massacred" (Minwalla, 1990).

13. John Paul II's seven-day visit to the United States started on October 1, 1977. It included six eastern and midwestern cities and

required the collaboration of the church and the issuing of 14,000 press credentials. Despite a scuffle about the role of women in the church, the visit proceeded in a climate of adulation. It was the leading story on the nightly news. In New York, the visit (to Harlem, to New York stadium, to Madison Square Garden) was covered live for twenty-one hours.

14. John Paul II's prayer for world peace, which opened the Marian Year, took place in the Basilica of Saint Mary Major in Rome on June 6, 1989, and was relayed by RAI to sixteen Marian sanctuaries around the planet, including Lourdes, Fatima, Czestochowa, Guadalupe, Bombay, Manila, and Dakar. Eighteen satellites and thirty relays permitted simultaneous recitation of the rosary by one and one-half million people in twenty countries. Hickey (1987) estimated an audience of one billion; but see Mytton (1991).

15. Barber (1980) reminds us that media events as teacher have an American precedent in the mixture of pedagogy, politics, and titillation which characterized the Chautauqua movement. See note 6, Chapter 3.

16. The visual and verbal aspects of the two broadcasts are analyzed thoroughly in Serr (1984).

17. On monuments, public places, and collective memory, see Innis (1951), Lasswell (1979), Mosse (1980), and Nora (1984).

18. As shown by Eliseo Veron (1981), news broadcasts are themselves submitted to a process of fictionalization, turned into events in their own right, and endowed with an interactive space and a temporal continuity. They still rely on frontal address, but often use it as the prelude to an intricate series of shots and reverse shots.

5. Celebrating Media Events

1. Richard Nixon gave his resignation speech at 11:30 a.m., on Friday, August 9, 1974. Despite the daytime hour, his address was viewed by a huge audience, estimated at 60 percent of the population. That evening the three American networks produced prime-time specials on the subject (*Broadcasting*, August 12, 1974).

2. President Kennedy's funeral took place on November 25, 1963. The broadcast lasted for seven hours and fourteen minutes, beginning at 9:00 a.m. (*Broadcasting*, December 2, 1963; cited in Russo, 1983, based on Nielsen and other data).

3. Like political conventions, the Olympic Games, and the royal family, the space program has provided a steady supply of media events, beginning with the fifteen-minute flight of Alan Shepard on May 5, 1961. The first live moon pictures were broadcast on March 23, 1965. We are especially concerned here with the Apollo XI mission that began with the blast-off from Cape Kennedy at 9:32 a.m. on July 16, 1969, and climaxed in the moon walks on July 20 and the splashdown on July 24. The blast-off was given two hours of live coverage, the splashdown four hours. The telecasts were viewed in some 40–45 percent of TV homes (*Broadcasting*, July 21 and 28, 1969). Europe, Latin America, and Japan relayed the American coverage.

4. Unless otherwise noted, viewing figures are from publications and personal communications of the A. C. Nielsen Company.

5. The 1990 Super Bowl, for example, was broadcast on January 28 from 5:00 to 9:00 p.m. on CBS and included a postgame show. According to *Broadcasting*, it reached 109 million viewers in the United States. Its rating of 39 percent was one of the lowest in the history of the Super Bowl.

6. The Senate Select Committee on Presidential Campaign Activities met from May 17 to August 7, 1973; by early August 70 percent of Americans had watched some portion of the hearings. Somewhat less attention was given to the hearings of the House Judiciary Committee on Presidential Impeachment, which met from July 24–29, 1974. Daily audiences for the live broadcasts—which rotated among the three networks on a daily basis and were rebroadcast in the evening on the Public Broadcasting System—ranged from 8.2 percent to 11.9 percent, competing favorably with scheduled daytime entertainment (Lang and Lang, 1983).

7. The Los Angeles Olympic Games (July 28–August 12, 1984) were broadcast over 16 days and 180 hours in the United States. They

were broadcast worldwide through international agreements and satellite relays (*Broadcasting*, August 20, 1984). Much dissatisfaction was expressed abroad concerning ABC's parochial emphasis on events in which the United States participated. Four years later, the Seoul Olympics (September 19–October 2, 1988) also broadcast some 180 hours according to *Le Monde*, of which about 42 hours were featured on prime time in the United States on the NBC network and were viewed by an average of 18 percent of Americans (*Variety*, September 28 and October 5, 1988). Increasingly, the Olympic Games are dependent on income from franchises given to international broadcasters. Under the presidency of Juan Antonio Samaranch, the IOC board's composition has been transformed through the replacement of aristocrats by businessmen, managers, and international lawyers.

8. The so-called Oscar ceremony began in 1928 as a banquet in a Los Angeles hotel. In 1944 it moved to a theater setting, and since 1966 it has been settled in Los Angeles' largest theater. The ceremony underwent a major transformation with the introduction of television in 1952, gradually expanding from initial broadcasts in Los Angeles and New York to its present scale. The Academy Awards on March 29, 1989, for example, were broadcast on the ABC network and received a rating of 29.8 (*Variety*, April 15, 1989).

9. In other countries it is not at all taken for granted that television will provide simultaneous coverage of an event that viewers may be eager to attend. Eastern bloc nations frequently broadcast ceremonial events but are far less likely to risk photographing the possible miscarriage of a space missile, for example (Lendvay, Tolgyesi, and Tomka, 1982). Instead, Eastern European events appear to have focused on Coronations—self-congratulatory ceremonies such as the reception after the cosmonauts' return from space—and on great folk celebrations such as May Day. On these festive occasions, the authors say, emphasis is placed on the use of television to augment and heighten civic holidays that call for mass participation "outside," at the procession, and to offer substitute

access to shut-ins and other unfortunates. Given the speed of secularization and the consequent withering of the religious calendar, such events are anticipated as markers of the seasons and of continuity with the (recent) past. Of course, the live broadcasts of the revolutionary events in Eastern Europe in the fall of 1989 changed all this, at least momentarily.

10. Conducted two years after the event, a survey showed that one-third of the Israelis thought it "important" that they had viewed the Sadat visit to Jerusalem together with nonfamily others. The survey did not provide the actual number of those who viewed with others (Peled, 1979).

11. Recalling King's funeral, Carter (1990) noted that, unlike the funeral of John Kennedy, "King's passing brought out much disease and ill-will among its audience. After the announcement of his shooting, riots broke out in New York, Watts, and Detroit. These were the worst cases of civil unrest recorded in this country, both in terms of lives lost and property damaged. The funeral's telecast only exacerbated the unrest in many communities, if only for a short period of time."

12. From an interview conducted by the authors in Warsaw in 1980.

13. Lang and Lang (1953, pp. 43–49, 66–69) discuss the functions of bystanders and witnesses. See note 19 in Chapter 2.

14. The funeral of Enrico Berlinguer took place in June 1983 and was broadcast for three hours by RAI. Two million persons attended the event in Rome, and the television audience was estimated at 8.6 million, of whom about 5 million viewed the entire event (Servizio Opinioni della RAI; cited in Mancini, 1987).

15. The interplay of dominant and oppositional readings is vividly reported by a French journalist (Fauré, 1981) who was visiting the Smith family at their home in Croydon, England, during the royal wedding. Mother, sister, and daughter were riveted by the occasion. They offered one toast to the newlyweds and another to "innocence" (confident that Lady Di, at least, had hers), then served a wedding brunch using paper napkins embossed with the Union Jack. They commented to one another on the appearance,

weight, and age of Margaret Thatcher, Nancy Reagan, former prime minister Harold Macmillan, Princess Margaret, and the King of Tonga, and expressed sympathetic understanding over Diana's mixup of her husband's several names. "Best thing that could happen to England now. With all of our problems, it's good to get together for such an occasion," said Mrs. Smith. "Without monarchy, England would be chaos. Besides, England without monarchy wouldn't be England." Throughout all of this the son, disobeying his mother's command to dress up, was in and out of the room, up and down the stairs, back and forth to his hi-fi, obviously uninterested in the occasion. His mother reprimanded him with "I don't approve your mocking the queen." Voicing his opposition, he mocked Charles and Diana, too.

16. Blumer's (1939) phrase "elementary collective groupings" is per- haps the classic statement of these distinctions. For an analysis of the origins of mass psychology in the founding works of Le Bon, Tarde, and Freud, see Moscovici (1981). Compare Rothenbuhler's (1985) attempt to come to grips with some of the same problems: "Durkheim's notion of a public festival of solidarity was dependent on a crowd, on the tactile presence of a collectivity. Canetti . . . makes a more explicit and literal use of the sense of touch (it is implicit in Durkheim), claiming that it is the base of all social existence. But Canetti has abandoned this literal logic for a sym- bolic one; the development of society was the development of sym- bols of crowd and symbols of touch . . . I would propose to distin- guish between a crowd—which is a group of people mutually present, mutually influencing, and mutually oriented; a public— which is a group of people mutually influencing and commonly oriented; and a mass—which is a group of people commonly ori- ented . . . The crowd, the public and the mass have existed side by side for as long as the touch could be expressed symbolically. The media event works on this symbolic expression to transform mass into public, and to achieve the functions Durkheim expected of crowds." See also Handelman's (1990) distinction between the size of a mass audience and its fragmented, molecular character, particularly in the case of media events.

6. Shamanizing Media Events

1. This statement is overly simple, as we shall argue below, in that access to state television came rather late in the process, after the revolutionary "small media" were at work.
2. There is room for speculation that the playful involvement invited by "recreational" events may be more effective in diffusing their latent messages than "serious" statements of the same messages.
3. In fact, at the framing stage of transformative events, there is an allusion to the restoration of a familiar paradigm from an earlier time. The restorative reference is only one ingredient of a process of persuasion directed primarily toward the future.
4. Originally intended to celebrate the six hundredth anniversary of the Black Madonna in Jasna-Gora, John Paul II's second visit to Poland on June 16–23, 1983, was overshadowed by the ban on Solidarity, by Lech Walesa's house arrest, and by the state of martial law that had been imposed eighteen months before. The visit turned into a carefully calculated blend of challenge and caution, during which it became increasingly clear that the Pope was promoting the resurgence of Solidarity. It was estimated that 18 million people—half of the Polish population—gathered at various times during the visit, causing the Polish government to warn the church about the political turn of the event and twice causing Polish television to interrupt sound or visual coverage (*Newsweek*, June 27, 1983; *Time*, June 27, 1983; *Herald Tribune*, June 17, 1983; *Figaro*, June 17, 1983; *Le Monde*, June 17–22, 1983; *Liberation*, June 20–27, 1983). The Pope's third visit on June 8–14, 1987, was even more confrontational.
5. Among the newspaper reports we have examined, we find the concepts employed by Apple (1989) closest to our own, and we therefore quote him liberally. *Le Monde* reports as follows: "On Wednesday the 29th, the deputies to the federal assembly voted unanimously, as always, though it meant, this time, abolishing the leading role of the communist party . . . Attended by many deposed leaders of the PCT still entitled to their mandates as deputies, the parliament session was broadcast on television. It illus-

trated the disarray of the Czech political class, following the crisis of the last twelve days. Their voice often shaking with emotion, all speakers mentioned the 'seriousness of the situation' . . . Many of them—communists included—called for free elections" (Kaufmann, 1989). For another report on the same event, see note 7 below.

6. [Monday, November 27] "The general strike is a success before it has begun. Just before the strike, the anchorman announces that he is preparing to join in the strike, then, from the stroke of noon, they show city squares filled with people in Prague, in Bratislava, in Brno, in Ostrawa . . . A subtitle explains that 'reporting on the strike is television crews' contribution to the strike' (Ash, 1990, p. 106).

7. [Wednesday, November 29] "Then, the Federal Assembly. The women with putty faces, cheap perms and schoolmistresses' voices. The men in cheap suits with hair swept straight back from sweaty foreheads. The physiognomy of power for the last forty years. But at the end of the day they all vote 'Yes' to the prime minister's proposal . . . to delete the leading role of the party" (Ash, 1990, p. 111).

8. Dahrendorf (1990) believes that "thinkability" is a contributory cause in radical social change, too. Quoting a Polish commentator on the Eastern European revolutions who quipped, "It took a generation that did not know it could not be done," Dahrendorf observes that "older people had been discouraged by the experiences of 1956 and 1968 and other, smaller revolts; the young had a go at it because they did not realize that it was impossible to dislodge regimes, and so they dislodged them." Of course, Dahrendorf also credits Gorbachev for making these thoughts thinkable.

9. In his attempt to create common ground between Moslems and Jews, Sadat invoked the image of their common mythical ancestor, Abraham (Liebes-Plesner, 1984). But Abraham is not only a shared figure and, as such, a mediating device; he is called upon to illustrate the power of faith and the value of sacrifice. Abraham's response to God's request for the sacrifice of his son is what Turner

(1974) calls a root paradigm, a cultural model for action. Sadat directed the Israelis to follow in the steps of the patriarch, with a precise analogy in mind.

The model thus proposed not only echoes the centrality of Abraham to the Jewish and Moslem traditions, it also delineates a project. Israelis owe Sadat a sacrifice in exchange for the sacrifice he made by coming to see them, but in their sacrifice they will be enacting the norms of their Jewish faith. Going beyond cultural reference, collective memory provides the situation with a dynamic impetus.

The rhetoric of Sadat has an additional dimension, this time turned toward his home audience. Calling upon the Jews to conform to the teachings of their own scriptures, the Egyptian president assumed the stance of a prophet, of a messenger of God. In Jewish style, he required from the Jews fidelity to their own traditions; but to a Moslem ear, this exhortation sounded very much like a call for conversion, replicating Mohammed's famous address to the Jews of Medina and echoing the theological notion that Jews, though a people of the Book, have gone astray. In a remarkably ambiguous statement, Sadat anchored his project in the collective memories of two cultures simultaneously.

10. Remember that John Paul II's first visit to Poland came after a long freeze in the relations between Poland and the Vatican, during which Pope Paul VI was denied (in 1966) the opportunity of visiting Poland.

11. The suddenness and scope of these transformative events often evoke the quasi-millenarian language of conversion. Of course, the endorsement of the Pope's visit by the Marxist rulers of Poland could be explained away in terms of realpolitik: a dire economic situation threatened the Gierek government with a massive popular upheaval that might have led to the direct intervention of the Soviets, who had three divisions already stationed in Poland. That Polish leaders should choose to make concessions to popular sentiment in the symbolic domain of religion seemed innocuous enough under the circumstances. Nevertheless, these concessions were perceived as a reconciliatory sign that the authorities were

modifying their attitude toward the church, as if to enact the conversion announced in messianic poems of the nineteenth century that tell of the crucifixion of the Polish people and of their redemption as the collective prophet of a new Christian era (Adam Mickiewicz, *The Book of Polish Pilgrims;* cited in Jeanneney, 1987). CBS agreed that Sadat's trip to Jerusalem was a "miracle." His visit was not only a tactical move, a Canossa of sorts; it was an act of God, a conversion. Flying to Jerusalem was Sadat's "road to Damascus." Sadat himself eagerly used such metaphors, calling for a conversion of hearts and minds that would allow Israelis to enter the benign era to which he offered the key.

In a more subdued tone, the Watergate hearings resonated with scripture. Advocating restraint on executive power and rededication to good government, they were a rite of purification. Reliance on the religious language of miracles, mysteries, and conversions expressed the magnitude of the transformations witnessed.

12. The "trial" and execution of Nicolae and Elena Ceausescu took place on December 25, 1989. The secret proceedings, shot on a videocassette, were shown repeatedly in various edited, truncated, and reorganized versions with the effect of blurring the sequence of events, concealing the identity of the judges, and casting doubts on the time and mode of execution. The full ninety-minute document was broadcast on foreign stations only a few months later. In France it was shown in full on April 22, 1990.

13. The Watergate affair had a very different impact on symbolic space. The issue of the limits of privacy was repeatedly addressed throughout the affair, by everyone from Daniel Ellsberg to Richard Nixon. The hearings made it clear that the White House was not off limits to judicial and congressional control. Neither the President nor his subordinates could declare his office a sanctuary above the law. In an interesting symmetry, the illegal breach of privacy by the President's men—the breaking into Democratic headquarters in the Watergate building—was repaid by asserting the legality of invading the privacy of the President.

14. Dahrendorf (1990) *excludes* the Soviet Union from this reunion, even while regretting "poor Vladivostock, which may in fact be

more European than Yerevan or Baku." He argues that (1) it is too early to lie down with yesterday's lion; (2) the Soviet Union, a vast developing country, has a longer way to go to achieve modernity than its former satellites; and (3) Europe is a federation of relatively small nations and has no place for a superpower.

15. Cognitive and affective restructuring, says Wallace (1966; cited in Myerhoff, 1982) occurs through *dissociation* from familiar reference frames, and the newly acquired information is maintained through various operations of reinforcement. The neophyte in a rite of passage is radically removed from past knowledge and presented with new information while immersed in a state of suggestibility. This state is one in which "any given set of cognitive and affective elements can be restructured more rapidly and more extensively, the more the perceptual clues from the environment associated with . . . previous learning of other matters are excluded from awareness, and the more those clues which are directly relevant to the elements to be reorganized are 'presented'" (p. 240). The stages of this type of learning are (1) *anticipation*; (2) *separation* (through sensory deprivation, physical stress, and the like); (3) *suggestion* (high susceptibility associated with trance and characterized by dissociation); (4) *execution* (achievement of a new cognitive structure); (5) *maintenance* (through repetition or reinforcement); and eventually (6) *resynthesis*.

Television's role in anticipation and resynthesis has already been discussed in Chapter 2 in connection with the scripting of events. Separation—albeit described in more sociological terms—is one of the key concepts we have borrowed from Turner (1969, 1977) and Van Gennep (1909) when stressing the single-mindedness of the viewers of media events. Wallace's three next stages (suggestion, execution, maintenance) turn *rites de passage* into forms of brainwashing, perhaps correctly so. While major media events do create an increased suggestibility on the part of audiences whose excitement and exhilaration may resemble trance, we do not attribute their efficacy to Wallace's concept of dissociation. In media events, as we show in the present chapter, the new information is not so much imposed on the receiver as it is actively constructed by him;

resynthesis is at work throughout the event and is already present at the stage of anticipation.

16. Media events have much in common with the Turners' (1978) approach to the ceremonial pedagogy of Christian pilgrimages. Pilgrimages are optional; they have neither the overwhelming importance nor the constraining powers inherent in rites of passage. They are individual adventures, freely and voluntarily undertaken. Of course, this freedom is actively canalized, as Philip Elliott (1982) has noted. The Turners stress the manipulative dimension in pilgrimages; yet they also emphasize the largely unimposed restructuring taking place in the pilgrim's mind.

    As in Wallace's second phase, the Turners' pilgrimage starts with an act of *separation*. The pilgrim interrupts the regularity of normal duties, dissociates from familiar surroundings, temporarily severs affective and institutional ties. The decision to undertake the long journey to a shrine gives the pilgrim access to a deeper level of existence, placing him or her in a situation of *vacancy*, or suggestibility.

17. This is not gullibility, we insist; indeed, we want to distance ourselves from the scholarly weepers who stand ready to diagnose a sheeplike atrophy of the public's critical faculties whenever television or political spectacle is involved.

18. Despite obvious differences in language and focus, Sperber's (1975) cognitive approach to symbolism spells out many implications of Victor Turner's concept of "subjunctivity." Sperber posits the existence in our minds of a symbol-processing apparatus working alongside our conceptual apparatus and linked to it by a feedback mechanism. Many pieces of information are rejected by the conceptual apparatus as too obscure to be stated in regular propositional form, or as contradictory of propositions that are part of our general knowledge. In Israel of 1977, for example, the sight of an Arab head of state deplaning at the Tel Aviv Airport could not but have clashed with former cognitions.

    Owing to their controversial status, such tantalizing new propositions are put between brackets. Rejects of the cognitive process, they are fed to a second type of processing called *symbolic*. Memory is explored to try to locate representations that will regularize the status of the bracketed propositions, either by bringing them to completion or by reconciling the contradiction. If this quest succeeds, the propositions are unbracketed and fed back to the conceptual apparatus, which stocks them in the encyclopedic memory.

Sperber points out that while some representations only transit through the symbolic apparatus, some are so baffling to the very foundations of positive knowledge that they have no possibility of ever gaining admission. Unless discarded, they may forever be confined to the evocation-bracketing loop. When—like dogmas, articles of faith, and other typically ceremonial topics—they are too important to be simply forgotten, such pieces of information become permanent inmates of the symbolic process. Deliberately maintained on the list of cultural memoranda, but nevertheless too paradoxical to be submitted to straightforward processing, they become trademarks that immediately identify certain activities as symbolic.

Stressing the dependence of the symbolic process on the cognitive process, which it both caricatures and complements, Sperber touches on the difficult problem of "symbolic efficacy" when he argues that even if no feedback takes place from the symbolic to the cognitive—when the symbolic process goes around in circles, apparently feeding on itself—its activity is far from sterile. The multiplicity of evocations, the repeated exploration of individual and collective memory, articulates culture, resulting in the structuring of similarities and differences, consonances and dissonances.

Such systematic rearticulation of cultural contents, closely resembling the Lévi-Straussian concept of "savage thought," is one of the threads we follow in the present chapter to explain the power of media events. Note again how the notion of a cultural reorganization fits with Turner's notion of the "subjunctive mood" as an outpost of culture, a laboratory or a frontier, a testing ground for possibilities and comparabilities, a meeting point between what is known to be true and what ought to be true.

19. "But there is always the possibility, however distant it may seem at the moment, that the present atmosphere will evaporate . . . A lawyer who lived through the dismaying events of 21 years ago commented: 'I refuse to believe the game is won. July 1968 seemed like the season for democracy, too'" (Apple, 1989). Compare the Sadat event during which the then commander-in-chief of the Israeli army, Mordechai Gur, voiced a suspicion that the visit might be a trick, a Trojan horse.

20. Lévi-Strauss's suggestions about ceremonial efficacy find an extension in Handelman's (1990) theory of ceremonial occasions, including specifically those ceremonies that usher in change. He calls these modeling events and distinguishes them from events that "present" or "represent" the world. The latter focus on certain aspects of the value system of a society. They either celebrate them directly—in events that "present the world"—or comment on them by turning them upside down in what he calls representing events (explained below). Thus, Memorial Day in Yankee City (Warner, 1962) is an event that "presents," highlighting the social structure through display of social solidarity among all of the elements that make up the community, living and dead. Carnivals, on the other hand, are events that "represent." They declare a time-out from the social structure and invert the stratification system. Within the festival the poor become rich, the beggars kings, elders and children exchange roles, and so on.

"Events that model the world" point to the interdependence between the component parts of a social system and the laws of nature. They are complex simulations in which a change in one order is meant to have a counterpart in the other. Modeling events suggest the notion of quasi-magical control over the society that the model represents. Social laws and cosmic laws are part of a continuum, hence the dangers and consequences inherent in any social action. The reverse is also true: the ritual invocation of transcendent forces has consequences for social order. It is by virtue of such continuity that the shaman's cure—or modeling—acquires its efficacy.

21. Except for a commemorative dimension, which soon became sec-

ondary, the Korean family reunions did not start as a symbolic event. They became symbolic by turning actions into gestures, rather than the other way around. These gestures implicitly conveyed a proposition which contradicted the official belief that the suffering of the Korean people and the dismemberment of families were the responsibility of North Korea; that those problems which admitted solution would have to wait until reunification took place; and that until then, South Korea had to remain mobilized against communism.

22. The Korean event condensed two themes, both connected to the end of the postwar era, that were central to the history of South Korea during the years that followed.

The first—for which the reunion of families was often used as a metaphor—addressed the political issue of reunification with North Korea, a constant preoccupation expressed in a long series of often ambivalent initiatives. Most of these initiatives aborted, only to be reiterated in some new form. Humanitarian gestures were made and a telephone line was installed between Pyongyang and Seoul, but the Olympic Games of 1988 marked a return to cold war: North Korea organized its own parallel games. Nonetheless, one could sense a change in the South Korean government on the issue of reunification. In 1984 the South Korean Red Cross proposed talks with North Korea with a view to allowing members of families separated during the war to hold reunions and exchange mail. In 1987 South Korea lifted the existing ban on public discussion of reunification. Dissidents were allowed to discuss reunification, but not to meet with North Koreans. In 1989 South Korea's President Roh Tae-Woo proposed the creation of a Korean "commonwealth," with a program including reunion of the still separated families.

The second theme marked a shift from a concern with national issues to a new emphasis on individual rights linked to the development and democratization of society. This (comparatively) smooth transition apparently was facilitated by the impact of media events such as the visit of Pope John Paul II and the Olympics. The games were widely viewed to be South Korea's opportunity to affirm its new status, as Japan did during the Tokyo games of 1964. They aimed to display to the world the country's development and its progress toward political democracy.

23. The funeral of Martin Luther King, Jr., was not only a response to a tragedy, it included some elements of "transformative" events, especially the modeling aspect. "The prior state of affairs dictated that negroes were to pass away without question, and usually without concern from the majority population . . . 'shot,' as my mother used to say, 'like a dog in cold blood and broad daylight.' King was eulogized as a man whose dream could transform black dogs into black people and elevate this country into the free democratic state it kept claiming to be" (Carter, 1990). Because of the lack of consensus at the time of King's death, the effects of this modeling were far from immediate.

24. A few days later the *New York Times* reported that "the long session of the parliament, until recently a rubber stamp for the Communist Party, was carried live for the first time on television. Cameras played deliberately over the faces of disgraced party leaders . . . and also of members that dozed off or took to doodling" (Schmemann, 1989). For other descriptions of the same event, see notes 5 and 7.

25. Indeed, Machiavelli himself advised the prince "to keep the populace occupied during certain periods of the year with festivals and spectacles" (Wagner-Pacifici, 1986, p. 293).

26. Even in the case of this ostensibly deliberate action, Ash (1990) observed the considerable difficulty involved in translating the common goal into a specific program of action.

27. Guttman's (1977) study of the durability of Anwar el-Sadat's influence on Israeli public opinion shows that such transformations may be short-lived. For example, Israeli hopes for the possibility of "no more wars" soared after the visit (from a constant 10–20 percent over previous years to 54 percent during the visit) and cooled off to their previsit level after about two months. They peaked again, then dropped again, following the Camp David peace accord in September 1978 (Stone, 1982).

7. Reviewing Media Events

1. Extending Austin's (1962) reflection on individual speech acts to the realm of symbolic events, we might go one step further and distinguish between effects which are "illocutionary," that is, practically synonymous with the ceremonial utterance itself—such as "I pronounce you man and wife"—and effects of a more ordinary (or, as Austin would put it, "perlocutionary") kind. The latter effects are quite distinct from the symbolic utterances that provoke or trigger them.

2. It is not easy, nor is it useful, in some of these examples to separate the event from the live broadcasting of the event. At the very least, the vulnerability of the organizer is enhanced by the intention to broadcast live. Moreover, additional pressure is exerted by media organizations, which may threaten to withdraw coverage if the design of the event is seriously impaired.

3. When the Arab Rejection Front, shunning the high ambitions of the Egyptian leader, accused Sadat of having turned traitor to his original cause, he might have invoked Machiavelli and retorted that he was pursuing the same goals but replacing war with other means. By then, however, his gestures had acquired an independent existence. His was a typically Pirandellian fate.

4. The summit meeting between President Reagan and Secretary General Gorbachev took place November 19–21, 1985. Strictly speaking, this was not a live media event, yet the summit story monopolized regular news broadcasts and public affairs programs from November 15 to November 22. In the United States it led to a lengthening in the duration of news programs and the rescheduling of other programs. In a comparison of broadcasts in the United States, Italy, and Russia, Hallin and Mancini (1989) argue that such international programs are selectively adapted to the concerns of each of the countries involved.

5. The search for criteria by which to evaluate success is one of the preoccupations of broadcast journalists prior to a media event. See the discussion of this point in Chapter 3.

6. From Schneiderman (1986), in *Le Monde:* "Surely Léon Zitrone [the paradigmatic French presenter of media events] was born on a red carpet . . . Does he need to test the mikes? to clear his throat? He would never be so undistinguished as to count 'One, two, three,' which is what all his less classy colleagues would do. He religiously has to whisper, 'Mr. President? Mr. President? Mr. President?' At night his dreams must be filled with points of etiquette, his lips busy kissing ladies' hands, beginning, no need to say, from the ambassadorial rank up. No doubt he practices on his bed-lamp." More recently, Saddam Hussein's presenter-translator has been the butt of satirists.

7. Writing of the Pope's visit to Ireland, Sorohan (1979, p. 19) says:

"During early September, the building and assembly of the various pieces of equipment proceeded. The magnitude and complexity of the operation began to register with us and we were conscious that an operation of this size had been rarely undertaken anywhere in the world—at least to our knowledge, and under such short notice. We had now to redouble our efforts and strain technical ability to the hour to ensure that this operation would be a success, and were also aware that it could go the wrong way . . .

"All the plans were laid and ten days in advance of the visit, the massive rigs commenced in Dublin Airport, the Phoenix Park, Dublin, Drogheda, Knock, and Galway. Now people and equipment started arriving from overseas. They worked night and day, sometimes sleeping in sleeping bags in caravans, and sometimes working right through the night. The worry now became one of whether staff could stick this pace. Nobody complained and the huge operation was working with efficiency and purpose that baffled our visiting friends. They had understood the Irish to be a disorganized and undisciplined race and they freely admitted that they had doubted in advance that we could achieve what we had planned.

"Saturday morning, September 29, dawned. The moment of truth had come. Would this mammoth operation work? We had not long to wait. From 8 am the crews at Dublin Airport, Papal

Nunciature, and Phoenix Park were on standby. At 9:45 am, the Papal plane loomed out of the morning mist and the great visit had begun.

"Day after day, wherever the Pope went, RTE [Irish television] went. All through, people and equipment were being ferried back and forth across the country by truck, minibus, car, and helicopter, while the quality of the production continued without a hitch throughout as the scene shifted from Drogheda to the Dublin motorcade, the Aras, the Papal Nunciature and to Galway on the Sunday. From there to Knock, with still the same brilliant success. Would all the equipment moved from Drogheda and Dublin to Mayroot, Shannon, and Limerick on the Monday work? It did, without the slightest hitch, and as the Papal plane took off, RTE, for a relatively small broadcasting organisation, had pulled off a broadcasting miracle."

8. Analyzing the political use of ceremony for orchestrating consensus and the renewal of elites, Gross (1986) argues that consensus may hold society together but is not itself spontaneous; it has to be actively constructed. In describing the social engineering that actually went into the scripting and production of public events in recorded history, Gross proposes that these events (1) symbolize power in a manner designed to dazzle and intimidate a vast audience with the regalia of monarchy, clergy, and the like; (2) present the social order in hierarchical display, affording the sort of view stressed by Geertz (1980) in royal progresses—or, one might add, the sort of insight that Kremlin watchers look for; (3) channel the expression of loyalty through ritualized dialogue between the ongoing performance and the stylized response of the populace in pageant and decor; (4) evoke tradition by parading symbols of continuity; (5) emphasize solidarity by focusing on central values around which allegiance is mobilized; (6) engineer social and cultural change by public destruction of the idols of the old (iconoclasm) and by public veneration of the new.

Of course, the ceremonies promoting change in societies such as revolutionary France—to take an example studied by Gross, but also by others (Ozouf, 1976; Mosse, 1980)—were engineered by the new and powerful elites. Yet one may argue, as Lukes (1975) does, that ceremonies sometimes also celebrate or map social divisions, thus reconciling the idea of cultural performance with conflict theories of society. Sometimes societal alternatives too may be expressed in ceremonial form.

9. Such utopian experiments are also open to individual initiative. Recently, some of these satellite celebrations have begun to emanate from commercial producers, not governments. See Hickey's (1987) review of satellite ceremonies such as the 1985 Live Aid concert and the Pope's prayer for world peace on June 6, 1987. The latter was "the most ambitious and elaborate satellite interconnection in broadcast history: a million and a half people in twenty-six countries linked by eighteen satellites recited the rosary with the Pope, who was able to see worshippers responding at sites all over the planet." More than one billion people tuned in to their television set or radio for the event.

10. The Challenger take-off on January 26, 1986, went virtually unnoticed until the disaster at 11:39 a.m., six minutes into the flight. Then the crisis was covered live for more than five hours, with the daytime broadcast seen in 29 percent of TV homes (*Broadcasting*, February 3, 1986).

11. Something similar took place following Shimon Peres' visit to Morocco in June 1986. Heavily involved in the organization of the visit, Jewish leaders, both in Israel and abroad, used it as an occasion to denounce the cliché that the Jews of Middle Eastern and North African origin in Israel are almost always opposed to peace with the neighboring countries because of their "wide knowledge and consequent distrust of these countries." This cliché, current in Israeli circles (including the left, the pacifist movements, and the communities themselves), was challenged by the event. "Many among us," said a leader of the Orientals for Peace movement, "desire peace and welcome concessions that would lead to it." An unexpected effect of Peres' visit to Morocco was to support the emergence of a new leadership, in a bid to recast the image of Moroccan and "oriental" Jews in Israel.

12. On May 25, 1986, Sports Aid attempted to combine a campaign

aimed at fighting malnutrition in Africa with the simultaneous scheduling of marathon races in hundreds of cities across seventy-five countries. The organizers aimed for 20 to 40 million joggers, whose participating fees would be donated. Television coverage focused on London and New York, where the race ended at the United Nations building.

13. Another indication of this trend, related to the celebration of the centenary of the Statue of Liberty in July 1986, was the attempt sponsored by U.S. Supreme Court Justice Warren Burger to process the naturalization of immigrants all over the country in one enormous television ceremony.

14. See Florian Znaniecki in Turner (1974, p. 46).

15. Talking over the heads of intermediary organizations is one of the defining characteristics of mass society (Kornhauser, 1959). See the discussion below on disintermediation.

16. This process is reminiscent of the "narcotizing dysfunction" of Lazarsfeld and Merton (1948). See also Gerbner et al. (1979) on the role of television in the mainstreaming of political opinion; that is, the convergence of opinions that otherwise would be polarized.

17. The genre of election-night television stands midway between the Contest of presidential debates and the Coronation of presidential inaugurals. Its format was established as early as 1948 by the American networks (Russo, 1983). From the beginning, the show proved compelling enough to be commercially sponsored. With the subsequent addition of the computer, it has been exported around the democratic world. Even when the actual voting is over, the essence of the event is a dual Contest—between the candidates as the returns come in, and between the computer predictions and the ballot count—followed by the pronouncements of losers and winners. And even though election technology has reduced the number of hours it takes to count the ballots, the broadcasters have stepped up their dramatization of the process.

18. Certain events are hardly distinguishable from direct action. The broadcast of the Eastern European protest movements and the reunion of families during the Korean television campaign are the

most dramatic examples, but philanthropic marathons such as Kate Smith's wartime sing-in also make the point. These events benefit from the existence of an already committed audience, and the nature of the effect is probably better described as "activating" or "facilitating" action. Similar events, such as Live Aid for Africa or the crusade of the French comedian Coluche against hunger, have evoked this kind of response. Affirmative attitudes are immediately translated into the concrete actions of pledging money or writing checks. These are the sorts of measurable effects searched for—usually in vain—by empirical communications research. But see Ball-Rokeach, Rokeach, and Grube (1984) for a well-designed effort to study this process experimentally.

19. The most recent World Cup in soccer took place in Italy in June 1990. The "Mundiale" included fifty-two matches throughout the country, spread over one month, and called for the restructuring of twelve stadiums. RAI served as home broadcaster, providing feeds to 140 other broadcasting organizations. Given the number of programmed events, estimates of the size of the audience were astronomic (de Montezomolo, 1990).

20. The fact that televised papal trips have been turned into a systematic resource under John Paul II allows us to infer some of the effects of media events on at least one religion. They seem to pertain to the structure and hierarchy of the church and the place of religion in society, but also the nature of the liturgical experience.

21. In Nicaragua, for example, responses to the mass were interspersed with slogans, and the altar was dwarfed by the presence of revolutionary frescoes. It is difficult, if not impossible, for a religious event to address a society in open conflict without being co-opted in support of one of the parties. The rioting and violent repression occurring on the very site of the Pope's mass in Santiago, Chile, defied his "neither/nor" image of a church above all parties and swallowed the meaning of the event. At the other extreme, uncontrolled reverence may go too far and prove embarrassing, as when American fans of the Pope turned John Paul II into a Catholic version of Elvis Presley.

22. A recent study conducted among French television viewers shows

that media events such as the special addresses to the nation of General de Gaulle, the funeral of Kennedy, the visit of Sadat to Jerusalem, and the moon landings are among the few best-remembered television events. Foreign events, the authors suggest, are more durable when transmitted within the media event format (Cayrol, Bourdon, and Souchon, 1988).

23. President Reagan's inauguration took place on January 20, 1981, while American hostages were being released from Iran. Offering a dramatic background to the Washington ceremonies, the timing of this gesture by the Tehran regime was a deliberate rebuff to the efforts of President Carter toward a solution of the hostage crisis.

24. This theme of disintermediation is developed in Katz (1988) as a generic process in the emergence and adaptation of new media technologies in the context of social institutions. James Beniger (1986) has contributed to our thinking on this matter.

REFERENCES

Abeles, M. 1988. Modern political ritual: ethnography of an inauguration and a pilgrimage by President Mitterrand. *Current Anthropology* 29:391–399.

Adorno, T. W., and M. Horkheimer. 1973. The culture industry: enlightenment as mass deception. In J. Curran, M. Gurevitch, and J. Woolacott, eds. *Mass communication and society*. Beverly Hills: Sage.

Alberoni, F. 1983. *Falling in love*. New York: Random House.

Alexander, J. C. 1988. Culture and political crisis: "Watergate" and Durkheimian sociology. In J. C. Alexander, ed. *Durkheimian sociology: cultural studies*. New York: Cambridge University Press.

Allen, R. C. 1985. *Speaking of soap operas*. Chapel Hill: University of North Carolina Press.

Altman, R. 1986. Television/sound. In T. Modleski, ed. *Studies in entertainment: critical approaches to mass culture*. Bloomington: Indiana University Press.

Apple, R. W., Jr. 1989. The Czech riddle: who will lead?, and other articles. *New York Times*, November 26, 28, 29.

Arlen, M. 1979. The big parade. *New Yorker*, April 30, pp. 122–124.

Arnheim, R. 1944. World of the daytime serial. In P. F. Lazarsfeld and F. N. Stanton, eds. *Radio research: 1942–1943*. New York: Duell, Sloan & Pearce.

Aron, R. 1957. *German sociology*. London: Heinemann.

Ash, T. G. 1990. *The magic lantern: the revolution of '89 witnessed in Warsaw, Budapest, Berlin, and Prague*. New York: Random House.

Austin, J. L. 1962. *How to do things with words*. Oxford: Clarendon Press.

Bagehot, W. 1927. *The English constitution*. London: Oxford University Press.

Bakhtin, M. 1981. *The dialogic imagination: four essays*. Austin: University of Texas Press.

Ball-Rokeach, S. J. 1985. The origins of media system dependency: a sociological framework. *Communication Research* 12:485–510.

Ball-Rokeach, S. J., M. Rokeach, and J. W. Grube. 1984. *The Great American values test: influencing behavior and belief through television*. New York: Free Press.

Barber, J. D. 1965. Peer group discussion and recovery from the Kennedy assassination. In B. S. Greenberg and E. B. Parker, eds. *The Kennedy assassination and the American public: social communication in crisis*. Stanford: Stanford University Press.

———— 1980. *The pulse of politics: electing presidents in the media age*. New York: Norton.

Baudrillard, J. 1978. La précession des simulacres. *Traverses*, no. 10. Paris: Minuit.

Becker, H. 1987. The writing of science. *Contemporary Sociology* 2:149–171.

Beniger, J. 1986. *The control revolution: technological and economic origins of the information society*. Cambridge, Mass.: Harvard University Press.

Benjamin, W. 1968a. The work of art in the age of mechanical reproduction. In Hannah Arendt, ed. *Illuminations*. Trans. Harry Zohn. New York: Harcourt Brace Jovanovich.

———— 1968b. What is epic theater? In Hannah Arendt, ed. *Illuminations*. Trans. Harry Zohn. New York: Harcourt Brace Jovanovich.

Bettelheim, B. 1975. *The uses of enchantment: the meaning and importance of fairy tales*. New York: Knopf.

Blumer, H. 1939. Collective behavior. In A. M. Lee, ed. *New outline of the principles of sociology*. New York: Barnes and Noble. Reprint ed. 1946.

Blumler, J. G., and E. Katz, eds. 1974. *The uses of mass communication*. Beverly Hills: Sage.

Blumler, J. G., and D. McQuail. 1968. *Television in politics: its uses and influence*. London: Faber and Faber.

Blumler, J. G., M. Gurevitch, and E. Katz. 1985. Reaching out: a future for gratifications research. In K. E. Rosengren, L. A. Wenner, and P. Palmgreen, eds. *Media gratification research: current perspectives*. Beverly Hills: Sage.

Blumler, J. G., et al. 1971. Attitudes to the monarchy: their structure and development during a ceremonial occasion. *Political Studies* 19(2):149–171.

Bogart, L. 1956. *The age of television: a study of viewing habits and the impact of television on American life*. New York: F. Unger.

Bokser, B. M. 1984. *The origins of the seder: the Passover rite and early rabbinic Judaism*. Berkeley: University of California Press.

Boorstin, D. J. 1964. *The image: a guide to pseudo events in America*. New York: Harper & Row.

Boureau, A. 1989. Commémoration politique, mémoire religieuse, mémoire privée: les funérailles royales sous l'ancien régime. Colloque International, "Le geste Commémoratif." Lyon: Centre de Politologie Historique.

Braudel, F. 1985. *La dynamique du capitalisme*. Paris: Arthaud.

Braudy, L. 1982. Popular culture and personal time. *Yale Review* 71:481–498.

Breitrose, H. 1980. Monday night football. Unpublished. Institute for Communication Research, Stanford.

Briggs, A. 1979. *The history of broadcasting in the United Kingdom*. New York: Oxford University Press.

Brown, P. 1981. *The cult of the saints*. Chicago: University of Chicago Press.

Browne, N. 1984. The political economy of television's supertext. *Quarterly Review of Film Studies* 9(3):174–183.

Bryant, J., P. Comisky, and D. Zillman. 1977. Drama in sports commentary. *Journal of Communication* 27(3):140–149.

Caillois, R. 1961. *Man, play, and games*. New York: Free Press of Glencoe.

Cantor, M. G., and S. Pingree. 1983. *The soap opera*. Beverly Hills: Sage.

Cardiff, D., and P. Scannell. 1987. Broadcasting and national unity. In J. Curran, A. Smith, and P. Wingate, eds. *Impacts and influence*. London: Methuen.

Carter, A. 1990. The funeral of Martin Luther King, Jr., as media coronation. Unpublished. Annenberg School for Communication, University of Southern California, Los Angeles.

Cassata, M. B. 1983. *Life on daytime television: tuning-in American serial drama.* Norwood, N.J.: Ablex.

Cawelti, J. 1976. *Adventure, mystery, romance: formula stories as art and popular culture.* Chicago: University of Chicago Press.

Cayrol, R., J. Bourdon, and M. Souchon. 1988. Politique et télévision. Internal document. Ministère de la Recherche, Paris.

Centre d'Etudes d'Opinion. 1981. Les grands événements historiques à la télévision. *Cahiers de la Communication* (1)1:51–61.

Chaney, D. 1983. A symbolic mirror of ourselves: civic ritual in mass society. *Media, Culture, and Society* (5)3:119–135.

Cohen, N. 1978. President Sadat's visit to Jerusalem: broadcasting aspects. *EBU Review* 29:8–12.

Coleman, J. S. 1980. Authority systems. *Public Opinion Quarterly* 44:143–163.

Comiskey, P., J. Bryant, and D. Zillman. 1977. Commentary as a substitute for action. *Journal of Communication* 27(3):150–153.

Csikszentmihalyi, M., and R. W. Kubey. 1981. Television and the rest of life: a systematic comparison to subjective experience. *Public Opinion Quarterly* 45:317–328.

Dahrendorf, R. 1990. *Reflections on the revolution in Europe.* New York: Random House.

Da Matta, R. 1977. Constraints and license: a preliminary study of two Brazilian national rituals. In S. F. Moore and B. G. Myerhoff, eds. *Secular ritual.* Assen, Netherlands: Van Gorcum.

———— 1984. Carnival in multiple planes. In J. J. MacAloon, ed. *Rite Drama, Festival Spectacle: Rehearsals toward a Theory of Cultural Performance.* Philadelphia: ISHI.

Darnton, R. 1975. Writing news and telling stories. *Daedalus*, Spring, pp. 174–194.

Davidian, H. 1983. Khomeini's return to Iran. Unpublished. Annenberg School for Communication, University of Southern California, Los Angeles.

Davison, W. P. 1983. The third person effect in communication. *Public Opinion Quarterly* 47:1–15.

Dayan, D. 1975. The tutor code of classical cinema. In B. Nichols, ed. *Movies and methods*. Berkeley: University of California Press, pp. 438–451. Reprint ed. 1976.

Dayan, D., and E. Katz. 1982. Rituel publics à usage privé: métamorphose télévisée d'un mariage royal. *Les Annales: Economie, Société, Civilisation*. Abridged and revised in English as Electronic ceremonies: television performs a royal wedding. In M. Blonsky, ed. *On signs*. Baltimore: Johns Hopkins University Press. 1985.

——— 1987. Performing media events. In J. Curran, A. Smith, and P. Wingate, eds. *Impacts and influences*. London: Methuen.

——— 1988. Articulating consensus: the rhetoric and ritual of media events. In J. Alexander, ed. *Durkheimian sociology*. Cambridge: Cambridge University Press. (Earlier French version: La télévision et la rhétorique des grandes cérémonies. In M. Ferro, ed. *Film et histoire*. Paris: Presses de l'Ecole des Hautes Etudes, 1984.)

Dayan, D., E. Katz, and P. Kerns. 1984. Armchair pilgrimages: the trips of Pope John Paul II and their television public. *On Film* 13:25–34. Reprinted in M. Gurevitch and M. Levy, eds. *Mass communication review yearbook*. Vol. 5. Beverly Hills: Sage. 1985.

Dupront, A. 1973. Pèlerinages et lieux sacrés. In *Mélanges Fernand Braudel*. Toulouse: Privat.

Durkheim, E. 1915. *The elementary forms of the religious life: a study in religious sociology*. Trans. J. W. Swain. London: Allen & Unwin.

Eco, U. 1989. *The open work*. Trans. A. Cancogni. Cambridge, Mass.: Harvard University Press.

Edelman, M. J. 1964. *The symbolic uses of politics*. Urbana: University of Illinois Press.

——— 1989. *Constructing the political spectacle*. Chicago: University of Chicago Press.

Eisele, T. D. 1979. The eagle has landed. *Michigan Quarterly Review* 18(2):177–182.

Eisenstein, E. 1979. *The printing press as an agent of change: communications and cultural transformations in early modern Europe*. New York: Cambridge University Press.

Elliott, P. R. 1982. Press performance as political ritual. In D. C. Whitney et al., eds. *Mass communication review yearbook*. Vol. 3. Beverly Hills: Sage.

Epstein, E. J. 1973. *News from nowhere: television and the news*. New York: Vintage Books.

Fauré, M. 1981. Vu de chez les Smith à l'heure du breakfast. *Liberation*, July 30.

Feldman, S. 1981. John Paul II in Brazil: the Argentinian press narrative. Unpublished. Communications Institute, Hebrew University of Jerusalem.

Fiske, J., and J. Hartley. 1978. *Reading television*. London: Methuen.

Fogel, M. 1989. *Les cérémonies de l'information dans la France du XVIe au XVIIIe siècle*. Paris: Fayard.

Freud, S. 1939. *Moses and monotheism*. New York: Knopf.

Friendly, F. 1967. *Due to circumstances beyond our control*. New York: Vintage Books.

Gamson, W. A., and A. Modigliani. 1989. Media discourse and public opinion on nuclear power. *American Journal of Sociology* 95:1–37.

Gans, H. J. 1979. *Deciding what's news: a study of CBS Evening News, NBC Nightly News, Newsweek, and Time*. New York: Pantheon Books.

Geertz, C. 1973. *The interpretation of cultures*. New York: Basic Books.

——— 1980. Center, kings, and charisma. In J. Ben-David and T. Clark, eds. *Culture and its creators*. Chicago: University of Chicago Press.

Gerbner, G., L. Gross, N. Signorielli, M. Morgan, and M. Jackson-Beeck. 1979. The demonstration of power: violence profile no. 10. *Journal of Communication* 29(3):177–196.

Giesey, R. E. 1960. *The royal funeral ceremony in Renaissance France.* Geneva: Droz.

Gitlin, T. 1980. *The whole world is watching: mass media in the making and unmaking of the new left.* Berkeley: University of California Press.

Gleeson, P. 1979. The chieftains, Bernadette, and a choir of 6,000. *Irish Broadcasting Review,* pp. 42–43.

Goffman, E. 1974. *Frame analysis: an essay on the organization of experience.* Cambridge, Mass.: Harvard University Press.

Goodhardt, G. J., A. S. C. Ehrenberg, and M. A. Collins. 1987. *The television audience: patterns of viewing.* 2nd ed. Brookfield, Vt.: Gower.

Goody, J., and I. Watt. 1968. The consequences of literacy. In J. Goody, ed. *Literacy in traditional societies.* Cambridge: Cambridge University Press.

Gouldner, A. W. 1976. *The dialectics of ideology and technology.* London: Macmillan.

Graber, D. A. 1984. *Processing the news: how people tame the information tide.* New York: Longman.

Gramsci, A. 1971. *Selections from the prison notebooks of Antonio Gramsci.* New York: International Publishers.

Greenberg, B. S., and E. B. Parker, eds. 1965. *The Kennedy assassination and the American public: social communication in crisis.* Stanford: Stanford University Press.

Greimas, A. J. 1966. *Sémantique structurale.* Paris: Larousse.

Griffin-Beale, C. 1981. The royal wedding day on ITV. *Broadcast* (UK), July 27, no. 1118:15–17.

Gritti, J. 1966. Un récit de presse: les derniers jours de Jean XXIII. *Communications* 8:84–102.

Gross, E. 1986. The social construction of historical events through public dramas. *Symbolic Interaction* 9(2):179–200.

Guizzardi, G., ed. 1981. *La narrazione del carisma. I viaggi di Giovanni Paolo in televisione.* Rome: RAI (Radio Televisione Italiana).

Gurevitch, M. 1977. Television and politics. In *Broadcasting hand-*

book 1: *Mass communication and society*. Milton Keynes, England: Open University.

Gusfield, J. R., and J. Michalowicz. 1984. Secular symbolism: studies of ritual, ceremony, and the symbolic order in modern life. *Annual Review of Sociology* 10:417–435.

Guthrie, K., and S. Grand. 1988. Symbolic conquests in the age of television: an analysis of Pope John Paul II's visit to Los Angeles. Paper presented at the annual conference of the International Association of Mass Communication, Barcelona.

Guttman, L. 1977. The impact of Sadat in Jerusalem on the Israeli Jews. Research report. Israel Institute of Applied Social Research, Jerusalem.

———— 1978. In Israel, back to square one. *Public Opinion* 1:19–20.

Hall, S. 1977. Encoding/decoding. In D. Hobson, A. Lowe, and P. Willis, eds. *Culture, media, language*. London: Hutchinson.

Hallin, D. C. 1987. Hegemony: the American news media from Vietnam to El Salvador: a study of ideological change and its limits. In D. L. Paletz, ed. *Political Communication Research*. Norwood, N.J.: Ablex.

Hallin, D. C., and P. Mancini. 1984. Political structure and representational form in United States and Italian TV news. *Theory and Society* 13(6):829–859.

———— 1989. Summits and the constitution of an international and public sphere: the Reagan-Gorbachev meetings as televised media events. Padora: Cedam.

Handelman, D. 1990. *Models and mirrors: towards an anthropology of public events*. New York: Cambridge University Press.

Harkabi, J. 1977. *Arab strategies and Israeli responses*. New York: Free Press.

Herzog, H. 1941. On borrowed experience: an analysis of listening to daytime sketches. *Studies in Philosophy and Social Science* 9:45–65.

Hickey, N. 1987. The age of global TV. *TV Guide*, October 3, pp. 5–11.

Hirschman, A. O. 1970. *Exit, voice and loyalty: responses to decline in firms, organizations, and states*. Cambridge, Mass.: Harvard University Press.

Hobsbawm, E., and T. Ranger, eds. 1983. *The invention of tradition.* New York: Cambridge University Press.

Homans, G. C. 1961. *Social behavior: its elementary forms.* New York: Harcourt, Brace & World.

Hood, S. C. 1967. *A survey of television.* London: Heinemann.

Horkheimer, M., and T. W. Adorno. 1972. *Dialectic of enlightenment.* New York: Continuum.

Houston, B. 1984. Viewing television: the metapsychology of endless consumption. *Quarterly Review of Film Studies* 9(3):183–195.

Huizinga, J. 1950. *Homo ludens: a study of the play element in culture.* New York: Roy.

Hyman, H. H. 1974. Mass communication and socialization. In W. P. Davison and F. T. C. Yu, eds. *Mass communication research: major issues and future direction.* New York: Praeger.

Innis, H. A. 1951. *The bias of communication.* Toronto: University of Toronto Press.

Jakobson, R. 1960. Linguistics and poetics. In T. Sebeok, ed. *Style in language.* New York: Wiley.

James, W. 1917. The moral equivalent of war. In W. James, *Memories and studies.* New York: Longmans, Green.

Jeanneney, J. N. 1987. Concordances des temps. *Le Monde,* July 18.

Jun, S. H., and D. Dayan. 1986. An interactive media event: South Korea's televised "family reunion." *Journal of Communication* 36(2):73–82.

Kantorowicz, E. H. 1957. *The king's two bodies: a study in medieval political theology.* Princeton: Princeton University Press.

Katz, E. 1978. Sadat and Begin: astronauts? Bulletin. Annenberg School for Communication, University of Southern California, Los Angeles.

——— 1980a. On conceptualizing media effects. In T. McCormack, ed. *Studies in Communication.* Vol. 1, pp. 119–141. Greenwich, Conn.: JAI Press.

——— 1980b. Media events: the sense of occasion. *Studies in Visual Anthropology* 6:84–89.

——— 1981. Publicity and pluralistic ignorance: notes on the spiral of silence. In H. Baier, H. M. Kepplinger, and J. Reumann, eds. *Public opinion and social change*. Opladen: Westdeutscher Verlag.

———— 1987. Communication research since Lazarsfeld. *Public Opinion Quarterly* 51:S25–S45.

———— 1988. Disintermediation: cutting out the middleman. *Intermedia* 16:30–32.

———— 1990. Viewers work. Wilbur Schramm memorial lecture. Urbana: University of Illinois.

Katz, E., and D. Dayan. 1986. Contests, conquests, coronations: on media events and their heroes. In C. Graumann and S. Moscovici, eds. *Changing conceptions of leadership*. New York: Springer Verlag.

Katz, E., and S. Feldman. 1962. The Kennedy-Nixon debates: a survey of surveys. In S. Kraus, ed. *The great debates: background, perspectives, effects*. Bloomington: Indiana University Press.

Katz, E., H. Adoni, and P. Parness. 1977. Remembering the news: what the picture adds to recall. *Journalism Quarterly* 54:231–239.

Katz, E., D. Dayan, and E. Hauser. 1990. Reflections on the role of media in the Eastern European revolutions. Paper presented at the Twelfth World Congress of Sociology, Madrid.

Katz, E., D. Dayan, and P. Motyl. 1981. In defense of media events. In R. W. Haigh, G. Gerbner, and R. B. Byrne, eds. *Communication in the twenty-first century*. New York: Wiley.

———— 1983. Television diplomacy: Sadat in Jerusalem. In G. Gerbner and M. Seifert, eds. *World communications*. New York: Longman.

Katz, E., M. L. Levin, and H. Hamilton. 1963. Traditions of research on the diffusion of innovation. *American Sociological Review* 28:237–252.

Katz, E., P. M. Blau, M. L. Brown, and F. L. Strodtbeck. 1957. Leadership stability and social change; an experiment with small groups. *Sociometry* 20:36–50.

Katzman, N. 1972. Television soap operas: what's been going on anyway? *Public Opinion Quarterly* 36:200–211.

Kaufmann, S. 1989. Le poids d'août 1968. *Le Monde*, December 1.

Kerns, P. 1982. Papal visit to the U.S. as pilgrimage. Unpublished. Annenberg School for Communication, University of Southern California, Los Angeles.

Kertzer, D. L. 1988. *Rituals, politics, and power.* New Haven: Yale University Press.

Kornhauser, W. 1959. *The politics of mass society.* New York: Free Press of Glencoe.

Kraus, S., ed. 1962. *The great debate: background, perspectives, effects.* Bloomington: Indiana University Press.

Kubey, R. W., and M. Csikszentmihalyi. 1990. *Television and the quality of life: how viewing shapes everyday experience.* Hillsdale, N.J.: Erlbaum.

Lane, C. 1981. *The rites of ruler: ritual in industrial society—the Soviet case.* New York: Cambridge University Press.

Lang, G. E., and K. Lang. 1968. *Politics and television.* Chicago: Quadrangle Books.

Lang, K., and G. E. Lang. 1953. The unique perspective of television. *American Sociological Review* 18:3–12.

——— 1983. *The battle for public opinion.* New York: Columbia University Press.

Lasswell, H. D. 1979. *The signature of power: buildings, communication, and polity.* New Brunswick, N.J.: Transaction Press.

Lazarsfeld, P. F. 1948. Communication research and the social psychologist. In *Current trends in social psychology.* Pittsburgh: University of Pittsburgh Press.

Lazarsfeld, P. F., and R. K. Merton. 1948. Mass communication, popular taste, and organized social action. In L. Bryson, ed. *Communication of ideas,* pp. 95–118. New York: Harper & Row.

Lazarsfeld, P. F., and F. Stanton, eds. 1949. *Communication research.* New York: Harper.

Lendvay, J., J. Tolgyesi, and M. Tomka. 1982. First of May: a Hungarian media event. Paper presented at the World Congress of Sociology, Mexico City.

Levin, E. 1982. Election night broadcasts on Israeli television. Master's thesis, Communications Institute, Hebrew University of Jerusalem.

Lévi-Strauss, C. 1963. The effectiveness of symbols. In C. Lévi-Strauss, *Structural anthropology*. Vol. 1. New York: Basic Books.

Levy, M. 1981. Disdaining the news. *Journal of Communication* 31(3):24–31.

Lewis, A. 1978. Peace ritual in Israel: images of social order in the Middle East. Unpublished. International Seminar for Conflict Resolution, University of Haifa.

Lewis, L. 1929. *Myths after Lincoln*. New York: Harcourt Brace.

Liebes, T., and E. Katz. 1990. *The export of meaning: cross-cultural readings of Dallas*. New York: Oxford University Press.

Liebes-Plesner, T. 1984. Shades of meaning in President Sadat's Knesset speech. *Semiotica* 48(3/4):215–229.

Livingstone, S. 1990. *Making sense of television*. London: Pergamon Press.

Lowenthal, L. 1944. Biographies in popular magazines. In P. F. Lazarsfeld and F. N. Stanton, eds. *Radio research: 1942–1943*. New York: Duell, Sloan & Pearce.

Lukes, S. 1975. Political ritual and social integration. *Sociology* 9(2):289–308.

MacAloon, J., ed. 1984. *Rite, festival, spectacle, game*. Chicago: University of Chicago Press.

Mancini, P. 1987. Rito, leader, e mass media. In *Leadership e democrazia*. Padova: Cedam.

Marc, D. 1989. *Comic visions: television comedy and American culture*. Boston: Unwin Hyman.

Marin, L. 1981. *Le portrait du roi*. Paris: Minuit.

Martin, D. A. 1969. *The religious and the secular: studies in secularization*. London: Routledge and Kegan Paul.

McCormack, T. 1962. The context hypothesis and television learning. *Studies in Public Communication* no. 4, pp. 111–125.

McDougall, W. 1985. *The heavens and the earth: a political history of the space age*. New York: Basic Books.

McGuire, W. 1986. The myth of massive media impact. In G. Comstock, ed. *Public communication and behavior*. Orlando: Academic Press.

Mendelsohn, H. 1964. Listening to radio. In L. A. Dexter and D. M.

White, eds. *People, society, and mass communications*. Glencoe: Free Press.

Merei, F. 1949. Group leadership and institutionalization. *Human Relations* 3:23–39.

Merton, R. K. 1946. *Mass persuasion*. New York: Harper.

Metz, C. 1968. *Essais sur la signification au cinéma*. Paris: Klincksieck.

Meyrowitz, J. 1985. *No sense of place*. New York: Oxford University Press.

Mindak, W. H., and G. D. Hursch. 1965. Television's function on the assassination weekend. In B. S. Greenberg and E. B. Parker, eds. *The Kennedy assassination and the American public: social communication in crisis*. Stanford: Stanford University Press.

Minwalla, S. 1990. The assassination of Indira Gandhi. Unpublished. Annenberg School for Communication, University of Southern California, Los Angeles.

Missika, J. L., and D. Bregman. 1987. On framing the campaign: mass media roles in negotiating the meaning of the vote. *European Journal of Communication* 2(3):289–309.

Modleski, T. 1982. *Loving with a vengeance*. Hamden, Conn.: Action Books.

Molotch, H. L., and M. Lester. 1974. News as purposive behavior: on the strategic use of routine events, accidents, and scandals. *American Sociological Review* 39:101–113.

de Montclos, C. 1990. *Les voyages du pape Jean Paul II*. Paris: Le Centurion.

de Montezomolo, L. 1990. The effects of transnational information on the daily management of events. In P. L. Branzi, ed. *News in the age of satellite*. Rome: RAI.

Moore, S. F., and B. G. Myerhoff, eds. *Secular rituals*. Assen, Netherlands: Van Gorcum.

Morley, D. 1980. *The "nationwide" audience: structure and decoding*. Television monographs, no. 11. London: British Film Institute.

Morse, M. 1985. Talk, talk, talk: the space of discourse on television. *Screen* (26)2:2–17.

Moscovici, S. 1981. *L'âge des foules*. Paris: Fayard.

Mosse, G. 1975. *The nationalization of the masses: political symbolism and mass movements in Germany.* New York: H. Fertig.

———— 1980. *Masses and man: nationalist and fascist perceptions of reality.* New York: H. Fertig.

Myerhoff, B. G. 1977. We don't wrap herring in a printed page: fusion, fictions and continuity in secular ritual. In S. F. Moore and B. G. Myerhoff, eds. *Secular rituals.* Assen, Netherlands: Van Gorcum.

———— 1982. Rites of passage: Process and paradox. In V. Turner, ed. *Celebration.* Washington, D.C.: Smithsonian Institution.

Mytton, G. 1991. A billion viewers can't be right. *InterMedia* 19/8:10–12.

Nasser, M. 1979. Sadat's television manipulation. Unpublished. Annenberg School for Communication, University of Southern California, Los Angeles.

Nesiah, V. 1990. The Indo-Lanka peace accord: an analysis of a media event. Unpublished. Annenberg School for Communication, University of Southern California, Los Angeles.

Newcomb, H. 1974. *TV: the most popular art.* New York: Anchor.

Newcomb, H., and P. Hirsch. 1983. Television as a cultural forum: implications for research. *Quarterly Review of Film Studies* 8:48–55.

Newman, B. 1989. Switching channels: Czechoslovakia's TV in a flash became free as it covered uprising, and other articles. *Wall Street Journal,* November 27, December 5.

Nicolson, H. G. 1955. *Good behavior: being the study of certain types of civility.* London: Constable.

Noelle-Neumann, E. 1984. *The spiral of science: public opinion, our social skin.* Chicago: University of Chicago Press.

Nora, P. 1972. L'événement monstre. *Communications* 18:162–172.

————1984. Les lieux de mémoire. Paris: Gallimard.

Ozouf, M. 1976. *La fête révolutionnaire.* Paris: Gallimard.

Peacock, J. L. 1968. *Rites of modernization: symbolic and social aspects of Indonesian proletarian drama.* Chicago: University of Chicago Press.

Pearce, E. M. 1979. How RTV met demands of papal visit. *Irish Broadcasting Review*: 31–37.

Peirce, C. S. 1960–66. In C. Hartshorne and P. Weiss, eds. *Collected papers of Charles Sanders Peirce*. Cambridge, Mass.: Belknap Press of Harvard University Press.

Peled, T. 1979. Dynamics of public opinion from Sadat's visit to Jerusalem through President Carter's announcement of the Israeli-Egyptian agreement. Jerusalem: Israel Institute of Applied Social Research (research report for ABC News).

Phillips, D. 1983. The impact of mass media violence on U.S. homicides. *American Sociological Review* 48:560–568.

Propp, V. 1968. *Morphology of the folk-tale*. Austin: University of Texas Press.

Radway, J. A. 1984. *Reading the romance: women, patriarchy, and popular literature*. Chapel Hill: University of North Carolina Press.

Real, M. R. 1977. Reprint ed. 1982. The Superbowl: mythic spectacle. In H. Newcomb, ed. *Television: the critical view*, pp. 190–203. New York: Oxford University Press.

Reynolds, J. P. 1985. Television and worship. Unpublished. Annenberg School for Communication, University of Southern California, Los Angeles.

Riesman, D., R. Denny, and N. Glazer. 1950. *The lonely crowd*. New Haven: Yale University Press.

Rokeach, M., and S. J. Ball-Rokeach. 1989. Stability and change in American value priorities, 1968–1981. *American Psychologist* 44:775–784.

Rosengren, K. E., L. A. Wenner, and P. Palmgreen, eds. 1985. *Media gratification research: current perspectives*. Beverly Hills: Sage.

Rothenbuhler, E. 1985. Media events, civil religion, and social solidarity: the living room celebration of the Olympic Games. Ph.D. dissertation, Annenberg School for Communication, University of Southern California, Los Angeles.

——— 1988. The living room celebration of the Olympic Games. *Journal of Communication* 38:61–81.

———— 1989. Values and symbolism: public orientations to the Olympic media event. *Critical studies in mass communication*. Vol. 6, pp. 138–157.

Russo, M. A. 1983. CBS and the American political experience: a history of the CBS News special events and election units, 1952–1968. Ph.D. dissertation, New York University; Ann Arbor: University microfilm.

Salomon, G. 1979. *Interaction of media, cognition, and learning*. San Francisco: Jossey-Bass.

Schlesinger, P. 1978. *Putting reality together: BBC News*. London: Constable.

Schmemann, S. 1989. Czechoslovakia's moment in time. *New York Times*, November 29.

Schneiderman, D. 1986. Opinion page. *Le Monde*, July 20.

Schorr, D. 1976. Reality of "Network." *Rolling Stone*, December 16.

Schramm, W. 1965. Communication in crisis. In B. S. Greenberg and E. B. Parker, eds. *The Kennedy assassination and the American public: social communication in crisis*. Stanford: Stanford University Press.

Schudson, M. 1978. *Discovering the news: a social history of American newspapers*. New York: Basic Books.

Schwartz, B. 1983. The Whig conception of heroic leadership. *American Sociological Review* 48:18–33.

Searle, R. 1971. *Philosophy of language*. Oxford: Oxford University Press.

Seltz, H. A., and R. D. Yoakam. 1979. Production diary of the debates. In S. Kraus, ed. *The great debates: Carter vs. Ford, 1976*. Bloomington: Indiana University Press.

Serr, R. 1984. The royal wedding on BBC and ITV. Master's thesis, Communication Institute, Hebrew University of Jerusalem.

Shils, E. 1962. The theory of mass society. *Diogenes* 39:45–66.

———— 1975. *Center and periphery: essays in macrosociology*. Chicago: University of Chicago Press.

Shils, E., and M. Young. 1953. The meaning of the coronation. *Sociological Review* 1(1):68–81.

Shinar, D. 1990. Television and socio-political crisis: reflections on the Romanian revolution. Paper presented at the International Conference on Media in Crisis, Laval University, Quebec City.

Sigal, L. V. 1986. Sources make the news. In R. K. Manoff and M. Schudson, eds. *Reading the news*. New York: Pantheon.

Silverstone, R. 1981. *The message of television: myth and narrative in contemporary culture*. London: Heinemann.

Singer, M. 1984. *Man's glassy essence: explorations in semiotic anthropology*. Bloomington: Indiana University Press.

Sorohan, J. 1979. Pulling off a broadcasting miracle with nine weeks' notice. *Irish Broadcasting Review*: 46–47.

Sperber, D. 1975. *Rethinking symbolism*. Cambridge: Cambridge University Press.

Sreberny-Mohammadi, A. 1990. The power of tradition: communications and the Iranian revolution. *International Journal of Politics, Culture and Society* (3)3:341–371.

Stanford, D. H. 1979. The moonlanding: a psychoanalytical interpretation. *Michigan Quarterly Review* 18(2):220–229.

Steiner, G. 1963. *The people look at television: a study of audience attitudes*. New York: Knopf.

Stephenson, W. 1967. *The play theory of mass communication*. Chicago: University of Chicago Press.

Stone, R. A. 1982. *Social change in Israel: attitudes and events, 1967–1979*. With the collaboration of Louis Guttman and Shlomit Levy. New York: Praeger.

Tannenbaum, P. H. 1980. *The entertainment functions of television*. Hillsdale, N.J.: Erlbaum.

Taylor, E. 1989. *Prime-time families: television culture in postwar America*. Berkeley: University of California Press.

Thomas, W. I., and D. S. Thomas. 1928. *The child in America: behavior, problems and programs*. New York: Knopf.

Todorovic, A. 1988. The funeral of Marshal Tito. *European Broadcasting Union Review* 31:25–28.

Tuchman, G. 1978. *Making news: a study in the construction of reality*. New York: Free Press.

Turner, V. 1969. *The ritual process: structure and antistructure*. Ithaca: Cornell University Press. Reprint ed. 1977.

———— 1974. *Dramas, fields, and metaphors: symbolic action in human society.* Ithaca: Cornell University Press.

———— 1977. Process, system, and symbol. *Daedalus* 106:61–80.

———— 1985. Liminality, Kabbala, and the media. *Religion* 15:205–217.

Turner, V., and E. Turner. 1978. *Image and pilgrimage in Christian culture: anthropological perspectives.* New York: Columbia University Press.

Uplinger, H. 1989. Global TV: What follows live aid? *InterMedia* 17(6):17.

Van Gennep, A. 1909. *The rites of passage.* Trans. M. Wizedom and G. Caffee. London: Routledge & Kegan Paul.

Veron, E. 1981. *Construire l'événement: les médias et l'accident de Three Mile Island.* Paris: Minuit. (With the collaboration of J. Dana and A. F. de Ferrière.)

Vianello, R. 1986. The power politics of live television. *Journal of Film and Video* 37(3):26–40.

Wagner-Pacifici, R. E. 1986. *The Moro morality play: terrorism as social drama.* Chicago: University of Chicago Press.

Wallace, A. 1966. *Religion: an anthropological view.* New York: Random House.

Warner, W. L. 1962. *American life: dream and reality.* Chicago: University of Chicago Press.

Weber, M. 1946. *From Max Weber: essays in sociology.* New York: Oxford University Press.

White, H. 1973. *Metahistory: the historical imagination in nineteenth-century Europe.* Baltimore: Johns Hopkins University Press.

Williams, R. 1975. *Television: technology and cultural form.* New York: Schocken Books.

Wills, G. 1980. The greatest story every told. *Columbia Journalism Review* 18:25–33.

Wolfe, T. 1980. *The right stuff.* New York: Bantam Books.

Yerushalmi, H. Y. 1982. *Zakhor: Jewish history and Jewish memory.* Seattle: University of Washington Press.

Zelizer, B. 1981. The parameters of broadcast of Sadat's arrival in Jerusalem. Master's thesis, Communications Institute, Hebrew University of Jerusalem.

———— 1990. Covering the body: the Kennedy assassination and the establishment of journalistic authority. Ph.D. dissertation, Annenberg School for Communication, University of Pennsylvania.

———— In press. From home to public forum: media events and the public sphere. *Journal of Film and Video.*

Znaniecki, F. 1936. *The method of sociology.* New York: Farrar and Rhinehart.

ACKNOWLEDGMENTS

We have been working on this book intermittently since shortly after Anwar el-Sadat's journey to Jerusalem in 1977. In the process we have shifted focus many times. If our original interest was in "media diplomacy," we came to think of the project as "the live broadcasting of history," as "the high holidays of mass communication," as "ceremonial politics," as "Durkheim, live," as "the experience of not being there." At each of these turns we looked for help from others who had arrived before we did. Our debts are enormous, and we begin by thanking all who remain unmentioned, betrayed by our memory and the passage of years.

For sheer inspiration and tutelage, we are grateful to the late Victor Turner, whom we follow haltingly into the symbolics and functions of ceremony; to Kurt and Gladys Lang, who founded the study of media events; to Don Handelman, Ruth Katz, and George Mosse.

Our closest working associates and best critics were our students in Jerusalem and Los Angeles. They include Pierre Motyl (who was a full partner in the project in the early days, before he escaped into the jungle), Shaul Feldman, Suk-ho Jun, Paul Kerns, Esther Levin, Tamar Liebes, Eric Rothenbuhler, Ronnie Serr, Uri Shinar, Gabi Weimann, and Barbie Zelizer. Other students and colleagues contributed case-study material that is included in this book. Among these Don Handelman, Suk-ho Jun, Paul Kerns, Pierre Motyl, and Barbie Zelizer collaborated with us in writing papers from the project. Emily Hauser helped examine the role of the media in the East European revolutions of 1989. Jack Feldman, then of the National Opinion Research

Center, was a precursor of this group, having collaborated with Elihu Katz on an analysis of the Kennedy-Nixon debates of 1960.

There are certain colleagues whom we have consulted regularly, and their influence is evident throughout. For the privilege of this interaction—oral and written—we thank Jeffrey Alexander, Marshall Blonsky, Jay Blumler, Asa and Susan Briggs, Nick Browne, Michael Confino, Yaron Ezrahi, Bill Gibson, Ron Gottesman, Edward Gross, Dan Hallin, Ian Jarvie, Arnold Lewis, John MacAloon, Paolo Mancini, Serge Moscovici, Horace Newcomb, Michael Real, Michael Russo, Michael Schudson, Barry Schwartz, and Percy Tannenbaum. Michael Russo's dissertation deserves special mention.

It is too late, unfortunately, to ask Moise Dayan, Hilde Himmelweit, Beverle Houston, Katherine Kovacs, Nathan Leites, George McCune, Barbara Meyerhoff, Milton Rokeach, and Wilbur Schramm to look for their names here.

On our various travels to collect data and videotapes, we were given material and spiritual help by many people. Anthony Smith, a central figure in our enterprise, showed us how to view the royal wedding on his television set. John Grist, Stephen Hearst, Kenneth Lamb, Michael Lumley, and Peter Saynor— all then of the BBC—let us watch and talk to them at work. In Poland, we were given ideas and access to the televised coverage of the Pope by Bishop Dembrowski, Kristina Jung, Anna Wika, and by Poltel members Jacek Bukowski, Marek Janicki, and Jerzy Sinkiewicz. Karol Jakubowicz and Jerzy Mikulowski Pomorski offered academic wisdom. Thanks too to the Korean Broadcasting System for assistance with documenting the reunion event, and to Gabi Bar-Haim and Dov Shinar for helping us to think about Czechoslovakia and Romania. Hadassah Haas, Erving Offenbacher, and Naomi Tadmor aided in our consideration of holidays.

Colleagues who have given our ideas hearing and hospitality in seminars, meetings, and printed collections—and often have worked along similar lines—include Jeffrey Alexander, Sandra Ball-Rokeach, Marshall Blonsky, the late Richard Byrne, Muriel Cantor, James Curran, Herb Dordick, Marc Ferro, George Gerbner, Carl Graumann, Larry Gross, Gustavo Guizzardi, Sumiko Iwao, Edith Kurzweil, Christian Metz, Enrico Pace, Arnaud Sales, Erwin Scheuch, Daniel Schorr, Kim Schroder, Marsha Seifert, Lucien Sfez, Pauline Wingate, and Mauro Wolf. The resulting papers, in various forms, have all found their way into this book—for which we also thank the publishers. Full citations are included in the References section. We are particularly grateful to Random House, the *New York Times*, the *Irish Broadcasting Review*, and Shabnam Minwalla for their generous permission to quote at some length from various documents.

For support—material and spiritual—we thank the Annenberg School at the University of Southern California, under the deanship of Fred Williams and later under Peter Clarke and program director Susan Evans. The unflagging support of the school, and its generosity, made it possible for us to converge on Los Angeles at least once a year, to produce a new chapter and discard an older one. Carolyn Spicer, director of the Learning Center at the school, produced a Media Events Sampler, which has been widely viewed in its own right. Colleagues mused over our obsessive interest in our subject, but were continually encouraging: Sandra Ball-Rokeach, Jim Beniger, and Ev Rogers. We wore out generations of the school's secretaries, to whom we are grateful—especially to Rachel Osborn and Agnes Uy—but the crowning achievement is that of Jane Opperman, who typed the entire manuscript and gave research assistance, aided herself by Joe Chung.

In Jerusalem, the Guttman Institute of Applied Social

Research was our venue, and we thank Haya Gratch, in particular, for keeping up with our whirlwind meetings. Colleagues and co-workers at the Hebrew University, in communications, sociology, and political science, also provided approval and help; notable among them was Shosh Zilberberg.

In Paris, we had the unwavering support of Sol Dayan and Martha Zuber, and the encouragement of Jean Marc Ferry, Jacques Semélin, Isabelle Veyrat-Masson, and Dominique Wolton of the Centre National de la Recherche Scientifique, matched in the United States by that of Arnold and Ora Band, Kenneth Brecher, Joan Goldhamer, Carole Horne, Sara McCune, Ronnie Tarr, and Steve Weissmann.

Initial encouragement in the form of seed money and interest came from Lloyd Morrissett, president of the Markle Foundation, to whom we are grateful. David Davis, then of the Ford Foundation, supported a summer seminar that brought together many of the experts mentioned above, some of whom we never let out of sight. In the production phase, we had the support of the Annenberg School, the Guttman Institute, and the CNRS in Paris. For their insightful editorial suggestions, we particularly thank Michael Aronson, David Thorburn, and Vivian Wheeler.

From the moment long ago when we first began to talk about a book, Arthur Rosenthal, then of Harvard University Press, did everything he could to keep us going. So did Rachel Rosenblum, whom Daniel Dayan wishes to thank last. And most.

INDEX

Note: Italicized items are media events discussed in the text.